"THE DISSIDENTS"

ROSA MIRIAM ELIZALDE / LUIS BAEZ

"THE DISSIDENTS"

CUBAN STATE SECURITY AGENTS REVEAL THE TRUE STORY

EDITORA POLÍTICA/ LA HABANA, 2003

Translation: *ESTI*
Edition: *Iraida Aguirrechu* and *Martha Brancacho*
Cover design: *Eugenio Sagués*
Design and layout: *Eugenio Sagués, Alejandro Greenidge* and *Osvaldo Valdés*
Photographs: *Liborio Noval* and *Cuban State Security Agents*
Correction: *ESTI*
Composition: *Ramón Caballero*

ISBN 959-01-0548-3 (Spanish)
ISBN 959-01-0553-X

Editora Política
Fax: (537) 556896 / 556836
Email: edit63@enet.cu
Internet: www.pcc.cu
Belascoaín No. 864, Ciudad de La Habana, Cuba

*To the anonymous heroes who keep watch
in the shadows, inside and outside Cuba,
so that our light may shine forever.*

Without the help of friends who helped with the transcription of more than 60 hours of interviews, the editing of the texts, the search for additional information and the compilation and computer scanning of the documents, we could have never completed this book in 10 days. *The Dissidents* is a book by:

Saúl González, Katiusca Blanco, Aracelys Bedevia, Juana María Santoyo, Wanda Caso, Reynaldo Mavilio, Bárbara Benítez, Kenia Carrasco, Carlos Garriga, Aday del Sol, Yuniet Escobar, Gabriel Herrera, Daynet Rodríguez, Aliet Valdés, Juanita Carrasco, Ahmed Hourruitiner, Melvis Sarduy, Sonia López and Carlos Formoso. Also, Alejandra García Elizalde, Patricia Báez Rodríguez, Alejandra Báez Rodríguez, Mirtha Ramírez and Ángel García.

BY WAY OF A PROLOGUE

FELIPE PÉREZ ROQUE

Combatants of State Security, gathered with us here today; combatants of State Security, which in Cuba means the security of the people, the people in the government, the people in power, the people served by the State, a guarantee, as well, of their independence;

Comrades from the leadership of the Communist Party and the government;

Workers from the Editora Política publishing house, from the newspaper Juventud Rebelde, *all those who cooperated in this effort, and most especially, Rosa Miriam and Luis:*

I agree with Rosa Miriam and Luis that this book is the product not only of the talent of Luis and Rosa Miriam, of the special sensitivity and journalistic skill of Rosa Miriam, or the bloodhound's scent — as Tubal[1] described it — and knack for

---

1 Tubal Páez, well-known Cuban journalist and president of the Cuban Journalists Union (UPEC).

capturing the moment and the news so typical of Luis.

This is not only the hastily prepared book, written in barely a week, by a veteran journalist, a correspondent at the age of 25 at the Bay of Pigs, where a photograph of him as a young man in a militiaman's beret is kept as testimony of his constant presence on every front where the Cuban Revolution has been defended over the past four decades. I believe this is in fact the 14th book he has authored, the latest addition to a vast body of work that is essential reading to understand the history of the Cuban Revolution and its triumph over all obstacles and threats from abroad.

It is also the book by a young journalist, born when Luis was already a leading figure in Cuban journalism. It is the fruit of two generations that have become intertwined today in defense of the Revolution, of those who fought for the Revolution from the very outset and those who have benefited from its immense efforts to achieve social justice and who defend it today with the same conviction and commitment as their parents and grandparents.

It is also the work of Rosa Miriam, the author of previous books addressing some of the most pressing challenges and difficulties facing us today, such as prostitution, as well as the director of the newspaper of Cuban youth and of important spaces that the Revolution has succeeded in establishing on the Internet, overcoming material difficulties through the talent and commitment of its sons and daughters.

It is additionally, as they have said, a book by all of the people who participated in its transcription, edition and layout, helping to create a book that is really quite modest by material standards, yet with a quality of design that inspires readers to finish it in a single sitting.

It is the book, as they have said, of the combatants of State Security, the security of the people, the vigilance of the people, the intelligence of the people, which has succeeded in defeating the threats from abroad. It is their lives that are recounted here.

Because this book does much more than discuss their work; it discusses their lives, their problems, the ways they managed to cope with the incomprehension of their families and the rejection of their neighbors, the ways they recovered from moments of weakness to continue their work, so difficult and so crucial for the security of their people.

But this book is, above all, a book of the Cuban people, for it is the ongoing battle waged by the people, the epic feats they have achieved, that serve as its basis. This book, I believe, is yet another episode in the biblical battle between little David and the mighty giant Goliath. It is the portrait of a people who incarnate David in the 21st century, a people who have earned the title of combatants for life, as someone said in Juventud Rebelde *not long ago.*

As you read through the eight interviews in the book, the engrossing tales of these 12 comrades, sometimes with a knot in your throat, you are struck by a thought: it could very well have been the lives of others recounted here.

To some extent, fate has played its part here, within this whirlwind that has swept all of us up in the struggle to defend our Revolution. These are, after all, the lives of normal people, sons and daughters of the people, who never dreamed that one day they would be called upon to play this role. And when they have finished, they happily return — as if a weight had been lifted from their shoulders — to the normal life of workers, militia members, residents of their neighborhoods, members of our mass organizations, neighbors accepted in their communities as part of the history of anonymous heroes.

Now then, what other reflections are inspired by this book by Rosa Miriam, Luis and so many other comrades? What does this book clarify? This is an essential question, and one that I asked myself when I was invited to talk here today. There are a number of things clarified in this book, and much more forcefully than ever before; here we have the testimony of exceptional witnesses, because they were in fact participants in the stories recounted.

They are only a part of the larger story. The enemy must know that there are many others like them who continue to play this role today, who are receiving their money at this very moment; they could be participating in some meeting or other as we speak, and one day, when the time is right, they too will tell their stories.

The enemy must know that the adversity, the challenges, the formidable threats we have been forced to endure for decades, have only served to give our people greater wisdom and intelligence. We have been obliged to overcome our initial innocence, and this book is above all a testimony to the epic efforts of a people defending their right to self-determination. They have defended it through intelligence, skill, the relentless pursuit of information, the infiltration of enemy activity, and not through force.

This is not the story of a repressive regime that obtained confessions through torture; this is not the story of a country that used the methods employed in Latin America, in another era, by military dictatorships backed by the U.S. government.

In today's edition of Juventud Rebelde [June 24, 2003], there is an article by Rosa Miriam that tells the story of a young man whose parents were disappeared and murdered in Argentina, and who is now searching for his identity.

No one will ever be able to say that the Cuban Revolution was defended through the use of murder or kidnapping, or torture to obtain confessions. And that is because this Revolution emerged from a popular liberation war, in which the enemy was provided with medical treatment using our own supplies, and prisoners were fed before the guerrilla troops. Those were the ethics and principles passed down through the Revolution, which could therefore not be defended with the methods used by others.

The Revolution has, however, used the method of infiltrating the enemy; it has used intelligence, shrewdness, covert activity, but within certain limits that the Revolution has imposed on itself, out of respect for the integrity of the enemy, both physical and moral. As a result, no one will ever be able to write a book about the horrors perpetrated by the Cuban Revolution to defend itself.

It can be said, yes, that it applied its laws with the right of a nation forced to defend itself; that it imposed severe and rigorous justice, but always in full compliance with the country's institutions and laws, on those who collaborated with the aggressive power seeking to exterminate our people. But it can never be said that in order to defend itself, it used the same methods with which it was attacked.

This book, as a result, provides new arguments and sheds new light on truths that have already been exposed, as Tubal has noted.

The book clarifies how so-called "dissident groups" are formed in Cuba. The so-called "political parties" in Cuba are established through decisions made abroad, decisions made by the government of the United States. They do not come about through an autochthonous process, in response to the needs of the Cuban people. And thus we see parties and associations and abbreviations sprouting like mushrooms in the pages of this book, then gradually disappearing as we continue to read. Time and again we encounter the words: "They're all in Miami now." "They've gone to Miami." "They're in the United States now." Sometimes the entire leadership, or every last member of the group. Of course, that was often their real goal: a visa to emigrate to the United States.

Certain key words pop up again and again. Above all, the word "money". Conflicts over money, the pursuit of money, the desperation over money, the news that "more money is on the way." And then there are words like "greed", and "ambition", and "lack of ethics".

But above all, it becomes clear that despite more than two decades of concerted efforts and the resources used by the U.S. special services, the U.S. government, and the governments of *some of their allies, they have not succeeded, despite this over-whelming effort, in sowing the seeds in Cuba for a group that has actually endured. And so we watch as abbreviations appear and then disappear, because they have no real foundation or support.*

At times the name of a founding father of our independence is invoked; but three months later, the group no longer exists. It is futile to try to use the sacred name of Martí, or Maceo, or Agramonte; it simply rings false, there is no basis for it in our history. It is just not possible to appropriate the Revolution's history and its martyrs.

Another point eminently clarified is where the money comes from. First it is made clear that decisions about the groups are made by outside forces. It is the U.S. Interests Section that decides when a member of one group should switch to another, when a group with three members should join with a group with four members to form a federation, when these two groups should link up with a couple from another band and create an alliance. It's all invented, made up, fake. It would almost make you laugh, if it weren't for the fact that a nation's right to its very existence is at stake, if it weren't for the fact that this whole phony apparatus assembled from abroad is used to attack the Revolution and justify the blockade against the Cuban people.

And where does the money come from? It comes from abroad, and it's always U.S. dollars. And then you can't help but think about the father of our independence, José Martí, and the pilgrimage he made to collect money from the poor Cuban cigar rollers toiling in Tampa, in Central America, the funds used to fight for our independence gathered penny by penny through the voluntary contributions of the sons and daughters of the Cuban nation. And then you remember the young people known as the Centennial Generation, and as I look at Martha[2] sitting there,

---

2   Martha Rojas, the Cuban journalist who covered the trial of the participants in the attack on the Moncada and Carlos Manuel de Céspedes Garrisons.

it reminds me of how the money was raised to attack the Moncada garrison, the sacrifices made by those humble young men and women; you remember how one of them sold his photography equipment, how one of them sold his position as a delivery truck driver for a brewery, how one took his family's savings out of the bank to contribute to the cause of the Revolution. And you also remember the hundreds of thousands of people who sold and bought July 26 bonds, how the people contributed to that victory.

This new purported attempt to "liberate the people" is being carried out with money from abroad. Its eminently mercenary nature is like a mark branded on its forehead, which nothing and no one can conceal. Decisions are made from outside, it is financed from outside, and the money comes from the government that blockades and attacks our country. That is why there is no support from the Cuban population, no foundation, it is simply a means of making a living, and a way of serving the interests of a power bent on destroying the country.

And I am stunned, because for perhaps the first time ever, a retort has been issued against a book that hadn't even been launched yet.

One of the individuals very clearly depicted in the book — and this is only the beginning, this is just the first step in a process of exposing the full truth; Rosa Miriam and Luis have informed us that there will be a second edition published, there is much more to be said, because no one should doubt for a minute that we have not yet revealed everything we know, and every day we discover something new. In any event, one of these individuals was featured in a major newspaper, responding to a book that did not exist yet, because the book is just coming out today. It was a nervous, fearful retort, void of any real arguments, crudely worded, using facile insults and groundless attacks in an attempt to silence the truth revealed by these stories. And the truth is that the so-called "dissidents" in Cuba are a creation of the aggressive policy of the U.S. government and its special services. Their creation is in fact proclaimed in the Santa Fe Platform, drafted for Ronald Reagan's presidential campaign. They form part of the strategy crafted to obtain, through pressure and blackmail, the condemnation of Cuba in the Commission on Human Rights, which can then be used as justification for the blockade. And if they cannot manage to obtain a condemnation, they can at least manipulate the human rights issue.

The book makes all of this very clear, just as it exposes the identity of those who are "opposition" members one day and "exiles" the next. It recounts meetings held with the Miami terrorist mob, with individuals who recognized their own defeat, who recognized that they could not defeat the Revolution with weapons, on the battlefield, that they could not defeat the people who armed themselves as militia members to definitively rout them, and so now they have come to use new methods of subversion against the Revolution. These are the terrorists involved in the bombings, the murders that have brought mourning to so many Cuban families, like the families who received the scattered remains of their sons and daughters after a Cuban plane was blown up in mid-flight, and mourned their loss at a funeral service held here in this very place. It is these same terrorists who have now been transformed into the leaders from outside and the suppliers of money and material resources for the so-called "opposition" groups and "dissidents", who are nothing more than mercenaries working for a foreign power.

This is why the word "money" comes up over and over again, along with the word "bag" [referring to the gift bags given out at U.S. Interests Section functions]. The bags become an obsession; conflicts erupt over them. Mr. Cason decides that there will be only one bag per person for distribution — you could almost say he invented the ration system for handing out gift bags — and then there are complaints when there aren't enough to go around. It is quite a depressing spectacle, but it accurately illustrates the moral caliber of these people, their complete lack of convictions, goals and aspirations. It also illustrates the difference between them and us, because we do have convictions, we do defend utopian ideals, we do want a better country, and even more than that, a better world, because we consider the world to be our country. We have a legacy, we have values and ideas that signify more than money, and gift bags, and open passes to the Interests Section, and visa endorsements, the sale of visa endorsements, the power to give someone an endorsement to allow them to emigrate to the United States. We are the sons and daughters of a Revolution that has made us better men and women, capable of fighting for ideals even beyond our borders, capable of fighting not only for our own rights, but in fact even more so for the rights of others.

And so the book, through the testimonies of the comrades with us here today, paints a vivid portrait of the greed and intrigue that permeate all of the work carried out by this species created and financed from abroad, and treated by their masters as what they are, treated with the contempt of a master over his slaves, treated with the air of superiority of those who pay and thus know that they are in charge. And this is certainly not the way that the millions of Cubans who defend the Revolution understand the world.

There is a question we must ask ourselves: Will this book be known beyond the borders of Cuba? Will it grace the front pages of the newspapers that until now have only offered the version and the arguments of the other side? Will the Cuban people and the Cuban Revolution have the right for their version and their arguments, recounted here by their sons and daughters, to be heard by the rest of the world? Will this book enjoy the same front page coverage as the media campaigns waged against Cuba? Will Rosa Miriam and Luis have the opportunity to publish their views on the front pages of newspapers that have already printed a retort to a book that hadn't been launched yet? That is the question we need to ask now.

Will the Cuban people be able to see the truths told here, the testimonies of the comrades gathered here, come into the public light, and be acknowledged, or will they once again meet *with silence and manipulation? This is an important question, and it does not solely depend — I know this very well — on the efforts and the desire to reveal the truth of the news correspondents based here in Cuba. All too often, they can only watch as others decide that their work should not be published, or that changes must be made to an article because it is too favorable to Cuba — and these days, as they themselves explain, the "trend" is to be unfavorable.*

We will have to wait and see if this book is widely publicized, if it becomes a bestseller abroad, if newspapers print reviews of it, if television networks come to seek the truth and interview the people who have revealed this truth.

The suggestive title of "The Dissidents", in quotation marks, calls for a closer look at what the word "dissident" really means. According to the dictionary, a dissident is "one who disagrees or dissents." To dissent is "to refuse to conform to a common doctrine, belief or conduct."

This leads me to the conviction that we are the real dissidents. It is the people of Cuba who have dared to dissent from the commonly shared doctrine that this country should be a colony of the United States, that this country could not be an independent nation, that there was a manifest destiny that obliged a small country, located right next to a major power, to desist from the "insane" aspiration of its founding fathers to be neither a colony of Spain nor a part of the United States.

We are the ones who dissent from the current world order. In the past, we disagreed with and helped to fight colonialism, and apartheid; today, we disagree with neoliberalism, and the promotion of market forces and savage capitalism as the means of ensuring the development and the rights of the world's peoples.

Therefore we, the Cuban people, are the dissidents. We are the ones who refuse to conform with the uniform model of those who seek to impose a single system on the world, a single way of living, a single model of conduct.

There is yet another question brought up by this book, one that underlies it from start to finish. That question is: What is the real conflict exposed here? Is there a conflict between the government and the people in Cuba? Is there a conflict in Cuba between the authorities and these mercenary groups, an unknown minority with no support or basis in the population? Is this a problem between Cubans? No.

What is exposed here is a much deeper struggle, and it is the real struggle of a people, a nation, defending its right to self-determination, in the face of an imperial policy, a centuries-old attempt to enslave it and subjugate it to the designs of a super-power. That is what is exposed here.

What is at stake here is whether or not Cuba can be an independent country, and whether or not it can win the war being waged against it to take away its independence. And that is the grounds for the legitimacy of our battle and the legitimacy of the actions of the comrades who are here with us today.

Now then, the activity that was condemned recently in our courts — in the trials where prison sentences were handed down to mercenaries who consciously contributed to the declared policy of the government that subjects their country to a blockade and other forms of aggression, a policy aimed at a change in government here, as quickly as possible and by any means — such activity is not a crime only in Cuba. Here I have a definition of an organization subject to foreign control. It says, "An organization is subject to foreign control if it solicits or accepts financial contributions, loans, or support of any kind, directly or indirectly, from, or is affiliated directly or indirectly with, a foreign government or a political subdivision thereof, or an agent, agency or instrumentality of a foreign government."

And where did this definition come from? Is this Cuban law? No, this is from the Penal Code of the United States. And so, if the Penal Code of the United States establishes that it is against the law for an organization to solicit or accept financial contributions, loans, or support of any kind from a foreign government or an agency of that government, because this makes it an organiza-

tion subject to foreign control, or if the policies of that organization are determined or advised by a foreign government, then why would it not be against the law in Cuba as well? What I have read here is not Cuban law, it is U.S. law, the Penal Code of 2001, which also states that "whoever knowingly or willfully advocates, abets, advises, or teaches the duty, necessity, desirability, or propriety of overthrowing or destroying the government of the United States; or whoever, with intent to cause the overthrow or destruction of any such government, prints, publishes, edits, issues, circulates, sells, distributes, or publicly displays any written or printed matter advocating, advising, or teaching the duty, necessity, desirability, or propriety of overthrowing or destroying any government in the United States" is guilty of a crime.

So why should such a law not be decreed in Cuba, a small country subjected to constant aggression and hostility, a country that has endured hundreds of plots to assassinate its leaders, and has been forced to survive the blockade, biological warfare, armed invasion and terrorist attacks? The U.S. law, in fact, is much more restrictive than our own; I have not been quoting Cuban legislation here, but rather the legislation of the United States.

"Whoever prints, publishes, edits, issues, circulates, sells, distributes or" even "publicly displays any written or printed matter advocating, advising, or teaching the duty, necessity, desirability, or propriety of overthrowing or destroying any government in the United States." So why must we accept that they proclaim from over there that their policy is to destroy the Revolution, change the government, abolish the constitution and subject our country to the status of a colony once again?

That is what is at stake here, and our people are defending themselves, our people have managed to defend themselves over all these decades. That is what is happening, and this book is an honest and forceful testimony to that battle.

I believe, finally, that this effort carried out by Rosa Miriam and Luis has provided our people with a document that not only

has a value in the current circumstances, not only as an argu-
ment in the battle of ideas we are waging at this moment in our
history, not only as way of explaining our reasons, our rights, and
our dreams. This book has a further value, I think, because it will
help our children and future generations of Cubans to under-
stand how much it was necessary to struggle, how high a price XIII
had to be paid, how many sacrifices had to be made by their
parents and grandparents, in order to hand down to them a free
and sovereign country, so that never again would this country's
constitution include an amendment recognizing the right of the
U.S. government to intervene in Cuba when its interests are threat-
ened, or prohibiting Cuba from signing any kind of treaty with
another government, or prohibiting the Cuban government from
assuming any public debt beyond that authorized by the United
States, or establishing that the Isle of Pines is not part of Cuban
national territory — they wanted to turn it into a part of the United
States — or establishing Cuba's obligation to cede territory to
the United States for the establishment of naval bases, one of
which continues to occupy our national territory today.

So that this will never happen again in Cuba, so that the
Revolution that cost so much to bring to triumph and has cost so
much to defend until today, in the conditions of a unipolar world,
in the face of the betrayals of so many, in the midst of the emer-
gence of a world ruled by a single superpower, and when practi-
cally nobody — not even Cuba's friends — believed that our
country could overcome the disappearance of the Soviet Union,
the collapse of the socialist bloc, the enormous challenges of
the special period; when nobody believed the country could crown
the feat of having lived through these years of heroism, but also
of suffering for the Cuban people; when the Cuban economy was
paralyzed, when our people went hungry, but did not surrender;
when there were no medicines in the country, and the enemy
tried to use the shortages of medicines and of food as a weapon
of subversion here — and it is sickening to read the testimonies,
the attempt to create "independent pharmacies" and "indepen-

dent libraries" in the only country in the world where the people have the right to buy books at an accessible price, when everyone knows that books are a luxury of the rich in the rest of the world; when you consider all of this, you understand the value of the feat we have achieved, but which is still not finished. At this very moment, in fact, the Cuban Revolution is facing greater threats and danger than ever before.

We are here today for the launching of this book by Luis and Rosa Miriam and all the others who have been named here. This event could be considered yet another tribute, yet another show of admiration, sympathy, affection and respect for these men and women sitting here among us, combatants for life; women and men of the people, who were given a complex, dangerous and highly demanding task to carry out in the battle of the Revolution, and have fulfilled it with a high degree of integrity and honor. Today, as we express our admiration, affection and respect for you, our cherished comrades, I think it is also a time to reiterate our conviction that we are in the right, that our people will succeed in defending their rights, that the sacrifices imposed on you throughout all these years will not be in vain, just as the sacrifices of those who cannot be here today, because they have lost their lives along the way, were not in vain.

This is also a time to reiterate — to those who believe that our people can be fooled, that our people can be forced into surrender, that our people can be defeated — that we will pass down to the future generations, to our children and grandchildren, a free and independent country, a better country than the one our parents conquered and have defended for us.

Congratulations!   Thank you.[3]

---

3 Speech given by Felipe Pérez Roque, Minister of Foreign Affairs of the Republic of Cuba, at the launching of the book *"The Dissidents"*, held at the José Martí Memorial on June 24, 2003.

SHADOWS AMONG SHADOWS

"The Dissidents" is a book that was urgently asking to be written. The idea came to us shortly after the Minister of Foreign Relations of Cuba, Felipe Pérez Roque, held a press conference explaining the reasons that had led the Cuban government to charge and sentence as mercenaries those individuals who had collaborated, throughout the years, with U.S. agencies and terrorist organizations working, for the most part, from Miami.

During this press conference, the foreign minister revealed that a number of State Security agents who had infiltrated the mercenary groups had testified in their trials. The evidence presented by Cuba was irrefutable.

One week later, we found ourselves before the 12 agents who had revealed themselves after years of living in the ranks and files of the so-called "opposition", "internal dissidence movement", or "independent journalists and librarians", as they are called by the enemies of the Revolution.

We shan't be giving away the book's secrets. The stories told by these men and women give us the clearest possible picture of those who devote themselves to the game of the "opposition" in Cuba: hostages of the Miami mobsters and shameless employees of the U.S. Interests Section in Cuba, whose officials, while opening the doors of their homes and their stock-rooms to them, and perhaps for precisely this reason, showed them the most vicious disdain. Is it anything less than an insult to promote mad scrambles over gifts on official U.S. Interests Section premises? And to hand out a U.S. visa in exchange for written proof of counterrevolutionary behaviour?

We're not short of anecdotes. Although we worked for many exhausting days, sometimes in search of details that were apparently trivial, those interviewed were not only extraordinarily well-disposed to converse with us — we would tape and transcribe the material almost simultaneously — but were also responsible for making a great many of the documents presented in this book available to us.

Patiently, they helped us identify, in the jungle of photographs and documents, the characters you will find in these pages. The vast majority of photos showing parties and meetings attended by "dissidents" were taken by them, and they have an incalculable documentary value. Some of the photos were chosen because of their testimonial value, despite the fact that, technically, they leave much to be desired. They were taken during Cuban State Security operations.

Many of those interviewed knew each other from their work in the "dissident" community. Some had friendly relations, while others were rivals in groups notorious for constant quarrels among themselves. No one knew that they were really working for the same team, and finding this out was quite possibly the most poignant moment in a process that saw all manner of emotions: from those who would have liked to continue in the shadows, feeling that they were at their peak in their work as agents — this is the case of Orrio, Aleida and Odilia — to one who longed for a peaceful respite among his own, namely Baguer.

3

What was common to all was the intimate and profound relationship they had with the officials of the Ministry of the Interior supervising their work. These people — shadows among shadows — were responsible for weaving this extraordinary web that has finally allowed us to know the truth, without the enemy ever suspecting how vulnerable they were — and are — in the shadow of the eagle.

Havana, April 30, 2003

Today the so-called "dissidents", actually mercenaries on the payroll of Bush's Hitler-like government, are betraying not only their homeland, but all of humanity as well.

Fidel Castro
May 1, 2003

I ALWAYS KNEW I WAS NOT ALONE

She has a prodigious memory, trained by half a lifetime devoted to conspiratorial work. She can re-member exact dates, the content of documents, the apparel worn by people, the complete names of those individuals she met in so-called Cuban "opposition groups", and of American officials who knew her as one of the frequent visitors to the official headquarters of the U.S. Interests Section in Havana.

There are hundreds of pages on the Internet devoted to the dissident Aleida Godínez Soler, to her news re-ports, the declarations she made in Havana, to her long and active career as a counterrevolutionary. On the U.S. State Department website www.terrorismcentral.com, one can find articles of this nature: "The first National Conference of the Indepen-dent Worker's Confederation was held in the home of the active dissident and independent journalist Aleida Godínez… In the document that was drafted, the September Declaration, they criticized the human rights viola-

*tions endured by workers under the CTC, a communist organiza-
tion, member of the pro-Soviet World Federation of Trade Unions."*

*Despite this, we knew very little about this woman's back-
ground on beginning an interview shortly after the trial brought
against members of "dissident" organizations, her former colleagues. We knew only that she is Agent Vilma from the ranks
of State Security, and that she was born to a working class family.
Her mother was blacklisted by the Bureau for the Repression of
Communist Activities (Buró Represivo de Actividades
Anticomunistas, BRAC) during the Batista dictatorship, and when
this fact is mentioned, she smiles sadly. One can imagine what
suffering a "counterrevolutionary" daughter brought to a mother
persecuted by the sinister BRAC.*

6

AGENT VILMA

How did everything begin?
By chance. Certain circumstances led me to make ties to a counterrevolutionary in 1991, the first human rights activist in the province of Ciego de Ávila, where I was born. He told me about the
Cuban Committee for Human Rights, which was directed back
then and is still directed today by Gustavo Arcos Bergnes.

Who is this man who introduced you to the Arcos Bergnes group?
His name is Mario Fernández.

Who is he?
He's a pensioner. An elderly man, who "convinced" me join the
Committee, which I did, in January of 1992.

What had he done, before retiring?
He had always been a counterrevolutionary, really. He was someone who didn't share the ideas and principles of the Revolution,
and he'd been out of work for quite some time.

Where did he live?
In Ciego de Ávila. On Independence Street, between 10th and 11th,
in the Vista Alegre district.

And why did he approach you?
I worked for the Construction Materials Company in Ciego de Ávila, and I had to walk down Independence Street to get to work. I walked down that street everyday, and we would greet one another, we would speak a few words, and one fine day he spoke to me quite openly about the matter…

Why was that?
He was a singular individual. He had no inhibitions in speaking to you; he would say everything in a loud tone of voice without the slightest concern. He would speak to me about the Universal Declaration of Human Rights and how it was violated in Cuba, just like that, shamelessly. Seeing where this man was coming from, I went to consult an official of the Ministry of the Interior and I mentioned what was happening …

You simply went to the Ministry, just like that, to speak with whatever official you found there?
No. I had already collaborated a long time before that. My first involvement with State Security dates back to October 21, 1979, when I was still a student. I graduated in Economics in 1988, and at the time I met this man I was applying to start the long-distance course offered by the law school.

They gave you a green light…
Yes. I agreed to speak to him, to find out what it was he wanted, what his intentions were. And so, this way, I began to study this man. When we saw that this was going to work, I quit my job at the company and began acting as a full-fledged counterrevolutionary.

What was your job at the company?
I was a specialist in the Organization of Work and Wages department, until December of 1991, when Mario Fernández introduced me to the leaders of the so-called Cuban Committee for Human Rights. Through him, I met a man who has been living in Miami since March of 1994, who continues working for this organization there.

What is his name?
Felipe Alexis Morejón.

And who was he?
He was the delegate for the Cuban Committee for Human Rights in Ciego de Ávila. Through him, I met the counterrevolutionary Rodolfo Santos, a professional photographer, who works freelance. State Security had elaborated a plan for me to travel to Havana, after getting to know these people, and to try and establish links with a number of counterrevolutionaries, Vilma Fernández Batista and Pablo Reyes Martínez among them, who were members of the Cuban Civic Union, an organization that disappeared after both of them left the country. I finally made the trip and this led to my first direct contact with *Radio "Martí"*. When I returned to Ciego de Ávila, I was already known as a counterrevolutionary and had my first "war trophy"…

What was the contact with Radio "Martí" *like?*
It was the most fatuous, the most stupid thing in the world. Vilma said, "Here I have an activist who wants to share some information with you," and *Radio "Martí"* was already calling, delighted with what you can "report", without verifying the slightest detail, whether you are lying or telling the truth on the air.

Do you remember who you spoke with from Radio "Martí"?
How can I forget! I spoke with Juana Isa. I returned to Ciego de Ávila transformed into the spokesperson for the Cuban Committee for Human Rights in Ciego de Ávila. I was doing that for quite some time. When the telephone connections with the United States were cut in the early 90s, a Cuban who lives in Canada, Antonio Tang Báez, got in touch with me. He was the one who had the connections in *Radio "Martí"*, in the *Voice of the CID*, run by Hubert Matos, and in *La Cubanísima* as well. He used to phone from Montreal and then set up a conference call to connect us to Tomás Madrigal, from the station called *Independent and Democratic Cuba*. At times, he would put us through to Juana Isa herself.

Antonio Tang Báez

Born in Ciego de Ávila, and a cook by trade. He lives in Montreal, Canada. He defected in Canada in September of 1981 during a stopover on a tour of former socialist bloc countries. In Cuba, he had worked as head of personnel at the provincial Public Health unit in his native city.

On July 14 of 1985, journalist Michel Rousseau published an article in the *Journal de Montréal* which linked Tang Báez to activities against Canadian tourists perpetrated by Alpha 66.

That same year, he had collaborated in the elaboration of an assassination plot against President Fidel Castro organized by Alpha 66. He openly advocated the use of violence. On one of his frequent visits to Miami, he received military training to carry out terrorist acts.

He has systematic contact with members of counterrevolutionary groups within Cuba. He served as an intermediary between Elizardo Sampedro Marín and the head of the counterrevolutionary organization Alpha 66, Andrés Nazario Sargén.

He instructed Sampedro Marín to distribute faxes with threatening messages, which were also sent to the Mexican Embassy in Cuba. For these activities, Sampedro Marín was arrested on February 17, 2001 and sentenced to a four-year prison term.

Did they ask you to speak about anything in particular?
At the time, they were prioritizing the situation of prisoners sentenced for crimes against state security. They were extremely interested in the social situation in the country and their stance was very aggressive. The counterrevolutionaries in Miami were calling on people to paint anti-government banners, to sabotage installations, to bring about blackouts and water failures. It was a time when counterrevolutionaries were looking for a way to wear down the officials of State Security. They would paint a sign on one street corner, and when it was erased, they would put up another one to keep them running. Through this fellow in Canada, between August 1st of 1992 and August of 1993, I personally denounced 102 alleged human rights violations on *Radio "Martí"*.

Thanks to my frequent collaboration with this radio station, I grew closer and closer to the main counterrevolutionary leaders in Havana. I made contacts with the Cuban Christian Democratic Movement (Movimiento Cubano-Demócrata Cristiano), directed by a podiatrist, María Valdés Rosado; with the Maceo Movement for Dignity (Moviemiento Maceista por la Dignidad), headed by a woman who boasted of her links to the Cuban-American National Foundation (Fundación Nacional Cubanoamericana, FNCA), Ángela Herrera Carrillo. I also made contact with Osvaldo Payá Sardiñas, main leader of the Christian Liberation Movement (Movimiento Cristiano Liberación). In brief, with the entire so-called "opposition" in Havana.

You would show up, just like that, without further introduction, and they would welcome you?
It was very strange, because every time I showed up before them, they would greet me with open arms. I was someone new, who could expand their movement toward the rest of the country. All of those delegations asked me for some kind of support, to establish branches in the province of Ciego de Ávila and Camagüey. The Committee for Human Rights already had a branch in Ciego de Ávila, it had been one of the first counterrevolutionary organizations and it apparently had members throughout the country — you know, a handful of people here and there — and all of them were anxiously looking for collaborators. I was delighted to do it, I gave them the support they asked for, on behalf of State Security.

It was a time of very intense labor, when we founded the delegations for the Cuban Christian Democratic Movement, the Maceo Movement, and continued supporting the Cuban Committee for Human Rights. There was a time, between 1992 and 1994, when I got to be the director of all these organizations in Ciego de Ávila.

How many members were under your leadership?
There were 11 members in the delegation for the Cuban Christian Democratic Movement. Eight out of those 11 members were trying to leave the country and, in fact, they're not in Cuba at the moment. Of the remaining three, I later discovered that one of them was an agent who was working for us. The same was true in other

movements. The group that had the most members was the Cuban Committee for Human Rights, with something like 15 or 20 people. All of them left the country during those years. The counterrevolutionaries that make up the organization today are new members.

Enrique Blanco Rodríguez

Representative and spokesperson for the counterrevolutionary organization known as Independent and Democratic Cuba (Cuba Independiente y Democrática, CID), headed by Hubert Matos Benítez.

In the 1990s, he created the so-called Operation Liborio, with the aim of sending medicines to counterrevolutionaries and their families in Cuba, an activity that continues to this day.

He has ties to leaders of counterrevolutionary organizations on the island, particularly with Roberto de Miranda Hernández, of the "Independent" Teachers Association of Cuba, whom he supplies with medicines and money.

What things would they do to "score points" within the movement?
In 1994, an operation was carried out in the province, because the anti-government signs were getting out of hand and there were violent plans in the making. One of those counterrevolutionaries, José Carlos Morgado Hernández, told me they were going to bomb the electrical registers in the provincial capital, Ciego de Ávila. He even invited me to see the places they were going to bomb. I remember getting on the back of his bicycle and he went about showing me, one by one, the places they were most probably going to sabotage. He showed me the electrical register located on Simon Reyes Street, between Independence and Libertad, one of the busiest zones in the city. I was shocked. By the details he was giving me, it was obvious they were really preparing themselves for this. State Security had to intervene. All of them were arrested, including me. Of course, that "repressive action taken by the Castro regime" was immediately denounced in *Disidente* magazine, published in Puerto Rico.

How long were you detained for?
Six or seven days.

Did they find the explosives?
They never found them, although they suspected they were going
to be home-made. They had to take swift action in any event. It
was clear they were willing to do anything to attract attention. The
Cuban Committee for Human Rights made me leave the group,
because they got quite a scare. They immediately published a
communiqué disassociating themselves from the sabotage plans,
which was signed by Jesús Alberto Sotuyo Zamora and Roxana
Valdivia Castilla. The operation was carried out well, and my prestige was left intact. I still have a handwritten declaration, in a center
page of a school notebook, where one of the members of the Cuban Committee for Human Rights accuses Pedro Argüelles Morán,
who is now in prison, of being the one responsible for the anti-
government signs that were put up in Ciego de Ávila. He did it in a
shameless manner, as well.

*What ties did the Cuban-American National Foundation have
with these people?*
At the time, the public stance of the Foundation was very aggressive. The instructions were received through the radio — as we
know there are more than a thousand hours devoted to anti-Cuban broadcasts a week — and these called on Cubans to practice civil disobedience. I remember the slogans perfectly well: "Cuban, rebel!", "Cuban, protest, put up banners, sabotage…"

Do you remember one voice in particular?
That of Ninoska Pérez. The station *Independent and Democratic
Cuba* was also constantly exhorting members of the military to
rebel. The extremely few members of the "opposition" groups, all
of whom were of a very low moral caliber and whose main interest
was in making enough noise to be given a visa to the United States,
all realized what the instructions were about: violent action. After
the operation and others that frustrated attacks on the population
— many of these terrorist designs were neutralized while still in an

embryonic stage — their tactics changed, or, at the very least, their discourse changed. They went from aggressive language to pacifistic blather, they began drafting documents, petitions, demands…

What did you do then?
I was involved with the Cuban Christian Democratic Movement and they invited me to join the so-called Cuban Council, which I didn't join, on instructions from State Security.

Center for a Free Cuba

The so-called Center for a Free Cuba, based in Washington D.C., was founded by counterrevolutionary Frank Calzón in October of 1997, with the explicit aim of working toward the overthrow of the Cuban Revolution.

The Center for a Free Cuba carries out its anti-Cuban programs with funding from the U.S. Agency for International Development (USAID) and the National Endowment for Democracy (NED), as well as from private donations.

In October of 1997, in order to carry out its subversive plans against Cuba, the organization received more than 200,000 dollars as private donations from the Cuban-American community, 400,000 dollars from USAID and 15,000 from the NED. In the year 2000, it was given a budget of 1,450,000 dollars by USAID to execute its plans, and in 2002, it received another 2,249,709 dollars from the same agency.

All of its programs have been aimed at spreading counterrevolutionary propaganda in Cuba with regard to a supposed political transition and stimulating a market economy, as well as giving support to internal counterrevolutionary groups and encouraging the international community to play an active role in the promotion of subversive activities on the island.

The material aid given to the counterrevolutionary groups has included personal computers, laptops, typewriters, fax machines, photocopiers, shortwave radios, cameras, tape recorders and other office supplies, as well as medicine, food and clothing.

I continued with my trips to Havana to visit the counterrevolutionaries. In March of 1995, the Cuban newspaper *Granma* published a document that Joseph Sullivan, the head of the U.S. Interests Section at the time, had sent to the U.S. State Department. It described the corruption within the Cuban Committee for Human Rights, with regard to the sale of endorsements for visas to leave the country. There, I found myself involved in an incident that exemplifies how corrupt the Committee was.

What happened?
I had met a family from La Guajira district, in Ciego de Ávila. The head of the household, Gabriel Martín Ferras, was in jail, serving a nine or ten year sentence. Among the instructions I had received from the Committee was that of visiting the jails and giving the inmates a bit of sugar, some ground cereal… And, of course, to try to gather information that we could later use in the enemy radio broadcasts. Martín Ferras' son, Eber, approached me and told me he wanted to leave the country. "No problem," I told him, "I'll recommend you and you can leave. You're the son of a prisoner." At the time, I could make those recommendations because I had contacts in the U.S. Interests Section, thanks to my ties to Aida Valdés Santana, leader of the Cuban Committee for Human Rights. She could get people out of the country through the Interests Section's refugee program. She had told me, "Recommend anyone who wants to leave the country, and they can leave."

What does Felipe Alexis Morejón do to try and eliminate me as leader of the counterrevolution in Ciego de Ávila? He travels to Havana and takes the form I had given Eber to Gustavo Arcos, and tells the president of the Committee that I had charged him for the service. First he tells him I charged him 2,000 Cuban pesos, then that it was actually 5,000, and then that it was 10,000. Of course, I hadn't charged him a cent, but because of what had been published in *Granma*, he took advantage of that to try and discredit me…In other words, he was using against me what they knew was absolutely true: that many of the "opposition" leaders were in fact mobsters who used their ties to the Interests Section to get rich.

How many endorsements did you give?
Many, always in consultation with my superiors. In a sense, it was doing something morally right in an immoral context to recommend someone you knew was not a member of the "opposition", but rather wanted to emigrate to the United States for family or economic interests, and had no chance of obtaining a visa from the United States through the regular channels.

What happened to Aida Valdés Santana?
She was expelled from the Cuban Committee for Human Rights, because she had made a fortune selling fraudulent endorsements. They had used the same argument against me, to try to discredit my leadership in Ciego de Ávila, because I was the person who could mobilize people, who got instructions from Havana and set down the law about what could be done, because I worked to get rid of the practice of putting up signs, of sabotage, to move towards monitoring human rights violations. I turned them into distributors of the UN Universal Declaration of Human Rights, which is, after all, a document ratified by Cuba, and it is not illegal to carry that document. Even though, for me, it was a time of great tension within the Committee, after the accusation of corruption published by *Granma* there was a period of calm. The whole business of visa endorsements came to an end, for the crooks in the "opposition" and the refugee program office as well. The Americans found themselves backed up against the wall, and had to start granting visas to those wishing to leave through the regular channels. They couldn't show the world that there were victims of political persecution in Cuba. Since we were partners in "misfortune", State Security asked me to strengthen my ties to Aida Valdés Santana, who wanted to go on with the "struggle" and was putting together a trade union organization: the Cuban Workers Coordinator. I went on to lead this movement in the central region of the country, in Sancti Spíritus, Ciego de Ávila, Camagüey, Santa Clara and part of Las Tunas.

If you weren't working, how did you support yourself?
I was making a living out of this, of course. Although, when I was in

Ciego de Ávila, the money being sent from Havana, home of the "sacred cows", was a very modest sum.

You were also involved in the creation of the Cuban Christian Democratic Party?

Yes. Parties with one or two members, often factions that had broken off from other organizations, where everyone wanted to be the leader, this was something you saw everyday. One day in June, I was here in Havana and was called on by María Valdés Rosado, along with Jesús Rafael Castillo Álvarez, a lawyer from the Agramonte Movement (Corriente Agramontista) led by René Gómez Manzano. They invited me to read a series of documents and to give them an opinion, based on my knowledge of the law. The meeting took place at 264 Jesús María Street. All of a sudden, I found myself reading the charter of the Cuban Christian Democratic Party, and some days later I ended up in the middle of a State Security operation. I was taken to Villa Marista with the other three members of this brand-new party of the "masses". Of course, I behaved just like the other counterrevolutionaries, or worse: I kicked the door, demanded aspirin, made a big scene. It was a huge shock for my family. It was the first time my mother disowned me. She told me she never wanted to hear from me again. It was terrible.

Why was that meeting broken up?

Oh, because when that famous little party was inaugurated, the first action on the agenda was that of breaking into the Argentine embassy. You're lucky to hear the true version of events, because, until now, there have been a number of different versions. The four of us who had founded the party were going to walk into the Argentine embassy with official passes, and, once inside, we would refuse to leave, unless they granted us political asylum. The aim was to create a scandal. The problem was that there were disagreements during the meeting. I said I would not participate for the very simple reason that if the Argentines went insane and granted us the visas, I would be stuck. I didn't want to leave under any circumstances. I told them they could count on my support, but from the outside, through the press. In the end, the intervention of the Cuban authorities prevented an act that could have had serious consequences.

When you speak about contacting the press…
To get a scandal going. You know that one thing goes with the other: the foreign press goes after these little scandals like vultures. That's how they get publicized. And don't forget, this was taking place during the so-called crisis of the embassies. Another provocation of that sort had to be avoided.

When did you make direct ties to the U.S. Interests Section?
The Party was founded on June 17 of 1995, and the break-in into the Argentine embassy was going to be carried out in September. It's interesting that when Jesús Rafael Castillo took the Party's charter to have it registered in the Associations Registry of the Ministry of Justice, he told me, "Aleida, the next step to take here is to present the party to the U.S. Interests Section," and I answered, "Listen, that I'm game for." "You're no dummy," he answered, "you won't go into the Argentine embassy, but you'll go to the Interests Section." "They're two very different things," I told him. On the June 20, 1995, at ten in the morning, I walked into the Interests Section for the first time. We were received by Christopher Sibila, who was a CIA official, someone who didn't make an effort to conceal himself. They congratulated us on the creation of the Cuban Christian Democratic Party. When I mentioned I was studying law, he wanted me to meet an official called Charles O. Blaha, who they told me was studying the Cuban constitutions. That was my first day in the Interests Section.

How did you get in?
Easily. Castillo had an open pass for two. We arrived and went in. We presented our ID cards at the Cuban post and the doors of the Interests Section were already open for Agent Vilma.

That was the first time you went in. When was the last?
March 14, 2003, the day I participated in the Journalistic Ethics Workshop, in the home of James Cason.

How many times did you go into the U.S. Interests Section?
I lost count. The arrival of Robin Diane Meyer, as second secretary of the Interests Section for political and economic affairs, was very important for me. She was very active, to the extent of calling herself "the godmother of the opposition." She would take care of

everyone, she would travel through the provinces, she would hand out literature. She was the one who asked me to distance myself from the Cuban Workers Coordinator, headed by Aida Valdés Santana, and to found a trade union organization. She felt that my talent was in uniting workers. I tried to hold her off a bit, to gain time: I told her that I had to think about it, that perhaps I would do it later on, that I was still young, that it required a lot of dedication… Nevertheless, from that point on, she started handing me trade union literature: how to put together a union, how to direct a meeting. She was paving the road toward what she had in mind for me without hiding it one bit. This woman had many meetings with me. During the two years she was in Cuba, we saw each other around 100 times.

These meetings were always held at the Interests Section?
Sometimes they were held in the Interests Section, at others they were held in her home on 7th Avenue and 66th Street, in Miramar (a neighborhood of Havana). At other times, she would travel to Ciego de Ávila with the pretext of monitoring the famous Refugee Program. I had already been in contact with her before going to the U.S. Interests Section for the first time. I remember that on one occasion, on June 23, 1995, she showed up in Ciego de Ávila with Victor Vockerodt, who would later become the second secretary. This man had been sent to Cuba by the U.S. State Department to monitor the rafters. I remember they got there on a Thursday, I'll never forget it. At the time, Orson Vila had been arrested in Camagüey, for making political speeches while preaching the bible. His family had refused to have any contact with the U.S. officials, even though the latter wanted to see them. They ended up showing up there. During this visit, Meyer said to me, "Aleida, I've come all this way because I need your help. The only one who can get me to speak to a member of that family is you."

In the midst of all this, I had surgery on both eyes for glaucoma — incidentally, I had to tape millions of reports because I wasn't able to write, and I had to memorize the news to recite it over the phone to Juana Isa. In the end, I went out to look for someone from the family on the back of a bicycle, so as not to attract attention, and they went in a rented car. In other words, they didn't come in a diplomatic vehicle, but as though they were mere tourists. I finally found the person, and it was very funny to see the two Americans hiding behind a tree, in the dark of night — it must have been around nine — so they could meet with the family through a kind of ambush, and so no one could catch them in the act.

They spent that day in Ciego de Ávila. Meyer ate and took a bath at my house. Victor climbed a tree in the backyard and knocked down some coconuts. She wanted to have rum and coconut juice and I told her, "No, please, if you get sick here you're going to get me in a real mess with State Security." And the best part about it is that what I was saying was true.

Just look at the level of intimacy this woman was trying to develop with me: I had first met her on March 16, 1995, and three months later she was already staying over at my place. I met her at a gathering they had put together for members of the "opposition", at the home of an Interests Section official. The vast majority of the "opposition" members who were there that day are now living in the United States.

Did the U.S. Interests Section officials ask for any information in particular?

The oil issue was always an interest of Robin Diane Meyer's, from the very first to the very last day that we saw each other. She was always interested to know about the oil deposits and about tourism, which was already standing out as the industry that was getting us out of the economic crisis. Don't forget I was living in an area that was being developed for tourism. She, and those who came after her, went crazy over information about tourism. They wanted to know the number of workers in the industry, and of those workers, how many were men and how many were women. How old they were, what political affiliations they had, if they were all Party members, if there were many retired members of the Armed Forces and the Ministry of the Interior, how many visitors the facilities had, what food they offered, what the workers ate there, if they had transportation, what salaries they earned.

During those meetings, aside from handing them the denunciations we had compiled between one visit and another, they would ask about education and about other issues, such as the metallurgical industry, the sugar industry. They would suggest the topics of discussion. That didn't change much throughout the years. Last December, Susan Archer, second secretary for political affairs, asked me to write about child labor in Cuba. We had to carry out an investigation into secondary school students working in the countryside, the ages, the number of students per classroom and school, the agricultural activities they were carrying out, the supposed salaries they should have earned. This was done to put together a statistical analysis aimed at slandering the work-study system, and to present it as a kind of child labor system.

During that meeting, she gave me a printed copy of the Statistical Yearbook of Cuba and later on she gave me a digital copy. She warned me that I couldn't rely on it much because Cuba published year-old statistics and made reports using the numbers it found convenient. She also wanted to know about people's opinions, why people went on marches and the like. For example, Robin Diane Meyer couldn't understand why, during those difficult years of 1995 and 1996, people still showed up for the marches, if, according to us, the Cuban people did not support Castro. She would ask me about this, and give me speeches about the unions. And I was always putting it off. We ended our meetings with the same words on more than one occasion: "Hey, what about the unions, when are you going to get started?" And I would say, "A little later on." Two years went by like this, until she was expelled from the country in August of 1996. That's when Timothy P. Brown arrived.

Tell us how a "dissident" can obtain an open pass to go into the Interests Section.

I obtained a pass to the Interests Section in 1995, and that gave me free access to the offices, on any day or at any time I wanted to go there. I could take three other people with me. I still have that pass. Of course, you have to earn the pass. There was a time when we had to work on my front as a "dissident" and to try, through contacts and many, many meetings with them, to strengthen our façade there and make inroads.

How did you strengthen that façade? What are the prerequisites to be considered a "dissident" by the officials of the Interests Section?

Persisting a lot, paying them many visits, telling them what they wanted to hear, procuring the information they requested. You can hardly imagine how hard my State Security official worked. They would ask me for information on the oil industry, and my official would hand me a folder: "Give them this." And they would go away very satisfied. Well, that was our case, because in the case of those who have now been sentenced, they would be asked for the same things and they were capable of writing and saying anything. They're where they are for a reason.

Satisfying these prerequisites also means being constantly invited to their work lunches and breakfasts, to their receptions, and, of course, to meetings with U.S. political figures who visit the country. Even when they come for other reasons, the officials at the Interests Section always organize a meeting with the "dissidents".

I remember that in July of 1995, when Anne W. Patterson came to Cuba — she was the undersecretary of state for Caribbean affairs — we held a meeting that just happened to be attended by Agent Tania and Reynaldo Cozano, Félix Bonne Carcassés, Georgina de las Mercedes Corvo Jiménez, Ruben Ruíz Armenteros, and yours truly, Aleida Godínez. This meeting was held at Robin Diane Meyer's home, on 7th Avenue and 66th Street. It took place on July 18, 1995, and as far as I recall, it was the very first time that a U.S. official openly spoke to us about providing material aid. Patterson asked us what we needed without beating around the bush. I recall that the answer was typically Cuban: "Well, look, when Napoleon was waging war, someone asked him what he needed to win it. He answered that only three things were needed: money, money and more money, and that's also what we need, money, because without money and without resources we can't do anything." After that meeting, money did start showing up, lots of it.

Why did you move to Havana?
I couldn't continue living in Ciego de Ávila. I had serious personal problems. My mom couldn't understand my counterrevolutionary behavior and I had to leave because it was hell living there. Of course, when I moved out here, my ties to the U.S. Interests Section grew stronger and stronger. We would have a meeting a month at the very least, when I would deliver all of the information I had gathered, all of the denunciations of human rights violations and all of the information they were asking for.

Do you recall one incident in particular from that time?
After they had expelled Robin Diane Meyer, we had contact with an official named Ryan M. Dooley, from the political section. He was so overbearing that some of the counterrevolutionaries got together and sent a letter to the State Department, complaining about his attitude. He would mistreat people. He would tell us we were showing up without bringing him what he wanted. I had a big fight with him. I was in the office of the consul for refugees, who was also asking for information.

What happened with Dooley?
I'm sitting in the office of the consul and he tells me to wait there. He gets on the phone and speaks with another American official in English, and tells him I'm sitting there in his office. That was in September. The man tells him to ask me to come back on October 18 to meet with him. That's what I did. But once I'm inside

the Interests Section, the hours go by and the man doesn't come down to see me. At noon he shows up and asks me, rather rudely, what I want. I told him that I didn't want anything, that I was there because he had sent for me. Immediately, he wanted to know what I had brought, and I told him that I hadn't brought anything. Do you know what that man said to me? Never to forget that if we went there, it was to deliver information. I bit down on my tongue, and answered that I'd never had the pleasure of speaking to him before, and "if you don't tell me what sort of information you want, I can't bring it to you." He was in Havana for something like five months. He mistreated a lot of people, he was very ill-mannered, and then that letter was sent to the State Department. I didn't take part in that because I was in Ciego de Ávila, but had I been there I would have signed that letter to have him kicked out, because he was a real jerk.

At the time, you were putting together your own party?
In July of 1998, at the request of my comrades in State Security, I founded the National Cuban Opposition Foundation (Fundación Nacional Cubano Opositora). I was already settled in Havana and had close ties to a number of counterrevolutionary leaders, who helped me with this project.

In truth, I could do everything from home. On August 23, 1999, we submitted a letter to the Office of Public Services of the Council of State, in which we asked for the release of a number of prisoners and the legalization of the human rights organizations. From that point on, we started gathering signatures and organizing ourselves in Havana. Though I was fairly well known because of my work in Ciego de Ávila, I needed to create my own space in the capital to maintain and to strengthen my ties to the Interests Section. From this point on, the toughest time began for me with the Interests Section, the time I grew very close to the main officials there and I began to receive money, handfuls of money.

Frank Calzón (I)

Until 1997, Frank Calzón, a citizen of the United States — though Cuban by birth — was the official director of the Cuban programs run by the counterrevolutionary organization Freedom House.

In July of 1995, U.S. citizens Adams Rosh Davison and George Erwin Sledge arrived in Cuba, sent by Calzón, with instructions to establish contact with leaders of counterrevolutionary groups and to supply them with medicine, food and money.

In January of 1996, on Calzón's request, John Sweeney of the Heritage Foundation traveled to Cuba as a tourist, to provide financial aid to various mercenaries, one of whom was Martha Beatriz Roque, who received a sum of 500 dollars on this occasion.

In April of 1996, Jozsed Szajer, a Hungarian dissident and leader of the parliamentary group known as Fides, traveled to Cuba upon a similar request made by Calzón, to meet with the heads of counterrevolutionary organizations and to provide them with money, tape recorders and computer disks, all of them sent by Calzón. In August of 1997, American union activist David Norman Dorn was arrested in Cuba; although he had traveled to the country as a tourist, he delivered money to counterrevolutionaries at the request of Freedom House.

This emissary had received very precise instructions from Calzón about how to behave in Cuba so as not to attract the attention of the authorities. Dorn confessed to carrying out acts of espionage in Cuba, taking photographs of economic targets in Havana, Santiago de Cuba and Moa (in the province of Holguín). The authorities also seized from him a list of the counterrevolutionaries he had contacted and receipts for the money handed over to them.

Could you tell us about how you began to receive funding?
In February of 1999, an American named Robert Emmet got in touch with some relatives of mine — remember that no one could call my place in Ciego de Ávila, because my mom was furious and didn't want to know a thing about Miami, nor receive calls.

This man was a messenger of Frank Calzón, from the Center for a Free Cuba. He brought a package the size of a sofa, full of medicines, toiletries, radios, flashlights, cameras, everything. He asked me to take it to Raúl Rivero, whom I knew already. He also wanted to go to the Literacy Museum in Ciudad Libertad, but he asked my advice on how to dress, because he didn't want to attract attention. He walked around in shorts, dressed up as an American tourist. I told him this, and he put on a pair of pants and barely opened his mouth.

He gave me money, in two parts. I remember that every time he was going to give me money, he would excuse himself to go to the bathroom, because he carried it in a moneybelt inside his pants. He gave me 500 dollars in cash: first 300, then 200 more, afterwards. He told me he wanted me to buy a motorcycle, because he'd seen me arrive on a bicycle. He also sent 100 dollars to Raúl Rivero, a camera, rolls of film, pens…

Who was this man?
He introduced himself as a librarian. The "independent libraries" project was being developed. He was also interested in the "independent" press, and how it was coming along.

Why did he want to go the Literacy Museum?
I'm still asking myself that question. He wanted to know what education was like in Cuba; he came with the idea of going there and asked me to take him. At the museum, he asked for very precise details about how the literacy campaign had been carried out. If he wasn't faking it, he was very moved by what he saw. He even told me that literacy had been one of Castro's great achievements. I have a photo with him taken that day, on February 24. He wanted us to find out where the main leaders of the Revolution lived and take photographs of the outside of their homes. That's why he gave me the camera.

Did he mention one leader in particular?
Yes, Carlos Lage. People abroad were saying that Lage could replace Fidel.

Frank Calzón (II)

In June of the year 2000, Romanian citizen Cornel Ivanciuc and Polish citizen Anna Krystyna traveled to Cuba after meeting in Washington with Freedom House, the U.S. Agency for International Development (USAID) and the State Department. The aim of these meetings was to study aid for "independent libraries" in Cuba. During their stay in the United States, Calzón instructed them to travel to Cuba as emissaries. They brought material aid for a group of counterrevolutionaries in Cuba, a mission which was organized and funded by Freedom House.

In November of the year 2000, Lithuanian citizens Anda Celma and Vladis Abols received money and instructions from Frank Calzón and Robert Pontichera (program director at Freedom House) to travel to Cuba and obtain information on the situation of the opposition groups. For this mission, they were given a list of individuals to contact and asked to give a lecture in Cuba on the Transition Process in Lithuania.

These emissaries were contacted in Lithuania by Virginia Sullivan, a public relations expert from the Naturalization Bureau of Lithuania, who deals with the work agreements made between Freedom House and the Bureau.

In January of 2001, Czech citizens Ivan Pilip and Jan Bubenik traveled to Cuba as tourists and declared, on being detained by the authorities, that they had received instructions and funding from Freedom House, through the intermediary Robert Pontichera.

Pontichera paid all of the expenses for the trip in order to send material and financial aid to mercenaries living in the island and to obtain information on the political, economic and social situation in Cuba. He gave them a list with the names and addresses of the individuals to be contacted and 1,400 dollars to cover expenses, as well as a laptop computer with various accessories and floppy and compact disks for the people they would be meeting with. He also told them to take safety precautions in order to avoid being discovered by the Cuban authorities.

What did he tell you about Frank Calzón?
He came on his behalf. He gave me the numbers where I could

reach him, including his home number, and told me I could call him every Sunday. I memorized Calzón's number: 703-998-8384. Some months later, Calzón started sending me money regularly, through different messengers.

Who were these messengers? What were their names?
For instance, in August of 1999, he sent me 800 dollars with Rita Llanesa Campos, a nun from the Social Sisters order. She lived in Camagüey and, later on, she moved to Havana, and I would go and see her at the branch of the Order on 27th and L Streets, in Vedado. These remittances of money began to be systematic. She told me that she went to Miami and Washington every year, and that I could send Frank anything I wanted through her.

The counterrevolutionary Jesús Yanes Pelletier also brought me 200 dollars sent by Frank, on October 27, 1999 and November 2, 1999. He also brought me two wrist watches, a radio, office materials, medicine…

Did Calzón ask for anything in particular?
Not through Rita. Only on one occasion, over the phone, he asked me to send him the magazine *Vitral*, published by the Diocese of Pinar del Río, which Calzón and others in Miami praise for its stance against the Revolution. We would use a mailbox of ours and send him other things through it. He is very cautious. He doesn't trust anyone. He doesn't give out his phone numbers, or any information about himself, not a thing. He made an exception with me. We were in touch with one another until this past April 2. His last dispatch of money came on March 16. He sent me 100 dollars.

What was the last thing you spoke with him about?
He told me over the phone, "Listen, a 'cousin' of mine is heading there…" That was how he would refer to the "mules" who brought things. From that first encounter with the American onward, he never stopped sending me money. Never.

Do you recall him sending you other things?
Yes. In August of the year 2000, Douglas Schimmel came to Cuba; he was an American tourist. He came with a list of people he had

to deliver money to. He was detained by the authorities and he confessed to having met on July 24 , 2000 with Frank Calzón, who had given him the list of counterrevolutionaries who were to receive the money.

He was also told to take safety precautions so as not be discovered. Schimmel explained that he had held on to the money given to him by Calzón until he met all of the interested parties, with the idea of distributing it among those he liked best. The last day of his visit to Cuba, he decided to distribute it among Elizardo Sánchez, Raúl Rivero and Hilda Molina. He did not include Martha Beatriz, Gustavo Arcos, Osvaldo Payá and Rafael León Rodríguez. He also excluded Jesús Yanes Pelletier. He said they already had money and that they had also received medicine and other items.

Did you have any ties to the Cuban-American National Foundation?
I was present at a number of incidents linking counterrevolutionaries to the Cuban-American National Foundation and the Interests Section. For instance, on July 16, 1999 I attended the "fast" led by Oscar Elías Biscet. Michael Kozak, who was the head of the Interests Section at the time, showed up with a package containing medicines, juices, cooking oil and soap. During a conversation, Kozak and Biscet agreed that the latter would visit the U.S. Interests Section three days afterwards to send a fax to the Cuban-American National Foundation, in which he would report on the "fast". That same day, and in front of the American official, another counterrevolutionary, Ángel Moya, worked himself up and proposed launching a call to the Heads of State who would be attending the Ibero-American Summit that was about to be held in Havana. The aim was to get them to demand from the President of Cuba an "end to the dictatorship." That whole show, of course, had been cooked up in advance.

Out of curiosity: was there really a fast?
Of course not. People were eating, drinking, preparing chicken broths and the like. Kozak himself contributed to the whole farce.

Again out of curiosity: did the Americans instruct you to get in touch with international institutions in order to promote the actions of "dissidents"?

Look, I myself got in touch with the International Republican Institute. I would send them faxes from the Interests Section asking for medicines, and they would send them to me. The Americans have always offered us their computers, their faxes and all of their means of communication. They made all of that available for us to establish those links. Since this was becoming something very common, they ended up putting together a room with five computers with Internet access, within the consular office. Little by little, they stepped things up.

What does that mean?

They ended up institutionalizing the relationship and giving us instructions in no uncertain terms. They would speak openly about their interest in overthrowing the Cuban government.

Can you prove what you're claiming?

It's all written down, in the documents they would give us. For instance, I have a pamphlet called Resource Guide for the Transition. It's a manual, in two parts. First, they explain what a transition is and what must be done in the social and military spheres. The second part is a list of all the organizations that support countries at a "pre-transition" stage, and of those organizations that support countries at a "post-transition" stage. You can find telephone and fax numbers there, the names of people to contact. In short, everything. Robin Diane Meyer gave it to me as something of great importance and top secret, that I had to memorize and destroy. And, really, it was all so simplistic that it was very useful for my "opposition" work. So much so that I hid it from my own comrades in State Security, afraid that it would get lost.

How so?

After Meyer's visit to my home, State Security conducted a search on me. They warned me that they were coming to my place, because they were doing searches on all the main counterrevolutionary leaders. The dining room had caved in and we had three cubic meters of stone piled up there, to repair the roof. I started shoveling rocks until I was exhausted. I placed the book there and started piling all of the stone on top of it again.

Why did you do this?
It was a kind of Bible, that gathered all of the concepts they wanted to hear. Keeping up those two identities wasn't an easy thing. It's hard to want things to prosper in your country, to love the Revolution, and yet to have to assume a discourse completely foreign to you. I always had the book on hand to draft letters and to make sure to say the right things, during the meetings with American visitors and with representatives of the accredited diplomatic corps in Cuba.

What diplomats did you meet with?
Oh! I had interviews with officials from the embassies of Poland, the Czech Republic, Germany, Belgium, Portugal, Sweden, Holland, Canada, Spain... Some of them were a little more discrete, and would warn us that they had relations with the Cuban government. They wanted the information and they'd be happy to receive it, but they didn't go in over their heads. Others, like the Czechs, the Swedes and the Spanish, were very aggressive with the Cuban government.

At what time did you come into contact with Vicky Huddleston?
As soon as she became the head of the U.S. Interests Section, on September 30, 1999. She had two very clear objectives: to promote the groups internationally and to unite them. She went on like this until she became obsessed with the "Varela" Project. When she realized this project had far too many detractors, mainly among the chief leaders of the organizations, she toned down her language some. She even confided to me that Oswaldo Payá had lied to her.

In what sense?
When Payá informed her of his project, he told Vicky that he was going to present it in December. Nevertheless, without consulting

her, he made it public two days before the visit by former President Jimmy Carter, in May of 2002. From that point on, she began to pay attention to other "opposition" projects, like the Assembly to Promote Civil Society in Cuba (Asamblea para Promover la Sociedad Civil en Cuba).

What was the objective?
She began to talk more energetically about uniting the common elements of the organizations. In her speeches, she would say she felt happy about the strength of the opposition and of the unions, and that, despite the fact that there were different points of view, some views were also shared, and agreements could be reached. The joint declaration on the Cotonú Treaty shows that people got to exchange ideas. Payá was kept out of the loop. I'll tell you something I was told by those who attended the meeting of counterrevolutionary leaders with Vicente Fox. It was a very brief meeting, and when Fox left — Foreign Minister Jorge Castañeda had stayed behind — Payá took the seat where the Mexican president had been sitting. They say that Payá said, as a joke, "I'm sitting here because a president was sitting here just now, and I am the future president of Cuba." I don't know how he was spared a beating, because there was much rivalry there. Payá, with his "Varela" Project, and Martha Beatriz Roque, with her Assembly to Promote Civil Society in Cuba, they can't stand the sight of one another.

Vicky tried to reduce this rivalry that had been building up for some time, by trying to strengthen the Cuban Council. I argued with her because she wanted me to sign up to join this front, and I told her no, because the Cuban Council was going to end up in the Refugee Program, and I wanted to continue fighting in Cuba. And that's how it went down.

What organization were you representing at the time?
I was representing many counterrevolutionary groups. Since February of 2001, I was directing the National "Independent" Workers Confederation of Cuba (Confederación Obrera Nacional Independiente), with seven members on the national executive and delegations in nine different provinces; and the "Independent" In-

stitute of Socio-Economic Labor Research (Instituto de Investigaciones Sociolaborales Económicas Independiente), attached to the Workers Confederation, which has two associated projects:

the Institute and the Press Agency, which came to be directed by Alicia Zamora Labrada, who joined this group on the request of State Security to lend me support in my work.

Alicia Zamora Labrada

Who were their representatives in Miami?

That's a good question, get ready to hear some of these names. By the end of the year 2000, I began to establish ties with René Laureano Díaz Gónzalez, of the Miami-based terrorist organization called the Trade Union Federation of Cuban Electrical, Gas and Water Plants in Exile. He asked me to put together a delegation in Cuba, to oppose the Central Organization of Cuban Trade Unions (CTC). He would also send me money and propaganda put together in Florida.

Thanks to my position in the counterrevolutionary milieu, as well as my work with René Laureano, I made ties with Calixto Campos Corona, another notorious terrorist, and to Frank Hernández Trujillo, from the Dissidence Support Group (Grupo de Apoyo a la Disidencia, GAD), who has known ties to the U.S. special services. Also with Manuel Tamargo and Nelson Rodríguez, both of whom are from the GAD; Rosa Berre, from *Cubanet*; José Rivero, from *Carta de Cuba*; Juana Isa, Rolando Cartaza, José Luís Ramos and Amado Gil, all of them from *Radio "Martí"*; Angelica Mora, from the *Voice of America*; Jackie Figueroa, from *Channel 23* in Miami; and Gabriel Salvia, from the group known as Unwavering for Cuba's Freedom and Democracy (Plantados hasta la Libertad y la Democracia en Cuba).

Federated Union of Electrical, Gas and Water Plants of Cuba in Exile (FSPEGA)

Created by René Laureano Díaz González in the late 1990s.

Its other top leaders include Calixto Campos Corona (alias "Callin"), vice president, and Joel Brito.

Its offices are at 7175 SW 8th St., Suites 213-215, Miami FL 33144.

Its public face is that of a trade union organization whose mission is to support the establishment of independent unions and to provide financial aid to counterrevolutionaries in Cuba. In reality, it also plans terrorist attacks and attempts to carry them out.

It supplies money and computers to "dissidents" in Cuba. It also publishes a bi-monthly magazine, *Lux,* which often includes articles by various "independent journalists".

How did your relationship with Martha Beatriz Roque begin?
I knew her, but I never had a work relationship with her. She's a very gruff and difficult person, who's always insinuating her superiority and doesn't worry about the image she projects, something that Payá, on the other hand, is obsessed with. My relationship with her began precisely because of the tensions between them. One of the people closest to Payá, Rafael Ernesto Ávila Pérez, invented a project which he named the Opposition Resistance Platform (Plataforma de Resistencia de la Oposición, PRECIO), and he came to see me to get legal advice. It was crazy: I told him they were going to tear it apart in no time, that who could think of naming a party PRECIO (the Spanish word for "price"), that people were going to go around joking that the opposition had a price... In truth, it was a movement aimed at competing with Martha's Assembly, so I showed up at her house without prior notice — you had to ask for an interview with her. I knocked on her door and I was lucky enough to have her open it. I told her to read the document, that it had strong points and weak points, but that, in my opinion, it wasn't something that favored us. In short, I showed her loyalty. That's how the PRECIO platform ended up crushed and ridiculed.

Some time later, she called me up and invited me to her place, saying she had to talk to me. She told me that the Platform did not specify when the transition in Cuba was going to take place, or how it was going to be, whether blood was going to be shed or not. Remember that before creating the Assembly she founded the Cuban Institute of "Independent" Economists, which had a Statistics Office, responsible for surveying all of the "opposition" groups. It was the office that granted "legal" endorsement.

We have a press dispatch here that claims you were the right hand of Martha Beatriz. Is that so?
Yes, she started giving me important tasks. On July 10, 2002, the Permanent Trade Union Commission was founded within her Assembly, and she asked me to be president. At the time, the Assembly began to be organized into Commissions: the Press Commission, the Permanent Trade Union Commission, Public Relations, Coordination and Organization, Human Rights, Social Denunciations, and Historical Issues. Some didn't ever get to meet because of a lack of leadership. One fine day, Martha told me I had to take part in all of the commissions, because I was the fourth most important person in the group, and I told her to sign me up. Before directing the Trade Union Commission, they made me a member of the Public Relations Commission, which was in charge of visiting the diplomatic missions and presenting the Assembly project to them. I paid a visit to the embassies of Holland, Italy and Poland to carry out this task. The visit to the Spanish embassy was on October 31, 2002, at 11:00 in the morning. The meeting took place in the office of Ambassador Jesús García, who was very kind to us and even offered us use of the diplomatic pouch to send or receive whatever material we wanted.

Did you reap any economic benefit from these gatherings?
On October 29, 2002, at 11:30 in the morning, we met with the officials of the embassy of Holland. The ambassador gave Martha 1,500 dollars, as a first donation to distribute among people

affected by the hurricanes that had passed through Pinar del Río. We have the documents: Martha gave 100 Cuban pesos each (equivalent to four U.S. dollars) to seven of the victims.

We also visited the German embassy. The aim of these meetings was to bring them up to date on the work of the Assembly and to ask them for money. Martha was given a large quantity of clothing there, which was supposedly for the victims of the hurricanes, but never reached any of them. Martha distributed it among some of her friends, including Alicia Zamora Labrada, who got a very expensive sweater that had belonged to the German ambassador.

How was your relationship with her?
Actually, I did what I pleased. I would go to meetings only if I wanted to. Of course, if I didn't go to one meeting, it was because I went to three others. I always sought her respect: without yielding, but without offering too much resistance either. I managed to earn her trust. She would pay for my taxi, in dollars, to go to and from her house. I started living well. I was the one who was most well off out of all the people who worked under her. I started to become indispensable and she began to share many secrets with me. Where the money was coming from, for instance, who was sending it, the strategy of not keeping it all in her home… She ended up giving me the password for her personal computer so I could download her e-mails and keep her people informed.

Who was sending money to Martha Beatriz?
Frank Hernández Trujillo, Ángel Quesada, Ángel Hernández Carrillo, Silvia Iriondo, who was heavily involved in the kidnapping of Elián González. This woman, who calls herself a Catholic and a defender of human rights, has been sending me threatening messages, telling me she's going to kill me. Her organization was one of the co-sponsors of the demonstration held in Miami on March 29, the only one in the world held in favor of the war on Iraq, and the war against Cuba: "Iraq now, Cuba later," this was what the participants were saying.

Did you ever get to witness an exchange between Martha Beatriz and Silvia Iriondo?

They were very close. This past March 15, we were at the fast organized by Martha following the first arrests of the "dissidents", and she said to me, "I have to call Silvia and I'm going to put you in touch with her, because really, honey, you're my right hand, and no one knows what's going to happen here…" Up to that point, my relations with Iriondo had been through third parties. Martha introduced me to Silvia, who said, "Aleida, I can finally hear your voice." Of course, this left no doubts about her ties to leaders of the emigré community who are deeply involved in subversive plans against Cuba. Martha always denied having those ties. After that conversation, Martha herself told me that Silvia sent her a thousand dollars a month — which was a lie, because she was sending her much more. She also told me that ten members — all of them millionaires — of Women Against Repression (Mujeres ante la Represion, MAR), the organization led by Silvia, were funding her organization, and she didn't want the money to go away. And it came, just as they had said: 1,300 dollars.

This time, the money came straight to you?
Yes.

How was it sent?
Through Western Union, in several parts. That's how we got the proof we wanted, because we had no documental evidence for the rest of the money sent, although we knew it was coming, judging by her standard of living. When they put her in jail, I took command of the Assembly, until April 2, the night before the trials held on April 3. I was there up to the last moment, until I came out and said that I was Vilma.

Martha Beatriz has repeatedly denied having worked for the Interests Section…
Yes, but she was completely dependent on them. I remember a lunch organized by Martha on August 30, 2002, at Vicky Huddleston's residence...

Martha organized lunches at the official residence of the head of the U.S. Interests Section? How was that possible?
The justification was that her home had all of the necessary conditions, and we wouldn't be bothered there. On this occasion, the reason for the lunch was to show Vicky the Assembly's gratitude for the work she had done in Cuba. It was the end of her posting here, and she been named the new ambassador to Mali.

Martha introduced the members of the Assembly, and a number of them spoke openly about the need for funding and the support they had received from the officials of the Interests Section, and from Vicky in particular. There were all sorts of beverages at the lunch, and breaded shrimp, lobster, pizza, ham sandwiches, roast pork…And, to top it off, they handed each one of us a bag with radios, flashlights and other gifts. But because there were more bags than participants, a scuffle broke out as everyone scrambled to make off with as many gifts as possible. It was one of the most repugnant spectacles I have ever had to endure, and you can imagine how many of them I had to witness during all these years.

And Mister Cason?
He arrived in Cuba on September 9, 2002 and was meeting with the counterrevolutionaries a week later. Before making contact with the official authorities. He received us in two groups, on the 17th and 18th. I was in the second group. As was customary, radios and books were handed out, and his wife, who was very kind to us, was especially attentive to all of her guests.

In truth, his "official" presentation was made to us. At that meeting, Cason gave us details of his extremely long curriculum vitae and even made a bad joke: he said he had this very impressive résumé at the age of only 39. He was trying to make his speech a bit less boring, trying to win people over. He was referring to his years in the diplomatic service and everyone was laughing, because no one can serve 30 years in the diplomatic service and be 39 years old — he is actually 59 years old. That sort of thing.

MAR for Cuba

Established in 1994 as a result of the incident involving the tug-boat "13 de Marzo", with the objective of bringing together a group of women with links to the extreme right, many of them wives, widows or close relatives of the counterrevolutionaries that left Cuba at the time of the Revolution's coming to power, or of those who emigrated to the United States in subsequent years.

Its current president is Silvia Iriondo. She left Cuba in 1960. Her father was a member of the infiltration teams sent by the CIA during the early years of the Revolution. Her maiden name was Silvia Goudie Medina; she adopted her husband's last name, that of Andrés Iriondo Olazábal.

MAR for Cuba has its headquarters in Miami and representative branches in New York, New Jersey, Washington and Puerto Rico.

This organization promotes all campaigns against Cuba led by Cuban American right-wing extremists, primarily in the Human Rights Commission at Geneva, at Latin American Summits and during visits of Cuban officials to the United Nations.

They support and stimulate counterrevolutionary movements, calling for civil disobedience. They send financial aid and hundreds of documents in the mail — most of it subversive propaganda — to both private citizens and state institutions in Havana. Their members dress entirely in black to symbolize a constant state of mourning.

MAR for Cuba is part of the group of organizations of the extreme right that make up the so-called Cuban Patriotic Forum (Fórum Patriótico Cubano).

He asked us to introduce ourselves, one by one, and tell him about our main needs. When it was my turn, I spoke about my organization. I said that I had a library on labor issues, but that we had received hardly any books. Not a month passed and I was already receiving two boxes of books from the GAD, sent directly by Frank Hernández Trujillo. He was clearly fulfilling the agreement reached at the meeting with Cason.

He sent books only?
No. Resources started showing up. I asked for a computer, a laptop specifically. A young man showed up some time later and asked me if I was waiting for anything. I answered him, "I'm always waiting for something." And the laptop came, but it was somewhat beat up. Four or five days later, I sent a message to Frank ex- pressing my thanks, but telling him that the laptop wasn't working properly. He told me, "Take it to Gladys Linares, and I'll send you another one." Gladys is a counterrevolutionary who directs the Women's Humanitarian Front (Frente Femenino Humanitario), and she's the "depot" in Cuba for the packages sent by Hernández Trujillo.

But since I had written some reports using that laptop, as a precaution I took a screwdriver, removed the hard-drive and dropped it on the floor. I put it back in and the computer started up like nothing had happened. I took out the hard-drive once again and gave it one hell of a beating. I got an e-mail a month later from Frank, which said: "Aleida, I have the corpse in intensive therapy, but I don't know what's going on with the hard-drive, it's not waking up." Three or four months later, the other laptop arrived, a little beat up as well, but it wasn't anything serious.

Now you didn't have any choice…
I spoke with my official and we agreed to ask for another laptop, to see what happened. I wrote him again and I told him: "Frank, a million thanks, but this one came with a black screen." He said to me, "Listen, that's impossible, that laptop traveled in a diplomatic pouch." He told me to leave it with Gladys, and not to worry. On December 23, 2002, Nicholas J. Giacobbe, the second secretary in charge of culture and the press, called me up and asked me to go to the Interests Section. Nicholas showed up with a box full of packages of paper and a laptop, in its case, strapped over his shoulder. He hands it over to me, and tells me, "Take care of this one, it's the third one Frank has sent. Let's see if we're lucky." If Gladys is the head of the GAD's warehouse in Cuba, Nicholas is the head of supplies at the Interests Section. I could call him up at

10:00 in the morning and tell him I had run out of paper, and two or three hours later he would show up with everything I needed. Of course, they were things that we unfortunately lack in our own state companies.

Did you notice any difference in the treatment you got from Huddleston and from Cason?
There was no difference between the two, except that one was a woman and the other a man. Cason is one of the most aggressive U.S. officials that I have known. The first day that we met, he said he was leaving the doors of his home open to the "opposition" and that he was willing to collaborate, support, finance and serve in whatever was necessary. And he proved it. There were constant lunches, dinners, meetings and press conferences until March 14, when the Workshop on Journalistic Ethics was held there. The fast organized by Martha Beatriz, following the incarceration of Biscet, was pushed ahead by Ricardo Zuniga, the political/economic chief at the Interests Section, who called her up and asked her how long she was going to keep postponing it. They talked about this in front of me. She told me herself, "Honey, I don't have a choice, we're doing it on the 11th." And she told me I was in charge of the Workshop on Journalistic Ethics. The news about the fast carried out by six "dissidents" went around the world in 24 hours.

Were there any instructions given by the Interests Section?
Based on their instructions, a certificate of participation was given out at the fast. This was a double-edged sword, because people wanting to emigrate went to the fast in order to get their little piece of paper so they would later have something to show to the Refugee Program office, to verify their counterrevolutionary merits. Alicia was responsible for designing the certificates and printing up large quantities of them.

How was the Workshop on Ethics organized?
It was agreed upon at a meeting held in the home of Gonzalo Gallegos, first secretary for the press and culture at the Interests Section. We were called on to attend a lecture on journalism, given

by John Virtue, from the International Press Center of the International University of Florida. He gave a dissertation about the efforts his center was making to have the articles and pieces these elements were writing published in newspapers in Latin American countries, and to seek out economic resources to finance the work of "independent" journalists in Cuba. He sug- gested we concentrate on different issues of daily life in Cuba, not only on political ones. He told us that Fidel Castro had a lot of sympathizers in Latin America and that it was crucial to win over those hearts to our side.

He was the one that introduced the issue of journalistic ethics and he called us the "future children of the United States in a Cuba with a democratic press." They handed out certificates and envelopes containing books from *Cubanet*, another one on the Cuban public health system — you can well imagine what it said — notebooks, pens, and so on. Gallego offered his own home to hold the workshop on ethics there. They were thinking that at least 60 people were going to show up, but we only managed to gather together 34. Since there were far fewer people in the end than planned, the meeting was relocated to Cason's home.

What happened there?
We were received by Cason's assistant, Rebeca Tobey, who was keeping track of the people arriving, checking them off a list. In the end there were fewer "independent" journalists than accredited foreign journalists present. Everything was supervised by the second secretary for the press and culture, Nicholas J. Giacobbe. Three other Americans were at the workshop as observers: Gonzalo Gallegos, Cory Giacobbe — Ricardo Zuniga's assistant — and Zuniga himself, who was there only briefly.

Of course, before the "work sessions" began, Gonzalo Gallegos ratified their "willingness to collaborate with and support not only the 'independent' journalists, but all those who, in one way or another, defend their rights as citizens in this country full of restrictions and censorship."

Alpha 66

Founded in 1962 by CIA agent Antonio Veciana Blanch, in Puerto Rico. It was joined by a faction of the organization known as the Escambray 2nd National Front, put together a year earlier by Eloy Gutiérrez Menoyo in Key West, Florida. Its headquarters were relocated to Miami, where they remain to this day.

Its central office is located at 1714 W. Flagler St., Miami FL 33135, and it has two branch offices: one in New Jersey, P.O. Box 5293, West New York NJ 07093, fax number (201) 863-2630; and another in California, P.O. Box 6434, Torrence, CA 90504. It also has a website on the Internet: www.alpha66.org

It is known for its terrorist, paramilitary and subversive activities, and especially for executing armed infiltrations, attacks on targets located near Cuban coastlines, acts of sabotage, and organizing plots to assassinate Fidel Castro and other Cuban leaders.

In September of 1993, Cuban authorities arrested Mexican citizen Mario García Rubalcava, who was planning to carry out acts of terrorism against tourism facilities and assassinate the Cuban president. Rubalcalva later admitted having been trained by Andrés Nazario Sargén of Alpha 66.

It finances the radio station known as *The Voice of Alpha 66*, using it to incite violent acts within the national territory. In its search for internal representation, this organization has made ties to leaders and members of counterrevolutionary groups within the country, supporting them financially.

Agreements were reached pertaining to the supply of financial and material aid, and the manipulation of photographs, as well as the copyright violations surrounding these by foreign editors. The dangers of writing false interviews and intentionally provocative news were considered. There was a consensus on the excessive presence of *Radio "Martí"*. Someone even labeled the station as untruthful. Due to the criticisms, Nicholas J. Giacobbe promised to make a telephone call to the U.S. State Department to express the concerns of the participants. A little after 5:00 in the afternoon, Cason showed up. The meeting was already over, but we were still there. Gonzalo Gallegos and Nicholas J. Giacobbe informed him of what had taken place.

Elizardo Sánchez told a foreign correspondent that he could recognize State Security agents by the special way in which they moved their eyelids…
I don't recall wearing dark glasses to speak to him. How ridiculous! But one has to admit that Elizardo is a very capable individual, because he's always out and about in the street while everyone else is in jail.

One thing I can tell you, though, is that one of the things that's hurt the Americans the most is never having suspected us. They underestimate us far too much, and they're content if the people around them do the tasks they assign to them.

But you must have had difficult moments inside the Interests Section.
Yes. There were two historical moments in the Revolution that hit me hard. One of them was the kidnapping of Elián. Every time I visited the Interests Section they would tell me that what the Cuban government was saying was false, that they weren't kidnapping the child. The other was in September of 1998, when they handed me the press release that spoke about the arrest of our five brothers. I left with a headache. Any one of them could have been me.

When did Alicia Zamora start working for State Security?
She came at a time when I couldn't deal with so much at once. There was a lot of money at stake, a lot of contacts, things we couldn't lose. So she started playing a very important role as the director of the Lux Agency, whose magazine is published in Miami. The poor woman didn't know a thing about the press, but the important thing was to work at it.

Who recruited her?
She had been spying on me for some time, something like a year and a half. She was always breathing down my neck. I can't remember the number of times I thought of sitting down with her and

telling her the truth. But I couldn't do it. One fine day, she was called on to go to the Police Station. And she started saying horrible things about me, I was about to be put in jail… Can you believe she agreed to keep watch over me? I knew what she was doing, I waited for her, I sat across the street. She came out crying and I asked her why and she never told me the truth. But every time I left for a meeting, she would pick up a slip of paper, and write down the hour and minute. She was spying on me. I called my official and told him I couldn't go on living like this, that she was constantly on my back and I couldn't take it anymore. She would sometimes give me a little speech to get me out of that world. I invited her to a meeting without telling her the reason. She called the officials and told them what was happening. The official answered, "Go, that meeting's going to be really interesting." When we got there and she saw her official, who was also my official, she started to cry. The three of us hugged each other. From that point on, she didn't spy on me any longer. We gave her the Lux Agency, which played an important role, because we were channeling the information sent abroad, and we weren't competing with any other agencies because we dealt essentially with labor issues, although we would take on all sorts of other things also.

Has agent Vilma hugged her parents yet?
No. And let me give you an idea of how everything's gone down: My dad, who's 80 years old, lives in Ciego de Ávila. He was with my brothers the day they aired the interview on the Round Table — that's when he found out, and he said: "I've seen angels turn into devils, but I've never seen a devil turn into an angel." And he started crying. I haven't seen him, but I know he's doing fine.

This whole process has been very hard on my family. The day Fidel entered Havana, January 8, I had just turned four. My brother and I would build podiums out of cardboard and we would do everything we saw Fidel do. When the invasion of the Bay of Pigs took place, I wrote Fidel a letter and Celia Sánchez answered it. She asked me to be a good citizen, to study, to prepare myself. I've never forgotten her words.

Rodolfo Frómeta Caballero

Born in Guantánamo. He heads the terrorist organization known as Comandos F-4. He moved to the United States in 1968, and established ties with the organization Alpha 66.

In 1981, he traveled to Cuba as an émigré and attempted to organize clandestine cells within the country to carry out acts of sabotage, for which he was arrested and sentenced to a 10-year prison term. He returned to the United States at the end of his sentence in April of 1991.

On February 6, 1994, leading a commando composed of six members of Alpha 66, he was detained while attempting to infiltrate Cuba with a team of three men. The authorities seized from him a 16-foot boat carrying large quantities of weapons, ammunition, money and uniforms. He was set free.

In April of 1994, he founded the organization Comandos F-4, and was arrested in Miami on June 2 of that same year, along with Fausto Marimón, also a member of the Comandos, when he paid 5,000 dollars to an undercover FBI agent to purchase C-4 explosives, a grenade launcher, three light anti-tank missiles and a Stinger surface-to-air missile, among other materials. For this crime, he was sentenced to a 41-month prison term and two years of probation.

On April 26, 2001, Cuban authorities captured an armed commando off the northern coast of Villa Clara, made up of three counterrevolutionaries who had been members of Comandos F-4 and were planning to infiltrate our country to carry out acts of terrorism against tourism facilities in the City of Havana.

In September of 2002, Comandos F-4 allied itself to the Venezuelan Patriotic Junta, an organization headed by ex-captain Luis García Morales and made up of ex-military men, now residents of Miami, who had participated in a coup d'etat in that country. They plotted assassination attempts on Fidel Castro and Hugo Chávez.

Were you ever afraid of being discovered?
Never. Martha always said she could smell State Security a mile away, and of course, I would say the same thing. I always felt sure

about what I was doing and why I was doing it, and the officials that helped me throughout these years had a lot to do with this.

Did they ever reprimand you?
Yes. Once, without asking for permission, I went to the March of the Torches. I sat down at the corner of Prado and Colon. I wanted to see Fidel, even from a distance. When he walked by me, I was so moved that I couldn't help myself and I started yelling: "Fidel, Fidel, Fidel!" I yelled so much that he waved to me. My heart skipped a beat. When I realized what I had done, I said to myself: "Shit, I've given myself away!" Luckily, no one saw me.

46

What was your relationship with the officials like?
At difficult times, we would speak to one another even with our eyes. I always knew I was not alone in those groups and that my work was insignificant compared with the work of other people. Time proved me right.

Among the infiltrators, who gave you the biggest surprise?
Tania (Odilia Collazo). I was fond of her, but she was a real legend within the "dissident" movement, and it never crossed my mind that she could be one of us. There was some friction with Orrio in the Ethics Workshop, because I had instructions from Martha Beatriz to add a note on the fast to the final declaration. I was directing the workshop on behalf of the Assembly leadership and he was in charge of the technical side. We set down some boundaries. When the time came to record the conclusions of all the committees, he told me that the fast had nothing to do with that. I told him, "Listen, write whatever you please, but leave the fast in there." And look at that, I found out later he's one of us. It's been very emotional. I sometimes feel like I'm watching a movie, that someone else went through all this, and I have trouble, at times, tearing myself from the counterrevolutionary language of Aleida Godínez.

So who have we been speaking with, Aleida or Vilma?
With both of them.

MONEY IS THE FUEL OF DISSIDENCE

Otuardo Hernández's wife asks him why he didn't trust her. "It's been extremely difficult trying to explain to her the reasons that kept me from coming clean," he admits. Nor was it easy to go from an active professional life as a civil engineer to that of an apathetic and quarrelsome fish peddler, in a neighborhood of his hometown Camagüey where everyone looked down on him. Including his parents.

It is difficult to imagine Agent Yanier, these days, in his role as a daring "dissident", taking part on more than one occasion in boxing matches among the "independent journalists" whose greed for money and professional ambitions led them to end up in the police station. He is a quiet and discreet individual, who grows emotional when speaking about his family.

While we speak with him, Odilia Collazo (Tania) interrupts numerous times to show us a relevant document or to interject a comment. One can sense much love between him,

Odilia, and her husband Roberto Martínez, who is also an agent of Cuban State Security. "I came to know something I felt all along: it's hard to run into decent people among the counter-revolutionaries. I had the feeling that they were decent, and it was painful to think of them lost to the Revolution. Can you imagine how I feel right now?"

AGENT YANIER

How did this story begin for you?
It all started on June 19, 1999. I had to intervene in a labor issue that gradually became a political issue. I ended up with a work sanction; they cancelled the contract I had with the Municipal Housing Administration in Camagüey, where I was living, and kicked me out of the Communist Party of Cuba. A number of counterrevolutionaries began to approach me almost immediately.

Were you already working for State Security?
No. I told an official what was happening to me.

Which was?
Lázaro Bosq Hinojosa, an active member of the Cuban Human Rights Foundation in Camagüey, invited me to participate in meetings and other activities that were being held in his home. He was a neighbor of mine. This happened around the time of the protest march outside the Czech Embassy, and he wanted to denounce or take some sort of action against the government's response to the provocations that were being committed by the diplomats of that country.

Lázaro even made public threats against two officers of the Cuban Ministry of the Interior that we knew personally, and he even made threats against the wife and son of one of those officers. The decision was made for me to become a secret agent, to keep a close watch on the actions being organized by the counterrevolutionaries in Camagüey.

When did you join the ranks of State Security?
On March 6, 2001.

Why is that date important?
It's the day I joined the Cuban Human Rights Foundation of Camagüey. That day, they gave me a copy of the Universal Declaration of Human Rights and a number of pamphlets. That's where they told me what Cubanet was, they showed me an "independent library" and told me that they had ties to dissidents in Ciego de Ávila and other provinces. Since I had more of an education than most of them — I'm a civil engineer — and I had some experience in administration, I started moving up the ladder. By August I was already the "democratically" elected president.

What was that process like?
There were many quarrels between the Foundation in Camagüey and the national leadership, based in Ciego de Ávila, with Juan Carlos González Leyva as president. The quarrels were over money, recommendations to get a visa to travel to the United States, and recognition for actions they were promoting or carrying out. There was a lot of jealousy and there were many conflicts, surrounding some rather crazy plans of theirs.

What sort of crazy plans?
For instance, two members of the organization had the bright idea of showing up at José Martí Revolution Square, wearing blood-stained clothes. They were going to call on the foreign press, hand out pamphlets and unfold a counterrevolutionary banner. They would then take off in a car. They were speaking with so much conviction that other members bought the story and immediately wanted to join in. They said that they could count on the support of the U.S. Interests Section and, if everything went well, they would likely be included in the Refugee Program. They would dream up things of this sort, and then no one would actually do anything, but it got them all worked up.

How did you manage to penetrate that world?
I did it little by little, and studying the situation a lot. For instance, if they held a workshop on the problems of the Cuban sugar industry, I would prepare myself for the workshop so as to leave them breathless; likewise if it dealt with politics or history. I even took up studying journal-

ism, to put together my own speeches. I would show up to every single meeting and event. That earned me the trust of the leaders.

Can you think of a significant event that took place in the organization?

There was one that was crucial to the decision of making me president: the inauguration of the 20 de Mayo "Independent Library" in Sancti Spíritus, to which each of us had to donate a book. We met in the home of Lázaro with Juan Carlos Leyva to organize the trip; Juan Carlos was the national director of the Foundation. He lived in Ciego de Ávila and came to hand out forms to gather signatures for the "Varela" Project.

He told us, also, that the Foundation had received a number of donations and that, as president in Camagüey, I would have the doors open to me at the U.S. Interests Section, as well as those of other diplomatic missions.

The meeting took place in Sancti Spíritus?

The day before departing for Sancti Spíritus, the Camagüey group (10 members, counting myself) traveled to Ciego de Ávila, and we slept over at Juan Carlos' place to leave with him in the morning. At around five in the morning, Juan Carlos and Alejandro González Raga were detained in the street when they went off to look for another member of the group. Since they didn't come back and we didn't know what had happened to them, we almost cancelled the trip to Sancti Spíritus.

I took control, I made a lofty speech and I told the rest of the group, "We're leaving without them," and nine of us showed up at the house of the owner of the alleged "independent library", Blas Giraldo Reyes Rodríguez, but it had already been inaugurated and it had been something of a disaster, because no one had shown up and there were hardly any books there. To top things off, we'd arrived late, but, nevertheless, I made a statement, and we sang the national anthem with all of the doors and the windows open. In the middle of this, an old lady walked by and yelled at the neighbor: "Look at how drunk those people are, and it's so early in the morning!"

We'd traveled with merely 100 pesos. When we returned to

Juan Carlos' place, they had already let him go. I returned with an even firmer position within the group.

Angel Francisco D' Fana Serrano

Leader of the counterrevolutionary organization known as Unwavering for Freedom and Democracy in Cuba (Plantados Hasta la Libertad y la Democracia en Cuba).

For the activities he perpetrated in our country, he was arrested in 1962 and sentenced in Trial No. 458/62.

During his prison term, he approached the counterrevolutionary Hubert Matos and labeled himself an anticommunist revolutionary. He remained in prison until 1983, when he emigrated to the United States and became a member of the counterrevolutionary organization Independent and Democratic Cuba (Cuba Independiente y Democrática, CID).

In 1984 he moved to Venezuela and became the organizing secretary of the CID delegation in Caracas.

In 1986 he was designated a member of the public relations committee during the 7th CID Congress, held in Philadelphia. He began an intense recruiting campaign on *Radio CID*.

Through the radio station, he promoted actions against Cubans visiting the United States and encouraged the defection of Cuban sailors, diplomats, military personnel and artists.

In 1992, he was the director of anti-Cuban radio programs on the *Voice of the CID*, and he established ties with the ex-convicts' organization.

In mid-1995, he joined the CID executive and became known for his promotion of acts of protest and civil disobedience in Cuba, taking advantage of religious festivities such as San Lázaro's day, on December 17, employing alleged cells of the organization within the country.

In October of the same year, as a member of the CID leadership, he participated in the development of a new campaign aimed at carrying out acts of sabotage and terrorism, at establishing subversive groups in Cuba and utilizing all possible means to destabilize the country's internal order.

You spoke about disagreements…

Yes, there were differences between the groups in one province and another, within the groups themselves, and with the members of the national leadership. We were a handful of people fighting among ourselves.

This became unbearable when they announced that Juan Carlos was to travel to Havana to receive an award of 1,500 dollars in honor of his struggle for human rights in Cuba. The smell of money and the possibility of traveling to the United States turned the meetings into a battlefield, until the Foundation finally split up and everything went down the drain.

There were really that many fights?

They happened so often that they'd often kick us out of the house where we were having the meeting, and some people would end up throwing punches. I recall that once we had a serious quarrel because we were going to hand out a pamphlet explaining what the Foundation was about and someone with a bit of common sense asked us to throw it out because of the number of spelling mistakes in the text.

What was the main source of friction?

Everyone there knew that the leaders in Havana had many more opportunities for making money than the rest of the members. They would say that they were getting more money because they were the most persecuted of the group, which was a shameless lie. There was no such persecution. We would travel throughout the country and no one would bother us one bit, unless you tried to make a scandal or publicly conspire against the government, because, as everyone knows in Cuba, the streets belong to the revolutionaries.

That's why, when I became president of the Foundation, I always tried to avoid a scandal in the street, curbing aggressive acts and always avoiding public events. The Foundation started to fall apart bit by bit, until we were scarcely 10 members in total, and Lázaro Bosq asked me to travel to Ciego de Ávila to discuss the problems we had in the province with Juan Carlos. Since everything was going from bad to worse, the decision was made that aside from working in what was left of the Foundation, I had to join other organizations.

Which ones?
The Human Rights Party of Cuba, with Odilia Collazo as president. I joined as delegate of the province of Camagüey, in charge of gathering information and drafting reports on human rights violations in the province.

Since the party managed to gather 15 members who were instructed to avoid public provocations and to undertake peaceful activities instead, activities which often had to be invented because they had to prove they were doing something to get the famous endorsement for the visa somehow, bringing news about human rights violations became a business.

When things were getting out of hand — we had the enthusiastic support of the U.S. Interests Section, which was handing out very few visas through the regular channels, and favored those issued through the Refugee Program — we started telling people that this was not a travel agency, to discourage potential groups.

Why?
Many of the people that were coming to us had criminal records and had no jobs. The majority of the most enthusiastic members of these sorts of organizations are individuals who are socially very dangerous.

Of course, you were also an "independent journalist"…
Yes. On July of 2001 — I was not yet the president of the Foundation — Juan Carlos, Delio Requejo and Normando Hernández González asked me to join the College of "Independent" Journalists in Camagüey, of which Mario Enrique Mayo Hernández was also a member. Normando was the president of the school. The reason behind this was the fact I was collaborating with *Radio "Martí"* and had made ties with Frank Hernández Trujillo and his partner Ismael Hernández, and with Janisset Rivero and Ricardo Bofill. I had also done a few things for the *Voice of the CID*, particularly with Ángel D'Fana, from the ex-convicts organization.

Both Mayo and Normando were working for the College of "Independent" Journalists anonymously.

You told us earlier that you had graduated as an engineer. Did you ever take journalism classes anywhere?
Save for those superficial courses that they had given during the workshops held by the Foundation, I knew next to nothing of journalism.

How did the College work?

Everything was done at Normando's place, who lived in Vertientes. I would send out my reports over the phone. We agreed to meet every Tuesday to go over our work together and send it off to *Radio "Martí"*, the *Cuban New Press*, The *Foundation's Voice*…
We would make up the news.

> **World Federation of Cuban Ex-Political Prisoners (Federación Mundial de Ex-Presos Políticos Cubanos)**
>
> Established in 1983 and composed, from the time of its creation, of numerous organizations of former inmates acting independently of one another. Currently, it is a single organization that preserves the original name.
>
> Its headquarters are located at 3178 Coral Way, Miami, FL 33145.
>
> It is one of the organizations involved in a recent attempt to create a credit card aimed at facilitating financial support for counterrevolutionary groups within the country.
>
> Among its leaders, the most noteworthy is the terrorist René Cruz Cruz, who has organized acts of violence against Cuba and has close ties with Luis Posada Carriles and intimate involvement in his violent plots against Cuba and its leaders.

What sort of information would you send out?
For instance, we would say something like, "the quality of Cuban bread is poor," something which is not altogether false, for reasons we all know of, and we would find a way to make a scandal out of that, ending up in a denunciation against the "Castro regime".
Rolando Cartaya, who directs the program "Without Censors or Censorship" on *Radio "Martí"*, would constantly ask us to seek out information in the farmers markets, the hospitals, the schools, and to comment on that. Once, I wrote an article on the disparity

between the prices of things and the average income of people, which he absolutely loved. That one was published under my name, because not every article written is published using the author's real name — most of the names were made up. It was important to make it appear as though lots of people were collaborating with this counterrevolutionary radio station.

When did the payments begin?
I never received any money directly from them, but I did know that the Agency was receiving it. The whole time I worked with Normando and Mario Mayo, they mentioned only that I would receive five dollars, which I turned down.

Normando had already been told that he was being granted a visa and he was saving money for the trip. According to him, he still needed something like 400 more dollars, and I told him to forget about me, to finish saving up the money.

He was going to pay you just five dollars?
Yes, a month.

And how much was he making?
He never told me. When I became director of the Foundation I started distancing myself from the world of journalists, but the differences between Normando and Mario Mayo were too much. The main reason was the money, because when Mario found out how much Normando was making and that he was getting breadcrumbs in comparison, all hell broke lose. Then there was the accusation that Normando was jealous of Mayo, because he was a better writer. Each one accused the other of not knowing how to write.

How did that argument end up?
Mario opened up another press agency, called "Félix Varela".

How many press agencies were set up in Camagüey?
Just about anyone could open up a press agency. They were obsessed with getting the recommendation for the visa and with the money. That was the main objective of all those groups, because the oil that keeps the gears of the counterrevolution moving is money. As I told you, I saw a lot of fighting and a lot of hatred over a few lousy dollars.

Ramón Humberto Colás Castillo

A psychologist by profession, who held administrative positions in the public health sector, such as director of the Home for the Physically and Mentally Disabled in Las Tunas. He was a member of the Union of Young Communists (Unión de Jóvenes Comunistas, UJC) and later a member of the Communist Party of Cuba.

In 1994 he founded the counterrevolutionary organization known as the Jose Martí Revolutionary Party (Partido Revolucionario Martíano). He also became a member of the "Independent" Medical Association, and in 1996 he joined the Las Tunas branch of the Democratic Solidarity Party (Partido Solidaridad Democrática), which he headed up from June 12, 1997 onwards.

He founded and became director of the "independent libraries" project in Cuba. He emigrated to the United States in 2001.

Upon arrival, he was taken in by the Cuban Democratic Directorate (Directorio Democrático Cubano, DDC), and later went on to become a member of the Cuban-American National Foundation (Fundación Nacional Cubano Americana, FNCA), to which he currently belongs.

From the time of his arrival to the United States, he has approached government officials in search of funding for the "independent libraries" in Cuba, campaigns where he has met with considerable success.

In April of 2002, he traveled to Geneva as a representative of the DDC, and led a campaign against Cuba, along with other leaders of counterrevolutionary organizations, during the Committee on Human Rights sessions addressing supposed human rights violations in the island.

In July of that year, he returned to Geneva with Omár López Montenegro of the FNCA to seek recognition for his project within the United Nations system.

Some months later, in 2002, he held a meeting in Washington, D.C. with James Cason, the current head of the U.S. Interests Section in Cuba.

Presently, he serves as an announcer on the FNCA radio program.

And what did you do?
It was more comfortable for me to go over to Mario Mayo's place, who lived three blocks away from me, than to go all the way to Vertientes to send out information. So, I started to work for the "Félix Varela" Agency.

This Agency was also getting funding?
Not at first, no. Afterwards, they started getting it and he no longer wanted us to submit a complete story, but rather to give him the information verbally so that he could write up the story himself. He didn't have to pay us that way. He put his wife to work as a journalist so they would send him more money that he didn't have to split among the rest. Of course, things got ugly fairly quickly.

How did it happen?
It happened between Mario Mayo and Lázaro Bosq, who tried to kill Mario. He managed to break into his home and Mario accused him before a Cuban court. Lázaro was sanctioned. People started saying that Mario was an agent of State Security. I myself had a chat with him to get him to drop the charges, but Mario was unshakable.

Who were the representatives of these agencies in Miami?
Cartaya, from *Radio "Martí"*. We also had links with *Cubanet* and with the *Cuban New Press*.

Néstor Baguer would look over the articles you were sending to Cubanet?
Yes, and he never returned them to me. I would dictate them to him over the phone. He and Normando got along fairly well.

Were there other press agencies in the life of Agent Yanier?
Not journalistic agencies, no, but I did become involved with the "independent libraries" project. I set one up in my own home, which I called "Father Félix Varela Independent Library", and I went to the U.S. Interests Section to have it registered.

Let's take it one step at a time: Who suggested that you open a library? Where did you get the idea of registering it at the U.S. Interests Section?

The person that talked me into founding one was Gisela Delgado, Héctor Palacios' wife, whom I met in Havana during a trip I took along with Mario Mayo. She gave us some books, declarations of human rights, and she started sweet-talking us into thinking that we were going to get money, medicine, fax machines, computers, radios... she painted a very seductive picture.

At the time, the administration of the libraries project had undergone a division, one part was in Las Tunas and the other part in Havana. Ramón Colás was in charge in Las Tunas, and Gisela was in charge in Havana. Both called themselves directors.

Gisela Delgado proposed that I open up my own library in Camagüey in association with her and that I register it at the U.S. Interests Section. I hesitated because I was up to my head with work.

What other responsibilities did you have?

I was an "independent" journalist at the "Félix Varela" Agency, the president of the Cuban Human Rights Foundation in Camagüey and I had just become a partner of Odilia Collazo to be a delegate in her human rights monitoring office, and, on top of this, Gisela was asking me to represent the Camagüey branch of the "independent libraries". It was too much.

Nevertheless, Gisela called Odilia up to talk with her, but she wasn't home and she got a hold of Martha Beatriz Roque and registered me over the phone with her, although, in truth, they never actually made an official registration. Lastly, Gisela called the U.S. Interests Section and spoke with someone there for a while, she dictated all of my information and told me that the library had been registered, and that all I had to do now was show up there.

How did you manage?

When I returned to Camagüey, Mario Mayo told me that it was crazy, and asked me how I was going to take up the library project along with everything else, and started arguing against doing it, which strengthened the front I was putting up before everyone else. I had received instructions from an official not to become involved in that mess.

When we went back to Havana — Mario had been invited to lunch by the head of the U.S. Interests Section at the time, Vicky Huddleston — we explained to Gisela what the situation was. Nonetheless, I went with Mario to the U.S. Interests Section. There they gave us books, blank sheets of paper, envelopes, summaries of news published in the *Miami Herald*...I remember that around those days the fascist coup against Chávez had just happened and almost every article in the *Herald* dealt with that.

Why did they give you those documents?
I turned down the offer of being the representative of the "librarians" in Camagüey, but I did open up my own private library.

What books did you receive there?
Sketches of the United States, its government, its economy, speeches made by Bush, the sort of book no one was going to bother reading, but had to take anyways, if we wanted to receive other things as well.

Such as?
Westerns, dictionaries, children's books...

Did you receive instructions about the "independent libraries" at the U.S. Interests Section?
Yes, and they handed me a list of all the libraries in the country, which was a joke. Mario Mayo himself realized this, because Omar Darío showed up on the list. He told me, "Omar only has four books, and he doesn't lend them out." We were laughing at the people that showed up on there, from Camagüey. We knew them all.

Mario told me how Omar Darío would try to get books from the Interests Section that he could sell. Later on, Omar gave me his own version of events, in which he accused Mario of stealing a bunch of English-Spanish dictionaries in order to sell them. He had even asked to borrow one from Mario and he told him he had none left.

How many dictionaries did they give you?
They would hand out one per library. But there were times when they would let you go into the storage room to choose the books yourself. I didn't get that chance. Nevertheless, I had gotten instructions from Mario about what to do.

Which were…?
He told me, "If they let you into the storage room, look for a box and put all of the books that interest you inside it. Then, place all of the other books on top of those, the ones about the United States and human rights, which are the ones the U.S. Interests Section wants us to read in Cuba." He even told me not to worry about the dictionaries, because they were made with very light paper.

Mario Mayo went in there often, because he had a very good relationship with Vicky Huddleston.

Did they take books to your house?
The car from the U.S. Interests Section — a van that was driven by a Cuban — paid me a visit in Camagüey on three occasions and left me shipments of books.

When did you visit Odilia Collazo?
I went to hand her the reports on human rights violations. We got along well, and we organized a second meeting for me to submit new documents to her. I left somewhat confused from that other meeting…

Why is that?
There was a young man from Cienfuegos who was protesting because the television was on and Odilia was watching the Round Table.

She turned around and furiously told him, "Let me tell you something so you don't forget it: in this house we listen to Fidel's speeches and we watch the Open Forums and the Round Tables… Fidel doesn't lie in his speeches. I'm going to give you a piece of advice: try to watch the Round Tables and learn something from them. If the Americans don't miss a single one of them, and they've told me this themselves, do you think we're going to stay in the dark?"

The young man shrank back, and all of us there had to sit down to watch the Round Table with her. Until it was over. I don't recall what they were discussing, but I do remember her telling us, "You come to me with the truth and I will take you anywhere you please. I don't go along with lies."

Janisset Rivero Gutiérrez

Top leader of the counterrevolutionary organization known as the Cuban Democratic Directorate (Directorio Democrático Cubano, DDC).

She was born in Camagüey, Cuba, in 1969. She emigrated to Venezuela in 1983. There, she obtained a post-secondary degree in advertising at the University Institute of New Professions in Caracas.

In Venezuela, she established ties with former political prisoners and other counterrevolutionary sectors, and moved to Miami in July of 1990.

She was one of the founding members of the organization known as the Cuban Revolutionary Democratic Directorate (Directorio Revolucionario Democrático Cubano, DRDC), in September of 1990. In 1993, she served as the public relations secretary for that organization. She was elected national secretary of the directorate in August of 1995, at the organization's 3rd Congress.

Presently, she is the executive secretary of the organization. She also serves as a spokesperson for the Directorate, and makes radio and television appearances in Miami as part of her duties.

During the 4th Ibero-American Summit held in Chile in 1996, she traveled there as a representative of the DDC and took part in acts of propaganda directed against the Cuban delegation. As part of those activities, she established ties with Rafael Berastegui, a Cuban counterrevolutionary residing in Chile.

She is married to Orlando Gutiérrez, who is the president of the DDC.

She has ties in Cuba with the counterrevolutionary Roberto de Miranda Hernández, who receives money from her to promote his activities.

Did it worry you?
Just think of it! It was the last thing you could expect to hear in the home of a counterrevolutionary, one of the most renowned Cuban dissidents in the world. When I got to Camagüey I told my official, "Either this woman is working for G-2, or she's testing me. I'm not going to that place anymore. It's too much of a risk." My official,

who also had no idea that Odilia was Agent Tania, told me I had to go through that test and return.

Did you participate in any meetings with the head of the U.S. Interests Section, James Cason?

Not personally, but Normando did participate, in November of 2002, and I got to know how that went later on. It took place in Cason's home. Normando took part in a work meeting for the Assembly to Promote Civil Society in Cuba, which was run by Martha Beatriz Roque. Normando told the head of the U.S. Interests Section that it was very difficult for us to get denunciations of human rights "violations" to reach the capital. The decision was made to put together a list with all the phone numbers of all the "independent journalists" in the city of Havana.

An important activity was also held in Camagüey around that time, in support of the "Varela" Project.

What did it consist of?

On November 22, the diocesan priest Alberto Reyes Pías handed out the "Varela" Project during a religious youth group camping trip that was held in the town of Algarrobo, in Camagüey. He tried to get a debate going, which was not supported by some members of the Order of St. Theresa. Then news of this got out because some of the young people started handing out the propaganda about the "Varela" Project in Esmeralda, in the middle of the street, telling people that this was something good, because it was coming from the Church.

To top things off, James Cason himself traveled to Camagüey around the time this was happening, along with another Interests Section official, Francisco Daniel Sainz. They went to the home of Alberto Hernández Frómeta.

Do you remember the address…?

Dolores Betancourt Street, #115-a, in La Claridad District, in the city of Camagüey. Frómeta and his wife, Evelio Heredero, Eduardo Cedeño and others were there. They spoke of the "Varela" Project, which was a clear indication for us "dissidents" this was the priority of the U.S. Interests Section at that moment.

Do you recall any other indications?
Oscar Espino Chepe, a counterrevolutionary from Havana who had ties to a number of us in Camagüey, sent us a message telling us that he had recently put together a document, a preface to the "Varela" Project, in which he proposed 36 basic changes that would solve the problems of Cuba. This document was also going to be sent to the Cuban government and it was going to get a lot of publicity.

There was quite a bit of discussion around the "Varela" Project during the vigil promoted by the representative of the Cuban Christian Democratic Party, Dulce María Suárez Ramírez.

What did the vigil consist of?
It lasted an hour and a half, it was held in the home of Dulce María. It started at around 10:30 in the evening, and it was videotaped. It lasted exactly as long as the recording time of the videotape. Everything was done to put together a tape they wanted to send to the U.S. Interests Section. They were so worried about the filming of the event that they had to close the door because the streetlight was bothering them. They almost suffocated in there because of the heat. That happened at the beginning of February of this year.

And what was Normando doing around this time?
He had a very busy schedule. He had been instructed to put together the magazine *Luz Cubana* and he became partners with Ramón de Armas Guerrero, who was in charge of another press agency in Camagüey, known as El Mayor. They left for Havana and they got in touch with Raúl Rivero, Oscar Espinosa Chepe, René Gómez Manzano, Martha Beatriz, Hugo Araña, Omar Rodríguez Saludes, Tania Quintero, Ricardo González y Arnaldo Ramos Lauzerique.

Normando was saying that the magazine would be 70 pages long and that the technical advisor was going to be Raúl Rivero. They would have correspondents in a number of provinces and they would be affiliated with the Inter-American Press Society (SIP), during the first days of March. The *Nuevo Herald* would get the scoop on the launching.

Were they ever suspicious of you?
Yes, but that was normal. Everyone is suspicious of everyone else. They live in a relentless state of paranoia, and you gradually gain experience in dealing with that sort of situation. Furthermore, the support of your official is crucial. You feel that you are not alone, and that whatever conflicts arise can be turned around in our favor, if you are intelligent.

Hugo Araña

He comes from a petit-bourgeois family from Matanzas, the great majority of whom left the country at the time of the Revolution's triumph.

He participated in the sabotage carried out in Mantua, in Pinar del Rio, motivated by a profound resentment of the country's artistic sector. He was sentenced to a ten-year prison term for this crime, serving only seven years because of good behavior.

In 1998, he began to establish ties to counterrevolutionary groups, serving as an "independent correspondent".

What did your family think of your ties to the "dissidents"?
My mom, my dad and my brothers are die-hard revolutionaries. One day, my mom slapped me in the middle of the street because of something I had said. I had to lower my head and hold back my tears. It was a real hell trying to reconcile my life as an agent with my family life.

Why?
I had serious problems with my wife as well. She is a member of the Communist Party of Cuba. They wouldn't let me tell her anything, because she works in a branch of the Armed Forces, she had a lot of prestige, she was a member of the Provincial Union of Civilian Workers in the Revolutionary Armed Forces. She couldn't jump over to the other side just like that. It would have drawn too much attention. They didn't tell her a thing until March 30, three days before the trial. It was a very tense moment that had a happy ending.

Ninoska Pérez Castellón

Journalist and announcer of Cuban origins, residing in Miami. She was the official spokesperson of the Cuban-American National Foundation as well as a member of its board of directors and the director of *The Voice of the Foundation*. She received the "Journalist of the Year" award in 1996, given out by the National College of "Journalists of Cuba", based in southern Florida.

She is the daughter of Francisco (Paco) Pérez, a henchman of the sadly notorious motorized police of the Batista dictatorship.

Her resignation from the Cuban-American National Foundation in June of 2001 publicly revealed the internal conflicts in this organization. Apparently, her reason for resigning was FNCA chairman Mas Santos' support for holding the Latin Grammy Awards in Miami and allowing the participation of Cubans residing on the island, something that Ninoska Pérez was radically opposed to.

For some time now, the contradictions and ruptures within the Foundation have made themselves evident, especially since the time of the death of its director, Jorge Mas Canosa, in 1997, which has gradually led to the resignation of a number of its founding members.

What happened with your marriage?
We were separated for over a year. I spoke with my official, but he couldn't do anything for me. We ran the risk of losing everything we had accomplished until then. A great many meetings were held at my home, also. It is strategically located, in an alleyway, and it doesn't face the street. You have to walk down a passageway, go past two doors, and my place is at the back.

And your mother?
Two officials went to get her. She didn't give anyone a chance to speak and when she got into the car she starting saying she knew it all along, that she had told me again and again they were going to put me in jail, that I deserved it and that maybe this little scare would make me change my ideas… "Look at the sort of news I have to give his father on his birthday!" she said. She was extremely upset.

The officials thought it best not to tell her anything just then. They got to the house, where she thought they were holding me. When I went out to see her, I was very nervous and so I hid my hands behind my back so she wouldn't notice.

And what did she do?

She thought that I was handcuffed. She looked as though she was about to hit me, so the officials stood beside me. One of them said, "Ma'am, your son is no traitor, he's an agent of State Security."

Everyone started crying after that.

Aleida Godínez Soler.

Alicia Zamora Labrada.

Otuardo Hernández Rodríguez.

EMBAJADA DE SUIZA
SECCION DE INTERESES
ESTADOS UNIDOS DE AMERICA

P A S E

UNIDAD: _CONS_

NOMBRE: _Aleida Godinez Soler_

CANTIDAD DE PERSONAS _3_

FECHA: _Abierta_

HORA: _Abierta_

FIRMA: _____

The pass reads as follows:

EMBASSY OF SWITZERLAND
U.S. INTERESTS SECTION

PASS

UNIT: CONS
NAME: ALEIDA GODÍNEZ
SOLER
NUMBER OF PERSONS: 3
DATE: OPEN
TIME: OPEN
SIGNATURE:

De:Joelbrito@aol.com | **Bloquear dirección** | **Añadir a Libreta de direcciones**
Fecha:Mon, 16 Sep 2002 20:47:04 EDT
Asunto:Re: Aclarame esto
Para:aleida_godinez@yahoo.es

YO VOY A UNA REUNION DE LA FUNDACION AMERICANA PARA LA DEMOCRACIA
(NED),
DONDE VAN A ESTAR PRESENTES PERSONAS EU PUEDEN AYUDARNOS.
VOY A ENTREVISTARME CON FUNCIONARIOS DEL DEPARTAMENTO DE ESTADO, DE
TRABAJO,
CON LA AFLCIO, CON ALGUNOS INTEGRANTES DEL SUB COMITE DE RELACIONES
EXTERIORES DEL CONGRESO Y QUIZAS DEL SENADO.
EL DISCURSO TUYO DIRIGELO A LOS PARTICIPANTES EN LA REUNION DE ANALISTS
SOBRE
EL TEMA CUBANO, CONVOCADO POR LA NED.

Haga clic en una 🟢 para enviar un mensaje instantáneo a un amigo conectado 🟢 = Conectado, 🔴 = Sin conexión

Eliminar - Elija carpeta - Mover

Responder Responder a todos Reenviar como archivo adjunto Anterior |

E-mail written to Aleida Godínez by the counterrevolutionary Joel Brito, resident of Miami. He sends her instructions, and comments on his close ties to the Cuban-American National Foundation, as well as to officials of the U.S. Government.

he text of the e-mail reads as follows:

m going to a meeting of the National Endowment for Democracy (NED); ere'll be people that can be of help to us there. l be speaking to officials from the Department of State, the Department of Labor, with e AFL-CIO, with some members of the foreign relations sub-committee of the U.S. ongress and perhaps the Senate. You should direct your speech to the participants in e meeting addressing the Cuban issue, organized by NED.

MSN Hotmail - Mensaje

"Archer, Susan K" <ArcherSk2@state.gov>

Para :	Aleida Godínez <agodinez24@hotmail...
CC :	"Giacobbe, Nicholas J" <GiacobbeNJ@...
Asunto:	RE: Favor tuyo
Fecha t	Mon, 13 Jan 2003 12:00:15 -0500

Responder Responder a todos Reenviar Eliminar Colocar en carpeta... ▼ Versión compatible con la impresora

Hola Aleida,

Como tu sabes, Nick Giacobbe es el hombre con los "suministros"; he enviado
tu correo a el, para que el pueda ayudarte Con respeto al Anuario
Estadístico, todavía no hay los CDs – pero si tu quisieras una copie en
papel, Nick puede hacer un copie para ti también. Si no quieres esperar el
CD, habla con Nick. El AE es la unica fuente de datos sobre la educacion
que you tengo.

Saludos,

Susan

E-mail written by U.S. official Susan K. Archer, telling Aleida where she may get
a hold of the "supply-man": at the U.S. Interests Section. The computer
that Nick Giacobbe later delivers to Aleida was sent from Miami
by Frank Hernández Trujillo, using the diplomatic pouch of the Interests Section.

The text of the e-mail reads as follows:

Hello Aleida,

As you know, Nick Giacobbe is the "supply-man"; I've sent your e-mail to him, for him to be able to help you. With regards to the Statistical Yearbook, we still haven't got the CDs — but should you want a paper printout, Nick can make a copy for you as well. If you can't wait for the CD, talk to Nick. The SY is the only source of information on education that I have.

Regards,

Susan

Aleida Godínez, Oswaldo Payá and Félix Bonne in the home of James Cason, head of the U.S. Interests Section.

Víctor Rolando Arroyo, Vicky Huddleston, and Aleida Godínez, agent Vilma.

The staff of the "independent libraries" in Miami.
Standing in the middle is Janisset Rivero.

BIBLIOTECAS INDEPENDIENTES DE CUBA

1 Agosto /002
Sr. Enrique BLANco.

Te adjunto comprobantes que justi-
fican los gastos según el dinero
que has enviado y tus instrucciones
para entregarlo.

Quedan en fondo $160.00 US-
tos cuales estarán congelados hasta
recibir tus instrucciones

en saludos sinceros
tu amigo
Palacios
ciudad Habana

Encuentro Nacional de Bibliotecas Independientes de Cuba
Septiembre del 2001

The letter reads as follows:

INDEPENDENT LIBRARIES OF CUBA
August 1, 2002
Mr. Enrique Blanco,

I am including a report on the expenditures made following the delivery instructions you sent with the money.

There remain USD 160.00, which have been frozen pending further instructions from you.

Sincerely,

Your friend H. Palacios

Ciudad Habana, 12 de marzo del 2002

Por la presente se le entrega al Sr. Iván Hernández Carrillo
Coordinador de la Provincia Matanzas, treinta dolares (30.00 U
por el concepto de ayuda por el Proyecto de Bibliotecas Indepe
dientes en Cuba.

Recibe: Iván Hernández Carrillo   Entrega: Gisela Delgado Sabl

Ciudad Habana, 13 de marzo del 2002

Por medio de la presente se hace entrega de treinta dolares
30.00 US a la Sra. Julia Cecilia Delgado González, por concepto de ayuda de las Bibliotecas Independientes en Cuba.

Recibe: Julia cecilia Delgado   Entrega: Gisela Delgado Sabl

Receipt for money delivered in Cuba
to the mercenaries Iván Hernández and Julia Cecilia Delgado.

The receipt reads as follows:

City of Havana, March 12, 2002

The following certifies that the sum of thirty US dollars (USD 30.00) has been delivered to Mr. Iván Hernández Carrillo, Coordinator for the Province of Matanzas, as aid for the Independent Libraries Project in Cuba.

Received by: Iván Hernández Carrillo
Delivered by: Gisela Delgado Sablón

City of Havana, March 13, 2002

The following certifies that the sum of thirty US dollars (USD 30.00) has been delivered to Mrs. Julia Cecilia Delgado González, as aid for the Independent Libraries Project in Cuba.

Received by: Julia Cecilia Delgado
Delivered by: Gisela Delgado Sablón

Participants in the "fast":

1. Nelson Aguilar Ramírez
2. René Gómez Manzano
3. Martha Beatriz Roque
4. Félix Bonne
5. Elsa Morejón
6. Orlando Zapata Tamayo
7. Nelson Moliné Espino

Martha Beatriz hasn't lost a pound. This is con by Francisco Pijuán, the doctor for the "fast".

The "diet" of the fasters: among many other things, cream of asparagus soup.

The "fast": Bon apetit!

6.- Laura Álvarez Vargasç
   Rafael Ferro No.486
   Pinar del Rio
   CI 28031303853.. 100.00

7.- Tomás Pérez Morejòn
   Edificio No.81 ap. B9
   Calle Los Pinos y Vial Colón
   Reparto Hermanos Cruz
   Pinar del Río.
   CI 37091806349.. 100.00

8.- Diana Margarita Cantón Martinez
   Calle Los Pinos Edificio 111 Ap. A4 segundo Piso
   Reparto Hermanos Cruz. Pinar del Río
   CI 53061004771.. 100.00

9.- René Oñate Sixto
   Virtudes No.49 entre Recreo y Vélez Cabieles
   Pinar del Rio
   CI 61042205188.. 100.00

10.- Juana Martinez Ramos

11.- Jehanmys Medina Hernandez
   Emilio Núñez No.66 entre Cmdte. Pinares y
   Celestino Pacheco. Rpto. Carlos Manuel
   Pinar del Río.
   CI 78032601319.. 100.00

12.- Miguel Álvarez Morales
   Antonio Tarafa No.424
   Pinar del Rio
   Giro Postal No.1324906145
   Correo de 10 de Octubre y Princesa....................... 100.00

13.- Josvany Castelló Blanco
   Carretera La Coloma Km.6
   Pinar del Rio

Louis Nigro, Gonzalo Gallegos and Martha Beatriz during the "fast".
In the background, a refrigerator donated for the occasion by the U.S. Interests Section.

Martha Beatriz,

Te oí tu respuesta a los alegatos de Payá Sardiña que Ninoska nos dejó oir en su programa hace un rato. Comprendemos que no era aconsejable contestarle a ese señor y como dijiste aquí en el exilio hay opiniones de algunos líderes con quienes tampoco estás de acuerdo pero eso no quiere decir que los tengas que atacar pero al mismo tiempo deben respetar tu opinión. Obviamente ese hombre no tiene nada de caballeroso y sí mucho de dictador porque claramente no acepta que dentro y fuera de Cuba habemos mucho que jamás aceptaremos su PV. Pero bueno, no tomes a mal la insistencia de Ninoska, sabes muy bien su opinión acerca de ti y la que tiene de ese hombre, y por el otro lado estaba haciendo su trabajo de periodista.

Perdona pero a mí cuando oigo la vocesita de ese hombre se me revuelve el estómago, no creo que sea sincero, es más lo he visto perder los estribos cuando le insisten que responda claramente a una pregunta y es que él es tremendo demagogo, responde pero en realidad no responde y eso demuestra que sus respuestas no son sinceras. Y te digo cuando se trata de la libertad de Cuba tenemos que estar muy claro en nuestras posiciones y no tenemos que aceptar ninguna posición que no sea la recta para un verdadero cambio a la libertad plena de todos nosotros.

Así que el jueguito de Payá Sardiña no engaña a nadie. Por el otro lado considero que la asamblea que ustedes han organizado debe ser muy útil para penetrar el pueblo y crearles conciencia de los derechos universalmente aceptados y eventualmente cuando ese pueblo abra los ojos exigirá sus derechos a como sea.

Bueno, cuídate mucho y recibe mi afecto.

Mari

Mari Wetlago, from the group MAR for Cuba, comments on Martha Beatriz's opinions about Oswaldo Payá Sardiñas.

he letter reads as follows:

artha Beatriz,

ot to hear your response to Payá's allegations on Ninoska's program, which I was tening to a little while ago. We understand it was not advisable to give this man any sort answer and, like you said, that you also disagree with the views of some of the leaders exile here without having to attack them, and, at the same time, they have to respect ur opinion. Obviously, this man is more a dictator than a gentleman, because he clearly nnot stand the fact that there are many people both inside and outside of Cuba that will ver accept his Varela Project. In any event, don't take Ninoska's insistence to heart, you ow very well what she thinks of you and what she thinks of that man, and, besides, she as doing her job as a journalist.

u'll have to forgive me, but whenever I hear the man's voice, my stomach turns, I don't nk he's sincere, I've seen him lose his calm when someone asks him to make his point earer, he's a real demagogue, he'll answer you but, in truth, he's not answering a thing, d that goes to show you that his answers are not sincere. And let me tell you that when iba's freedom is at stake, we have to be very clear about our positions and we can't cept any position that's not aimed at a real change and at the total freedom of all bans.

, Payá's little game isn't fooling anyone. On the other hand, I think that the Assembly it you've organized is a powerful means of reaching people and making them conscious universally accepted human rights, and that, eventually, these people will open their es and demand their rights at any cost.

ke good care and accept my warm greetings.

ari

>From: "pedro corzo" <petercorzo@msn.com>
>To: "Martha Beatriz Roque Cabello" <mbroque17@hotmail.com>
>Subject: Re: Compressed
>Date: Sun, 9 Feb 2003 22:24:39 -0500
>
>Marta.
>Saludos, recibi lo que enviaste por el 24.
>Me alegra que te hayan llegado los calendarios de pared.
>Tratare de comunicarme con las oficinas de Diaz Balart y Ros lethinn. para
>las postales.
>Saludos Pedro.
>
>----- Original Message -----
>From: Martha Beatriz Roque Cabello
>Sent: Wednesday, February 05, 2003 2:19 am
>To: petercorzo@msn.com
>Subject: Re: Compressed
>
>Pedro:
>Si no resuelves habla con ileana Ross o Lincoln Díaz Balart para que te resuelvan. Hoy el
esposo de Bertha Antúnez me trajo 4 almanaques de tu parte. Los usamos hoy mismo en la
reunión de la Comisión de Historia. ¿recibiste lo que te envié del 24 de febrero?. Saludos mbrc.
>
>
> >From: "pedro corzo"
> >To: "Martha Beatriz Roque Cabello"
> >Subject: Re: Compressed
> >Date: Tue, 4 Feb 2003 22:11:08 -0500
> >
> >Marta.
> >Continua con las tarjetas. De no llamar la persona hablare con Ruano
> >para que busque otra via, si es posible. Tus calendarios grandes los tiene
> >Alpizar, la periodista de Placetas.
> >Un saludo Corzo.
> >

The intimate relationship between Martha Beatriz and U.S. Congress members
Ileana Ros-Lehtinen (a.k.a The Big Bad She-Wolf) and Lincoln Diaz-Balart.

The texts of the e-mails read as follows:

Marta,
Cheers, I got what you sent for the 24th.
Glad to know you've received the wall calendars.
I'll try to get in touch with the offices of Diaz Balart and Ros Lethinen to see about the cards.
Regards,
Pedro.

Pedro,

If you're still working on that, speak with Ileana Ross or Lincoln Diaz Balart to see if they can help you. Today, Bertha Antúnez's husband brought me the four calendars that you sent. We used them today during the meeting of the History Commission. Did you get what I sent you about the 24th? Regards, mbrc.

Marta,

Keep working on the cards. Should the person not get in touch with me, I'm going to speak with Ruano and ask him to look for another way, if possible. Your big calendars are with Alpizar, the journalist from Placetas.
Cheers, Corzo.

Western Union form (handwritten):

Beneficiario (Receiver)
- Nombre (First name): MARTHA BEATRIZ
- Apellido (Last name): ROQUE
- Dirección (Address): CALLE ESTE
- Ciudad (City): LA HABANA
- Teléfono (Telephone no.):

Remitente (Sender)
- Nombre (First name): MARIA
- Apellido (Last name): LUZ
- Dirección (Address):
- Ciudad (City): MIAMI

Monto anticipado (Amount expected): 300

Ciudad/Estado/Provincia/País de donde viene el dinero:
Número de control de transferencia (Money Transfer Control No.): 88298
Pregunta de identificación (Test Question):

NO ESCRIBA ABAJO / DO NOT WRITE BELOW
- Agencia: Arica
- Fecha: 8/02   Hora: 1:58
- Identificación:
- Tipo: C1   Fecha de expiración:
- Número: 4505160205
- Descripción física
- Número de control de transferencia: 88298 9416
- Número de cheque: Cantidad: 300

2001/12/21 15:17	MARTA BEATRIZ ROQUE CABELLO	MARIA S\TORANO PRIETO	KEY BISCAYNE FL33149 15 12-21 0154P EST		300.00
2001/12/21 15:24	MARTA BEATRIZ ROQUE CABELLO	LUZ\GOUDIE GOUDIE	KEY BISCAYNE FL33149 15 12-21 0159P EST		300.00
2001/12/21 15:33	MARTA BEATRIZ ROQUE CABELLO	MARIA E\COSCULLUELA BARRUECO	KEY BISCAYNE FL33149 15 12-21 0214P EST		300.00
2001/12/21 17:08	MARTA BEATRIZ ROQUE CABELLO	ENRIQUETA\LARREA	MIAMI FL33173 15 12-21 0342P EST		300.00
2001/12/21 17:15	MARTA BEATRIZ ROQUE CABELLO	MERCEDES\HERNANDEZ	MIAMI FL33173 15 12-21 0348P EST		300.00
2001/12/22 12:32	MARTA BEATRIZ ROQUE CABELLO	GLADYS A\AGUILERA	KEY BISCAYNE FL33149 15 12-22 1109A EST		300.00
2001/12/22 15:01	MARTA BEATRIZ ROQUE CABELLO	ELIA\TARAFA	KEY BISCAYNE FL33149 15 12-22 0129P EST		300.00
2001/12/28 14:57	MARTA BEATRIZ ROQUE CABELLO	ELEADOR\GOUDIE MEDINA	KEY BISCAYNE FL33149 15 12-28 0251P EST		300.00
2002/03/11 22:56	MARTA BEATRIZ ROQUE CABELLO	ISELA\FITERRE	MIAMI FL33174 15 03-11 0654P EST		200.00
2002/03/29 15:40	MARTA BEATRIZ ROQUE CABELLO	MARIA\HORVATH	MIAMI FL33183 15 03-29 0311P EST		300.00
			CORAL		

A list detailing Martha Beatriz's "allowance" and a receipt proving that she received the money.

A work lunch at the official residence of the head of the U.S. Interests Section. At the table, with Vicky Huddleston: Martha Beatriz, Julio de la Nuez Pitaluga, Gustavo Arcos Bergnes, Vladimiro Roca....

CUBAN TRADE AND MANAGEMENT CORPORATION
CUTISA
GERENCIA COMERCIAL

Ciudad de La Habana, 15 de diciembre del 2001.
"AÑO DE LA REVOLUCION VICTORIOSA EN EL NUEVO MILENIO"

AL   : Organo de Instrucción del Departamento de Seguridad del Estado.

Por medio de la presente, en respuesta a su solicitud, le certifico lo siguiente:

Que en nuestros puntos de venta la ciudadana **MARTHA BEATRIZ ROQUE**, con dirección particular Luis Estévez nro. 352, apto. 3, entre Cortina y Figueroa, Santos Suárez, Diez de Octubre, Ciudad de La Habana, con número telefónico 406821 y FAX 327636, ha realizado las siguientes compras, todas en moneda libremente convertible (USD):

1. *Factura nro. 23:*

- Fax Panasonic FP81 S/CONT	$ 167.00 usd
- Toner para fax KX-FA55	$ 30.50 usd
(aranceles)	$ 30.00 usd
Total	**$ 227.00 usd**

2. *Factura nro. 25:*

- 2 equipos Fax Panasonic FP81 S/CONT	$ 334.00 usd
- 2 Toner para fax KX-FA55	$ 61.00 usd
- Teléfono PANASONIC C/CONT	$ 45.00 usd
- 5 Casetes (microcintas) KX-T2390	$ 7.50 usd
(aranceles)	$ 67.00 usd
Total	**$ 514.50 usd**

3. *Factura nro. 52:*

- Computadora Personal GATE DISCOVERY PIII 850	$ 1010.00 usd
- Monitor SAMSUNG 550V	$ 210.00 usd
- Modem V90 56K.	$ 25.00 usd.
Total	**$ 1245.00 usd**

Total de efectivo pagado por la cliente	**$ 1986.50 usd**

Se anexan fotocopias de las facturas antes descritas.

Saludos cordiales,

Félix Quiñones
Vicepresidente Comercial
CUTISA

Some of Martha Beatriz's purchases, using "independent" money.

The document reads as follows:

CUBAN TRADE AND MANAGEMENT COORPORATION
CUTISA
COMMERCIAL OFFICE

City of Havana, December 15 of 2001
"Year of the Victorious Revolution in the New Millennium"

TO: Investigations Office of the Department of State Security

In response to your request, I certify that:

MARTHA BEATRIZ ROQUE, residing at 352 Luis Estevez, between Cortina and Figueroa Streets, Santos Suarez, Diez de Octubre, City of Havana, with telephone and fax numbers 406821 and 322636 respectively, has purchased the following items, in foreign exchange currency (USD):

1. Invoice no. 23:

Panasonic FP81 S/CONT Fax	USD 167.00
Toner for KX-FA55 Fax	USD 30.00
Duty	USD 30.00
Total:	USD 227.00

2. Invoice no. 25:

Panasonic FP81 S/CONT Fax (x 2)	USD 334.00
Toner for KX-FA55 Fax (x 2)	USD 61.00
PANASONIC C/CONT Telephone	USD 45.00
KX-T2190 Cartridges (x 5)	USD 7.50
Duty	USD 67.00
Total	USD 514.50

3. Invoice no. 52 :

GATE DISCOVERY PH1 850 Personal Computer	USD 1010.00
SAMSUNG 550 V Monitor	USD 210.00
V90 56 K Modem	USD 25.00
Total	USD 1245.00

Total paid by customer:	USD 1986.50

Photocopies of all listed invoices are included.

Vicky and Martha, in the shadow of their flag.

SRE
SECRETARIA DE RELACIONES EXTERIORES

Oficina de la Embajadora Especial para los
Derechos Humanos y la Democracia

EEDHD/0045/01

Tlatelolco, D.F., a 21 de febrero de 2001

Marta Beatriz Roque,
Grupo de los Cuatro.

     Con relación al 57° período de sesiones de la Comisión de Derechos Humanos de las Naciones Unidas y a fin de normar la posición del Gobierno de México en ese importante foro internacional respecto al tema de Cuba, mucho agradeceré a usted, de no mediar inconveniente, dar respuesta al cuestionario que se adjunta sobre la situación de los derechos humanos en ese país y hacerlo llegar a la Cancillería mexicana a través de la Embajada de México en Cuba.

     Aprovecho la oportunidad para reiterar a usted las seguridades de mi más atenta y distinguida consideración.

ATENTAMENTE,
La Embajadora Especial

Mariclaire Acosta

CAF/*

The text of the letter reads as follows:

Marta Beatriz Roque,
Group of Four.

Nearing the 57th period of sessions of the United Nations Commission on Human Rights, and with the aim of formalizing the position of the Mexican government with respect to Cuba in this important international forum, I would be very much indebted to you if you could fill out the questionnaire on the situation of human rights in Cuba, which I am enclosing, and have it reach the Mexican foreign affairs office through the Embassy of Mexico in Cuba at your earliest convenience.

I take this opportunity to extend my most sincere regards,

Sincerely,
Special Ambassador
Mariclaire Acosta

CUESTIONARIO RESPECTO A LA SITUACION
DE LOS DERECHOS HUMANOS EN CUBA

1. De acuerdo con los instrumentos internacionales de derechos humanos de los que Cuba es parte, ¿considera usted que se respetan los derechos humanos protegidos por dichos instrumentos? ¿Cuál es el grado de instrumentación de dichos instrumentos internacionales, cuáles derechos son respetados y en qué medida?

2. ¿Cuáles son los órganos encargados de la protección de los derechos humanos en Cuba? ¿Qué tan eficaces son éstos órganos en la tutela de los derechos humanos de los cubanos? ¿Cuál es su alcance y cuáles sus perspectivas en el corto y mediano plazos?

3. ¿Cómo se garantizan los derechos humanos en Cuba?

4. ¿Cuáles son los mecanismos jurídicos, administrativos y judiciales establecidos por el Estado para garantizar la protección de los derechos humanos?

5. ¿En que medida ha incorporado Cuba en su legislación nacional los estándares internacionales de protección a los derechos humanos?

6. ¿Considera usted que en el corto plazo el Estado cubano estaría en posibilidad de ser parte de algún otro instrumento internacional en materia de derechos humanos?

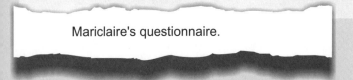

Mariclaire's questionnaire.

The document reads as follows:

QUESTIONNAIRE ON THE HUMAN RIGHTS SITUATION IN CUBA

1. Considering the international human rights instruments of which Cuba is a signatory, do you believe that the human rights protected by said instruments are respected in Cuba? To what extent are the said international instruments implemented, which rights are respected and in what measure?

2. Which institutions are in charge of protecting human rights in Cuba? How efficient are these institutions with regards to protecting the human rights of Cuban citizens? What is their scope of action and what are their short and long term prospects?

3. How are human rights guaranteed in Cuba?

4. What are the legal, administrative and juridical mechanisms established by the State to guarantee the protection of human rights?

5. To what extent has Cuba incorporated into its legislation the international standards established with respect to the protection of human rights?

6. Do you believe that the Cuban government will be in a position to join another international human rights instrument in the near future?

Ciudad de La Habana, 28 de febrero de 2001

Excma. Sra. Mariclaire Acosta
Embajadora Especial para los
Derechos Humanos y la Democracia
Secretaría de Relaciones Exteriores
Estados Unidos Mexicanos.

Excelentísima señora):

Adjunto encontrará respuesta al cuestionario enviado
por usted sobre la situación de los derechos humanos
en Cuba.
Debo aclararle que en el marco del conocimiento general de la grave situación en nuestro país por el
incumplimiento de lo establecido en la Declaración Universal de Derechos Humanos, ha sido muy
difícil restringirme sólo a estas preguntas.
No obstante, estamos en la mejor disposición de
mantener cualquier contacto que le permita tener
un mejor conocimiento del tema Cuba.
Agradezco su deferencia y le transmito mi más
alta consideración por su trabajo.

Atentamente,

Martha Beatriz Roque Cabello

The text of the letter reads as follows:

Your Excellency,

Enclosed you will find the completed questionnaire you sent, inquiring into the human rights situation in Cuba.
I must add that, parting from what we know about the serious situation our country faces due to the non-fulfillment of what is established in the Universal Declaration of Human Rights, it was very difficult to limit myself to answering the few questions included in the survey.
Having said this, we have every interest in maintaining whatever contact you might deem useful in becoming more informed about the situation in Cuba.
I thank you for your attention in this matter.

Sincerely,

Martha Beatriz Roque Cabello

The Boss ensures that his orders are carried out (declaration by Martha Beatriz to the foreign press and the U.S. Interests Section).

Martha Beatriz y Louis Nigro, Deputy Principal Officer of the U.S. Interests Section in Cuba.

I AM STILL INSIDE THE SKIN OF MY CHARACTER

MANUEL DAVID ORRIO DEL ROSARIO 67

He had polio as a child and walks with a limp as result. But this didn't stop him from riding all over Havana on his bicycle, his cane strapped on the side, visiting people and thinking over the article he would write that week for Cubanet, the Miami-based agency established to promote "independent journalism". "I was their star journalist," he mischievously declares, making it clear that he was fully aware of all the tricks behind this business.

He is driven and rigorous, painstakingly verifying information and dates. And all his careful research leads to the same conclusion: the dependence of these "independent" journalists on the money and the whispered instructions from the U.S. Interests Section. It doesn't take much to figure this out; and he is able to attest to the inner workings of the business of news, the profitability of relentless criticism of the Revolution, the dirty tricks aimed at denying the Cuban people of their daily needs, particularly in the most difficult years of the so-called Special Period.

Manuel David Orrio del Rosario, a 38-year-old accountant, toiled in a complex world where he had to struggle to avoid being shoved aside by the more ambitious, where he was obliged to undertake actions that did not always meet with the approval of his superiors, and where he had to study, like never before in his life, to learn everything possible about the inner workings behind the so-called "opposition" in Cuba, and above all, the opposition "journalists".

AGENT MIGUEL

How did you first come into contact with these counterrevolutionary elements?
Late in 1991 a friend asked me to go with her to the home of Elizardo Sánchez Santacruz, who was also a friend of hers. It turned out eventually that her friendship with him was a way to help her get a visa to the United States, something she finally managed to do. That was how I met this gentleman.

Did it go beyond simple greetings?
On that particular occasion, no. But on January 31, 1992, I went to a party at the house of some friends of mine, and something interesting happened.

What?
After I'd had a few drinks, I started chatting with Enrique Patterson, a former professor of the history of philosophy at the University of Havana. During the conversation he showed me a document outlining a democratic social program that had been released a few days earlier by a number of individuals, one of whom was Elizardo.

And why did he show this kind of trust in you?
I was with Elizardo's friend again, and she vouched for my trustworthiness.

Did you read the document?
Yes, I read it.

What did you think of it?
I found it interesting.

Did you meet again?
Yes, and I was also introduced to some other people.

Who were they?
Rolando Prats, the president of the Cuban Democratic Socialist Current (Corriente Socialista Democrática Cubana, CSDC), Carlos Jesús Menéndez, and others. Eventually, Prats moved permanently to the United States.

These meetings led to a kind of recruitment process. They were looking for new members for the group, and wanted people of a certain intellectual level. This started to worry me. I talked about it with a cousin of mine, who's an officer in the Ministry of the Interior, and I asked him what I should do.

What did he tell you?
He told me to write a report for State Security, and he would take care of getting it to them.

Did you get a response?
In February of '92, my cousin informed me that an officer specializing in this area was going to visit me. That was how the first interview came about.

What did they tell you?
They just asked me if I would be willing to cooperate with them.

What did you answer?
I told them that in principle, yes, but that I would give them a definitive answer later.

Why in principle?
At that particular point in time I was going through a really difficult period in my personal life. I had even stopped working in my profession.

What is your profession?
I'm an accountant?

Why did you leave your job?
Because of problems in the workplace.

What did you live on?
I was working as a night watchman in a farmer's market in Cerro

(a neighborhood in Havana). Just imagine, from an accountant to a night watchman! Aside from all my other problems.

What were those other problems?
My father had recently died, and I was in the middle of a long and drawn-out custody battle for my son. My life was a mess.

What did you decide in the end?
In September I called the officer and told him I was prepared to cooperate.

What led you to make this decision?
I had come to the conclusion that if I didn't get involved in a good cause, I was going to get completely lost in all the turmoil of my life.

What were the first tasks you were assigned?
Joining the Cuban Democratic Socialist Current (CSCD). I went to see Elizardo on October 25, and he informed me a few days later that I had been officially accepted into the organization. I will never forget the date: November 3, 1992.

During that period, important meetings were held every Thursday evening at Vladimiro Roca's house. By December 10 I was already involved in my first operations.

What were those first operations?
The CSDC carried out a variety of propaganda activities after Álvaro Prendes' defection from the ranks of the Revolution. In response, a series of acts of repudiation were held outside Vladimiro's house, and this led to fragmentation within the CSDC. I took advantage of this opportunity to gain a foothold within the organization.

I began to visit a number of people. I earned the trust of many of these individuals when they saw that in spite of facing a difficult situation, I didn't lose my nerve.

This paved the way for the executive of the CSDC to meet in my house on March 29, 1993. The meeting was authorized by State Security, which set up filming equipment.

Around this time, Prats went abroad. This led to conflicts within the Socialist Current. As would be expected, Prats used the trip to serve his own personal interests.

Could you expand on that?
It should be remembered that within the Cuban Democratic Socialist Current there was a marked struggle among Vladimiro, Elizardo and Prats. Each one represented a tendency. Prats started to make statements abroad against the blockade, and got a lot of publicity. He started to gain influence.

He even made statements in which he said that he would rather negotiate with a reformed communist party than with the extreme right-wing exile sector in Miami.

Elizardo, who is a chameleon, could not contain himself, and prepared a trip abroad as well. Vladimiro stayed behind in Havana, undermining the position of both Elizardo and Prats.

It was a very turbulent time. Full of intrigues. With time, I came to realize that this is what predominates in that world: intrigues, dishonesty, betrayal.

What happened when Elizardo returned?
When Elizardo got back from the United States, he prepared a file on Prats, portraying him as a social menace. He removed him from the presidency of the CSDC, named himself the new president, and took absolute control.

I confronted Elizardo on all of this, which made me a marked man as far as he was concerned. He set out to marginalize me.

It was a difficult period. It was around this time that I finally resolved the problem of the custody of my son. More than one person tried to convince me to use political manipulation to deal with this conflict, but I chose to find a solution through legal channels, like any average citizen of the Republic, without getting politics involved, which is what the counterrevolutionaries wanted me to do.

But it was becoming more difficult for me to get deeper into the group, because of the situation with Elizardo. That was when I discovered there was another possibility open to me; not even I could have guessed the way it would change my life.

72

Carlos Alberto Montaner

A Cuban, now living in Madrid, he calls himself president of the Cuban Liberal Union. He left Cuba on May 24, 1961, and in 1963 joined a select group created by the CIA and trained in Fort Benning, Washington.

In 1970, he moved to Spain, where he founded, with the financial support of the Central Intelligence Agency, the Playor publishing house and Firmas Press news agency, which publish anti-Cuban literature and supply biased information about Cuba to the Latin American, European and U.S. press. He also participates in propaganda campaigns against our country in the international media.

In August of 1990 he founded, in Madrid, the Cuban Democratic Platform (Plataforma Democrática Cubana), a coalition made up of the Cuban Liberal Union (Unión Liberal Cubana) and counterrevolutionary organizations such as the Social Democratic Coordinator (Coordinadora Socialdemócrata) and the Cuban Christian Democratic Party (Partido Demócrata Cristiano Cubano). This organization was created by the CIA to influence European and Latin American political sectors and to foster pressures against the island.

He backs the U.S. policy of tightening the blockade against Cuba, is against foreign investment in Cuba, and promotes the international isolation of our country.

In December of 1991, he organized a seminar called "The Present and Future of the Cuban Economy", aimed at discouraging foreign investors from entering into business with our country, and using veiled threats for this purpose.

He supports the activities of counterrevolutionary groups by sending them material supplies and communications equipment, as well as funding. He has even proposed that these items be sent to Cuba through the diplomatic pouch of the Spanish Embassy in Havana.

What was it?
Writing. I had always liked to write, but I had never pursued it before. I felt a need to express my views. Since I was still working as a night watchman, I had 12 hours every night to do whatever I wanted from an intellectual point of view.

What did you write about?
Economics and historical research.

When did you start out as a journalist?
On instructions from State Security, I joined the Cuban Association of "Independent Journalists" (APIC) in the summer of 1995. I was responsible for helping to revive the association, because it was almost non-existent at the time. I started to write about the economy, and had a few initial successes.

Who were your first contacts?
I took my first works to Néstor Baguer.

Once you were inside this world, what did you find?
A crazy world, full of gossip and intrigues. The ones who worked the least were the ones paid the most. The APIC offices were in the home of Yndamiro Restano, Sr., better known as Julio Suárez, who founded the association with Pablo Reyes in 1988. In fact, Robert Ménard, a representative of Reporters Without Borders, came to Havana to question Suárez about money that he was supposed to have distributed, but had kept for himself instead.

Did you have any contact with Ménard?
Not with him, but with one of his emissaries, a Canadian named Gregory Barker. I went around Havana with him, to put together a report. He conducted a very long interview with me, and kept pressing me about the situation of so-called prisoners of conscience. He told me that he had also visited Raúl Rivero and Jorge Olivera Castillo.

What happened later with Suárez?
At one point a plot emerged aimed at removing Baguer from the agency. Suárez harassed him relentlessly, and ended up calling a meeting to eliminate his rival.

Baguer found out and showed up at the meeting with a copy of the *Diario de las Américas* that contained a lengthy account of Suárez' activities as a prosecutor at the trials in the province of Matanzas during the first months after the triumph of the Revolution. According to the article, he had requested the death penalty for numerous individuals. The same newspaper also reported on the background of Elizardo, who had been a professor of Marxism, a Cuban diplomat, and above all, a fanatical extremist.

Did Baguer get kicked out in the end?
No way! When Baguer pulled out the newspaper, the meeting ended right then and there.

I understand that a pool of agencies was created.
Yes, on September 8, 1985, the day of Our Lady of Charity of El Cobre (the patroness of Cuba). They named it the Cuban Independent Press Agency. Its members included APIC. There were a very small number of journalists who had actually worked in the media, like Raúl Rivero, and a handful of pseudo-journalists. Incidentally, that night, Rivero received 100 dollars; he got roaring drunk and founded his own agency, Cuba Press.

Where did you publish your first work abroad?
In the *Nuevo Herald*.

What was it about?
It was a historical research piece on Eduardo Chibás.

When did you begin to be paid regularly?
In January of 1997, when I began to get a salary from *Cubanet*. That same year, I was also sent money by Frank Calzón, through Carlos Gerb, a U.S. citizen.

How much?
Frank sent me 100 dollars. My name started appearing on *Cubanet,* and as of May they were paying me 100 dollars a month. They also sent me a computer and a digital camera. I was paid more than the others were. This was *Cubanet*, and they considered me their star journalist.

How did you send in your work?

I dictated it over the phone to Rosa Berre, who was working as the director of *Cubanet.* We made contact twice a week, and every Wednesday I would submit three or four news stories, which weren't necessarily about the problems of the opposition, but also about Cuban society. I sent them articles, reports…

Brothers to the Rescue (Hermanos al Rescate, HAR)

Founded on May 15, 1991, under the pretext of aiding rafters. Its active leaders are José Basulto León, William Schuss and Arnaldo Iglesias, all former members of CIA infiltration teams and the 2506 Brigade.

This organization is primarily made up of pilots of Cuban origins, although it also includes pilots from Argentina, Peru, Venezuela, Mexico and the United States.

Its headquarters are located in Opalocka, and consist of a hangar rented at 5,000 dollars a month, a sum its members are able to pay thanks to the donations of various organizations, the Cuban-American National Foundation among them.

Under the cover of their activities in rescuing rafters, they carried out a survey of our coasts and the movement of Cuban vessels and tracked Cuban communications with the aim of supporting paramilitary groups and Cuban terrorists and drawing up plans to sabotage high-voltage towers within the country.

They have violated territorial borders and carried out extremely low flights over our territory, dropping propaganda leaflets in the northeast sector of the Cuban capital, in the hopes of provoking a direct confrontation between Cuba and the United States, and thus reverting whatever progress has been achieved in the relations between both nations. Repeated provocations of this nature were responsible for the downing of two light aircraft belonging to the Brothers to the Rescue organization on February 24, 1996, after the Cuban government had issued numerous warnings.

Where does Cubanet's *funding come from?*
From the National Endowment for Democracy.

In addition to Cubanet, *where else did you send your work?*
To *Radio "Martí".*

76 *How did you become connected with* Radio "Martí"*?*
Through Carlos Quintela, Rosa Berre's husband. I wrote them reports on the economy, agriculture, the sugar harvest.

Did you come to hold important positions within the dissident community?
Yes. I was the president of the Cuban "Independent Journalists" Cooperative and of the Cuban Federation of Journalists. I started out at the bottom, but I managed to earn a place for myself thanks to the quality of my work, the fact that I was a regular and reliable collaborator, and a series of landmarks that attracted attention.

For example…
In this milieu, it is taboo to criticize the opposition. I broke that rule, and I got into trouble for it.

What kind of trouble?
They threatened to beat me up.

Who?
Different elements tied to the dissident community. There were lists of people drawn up who were not supposed to be allowed to work as "independent journalists". It was really quite funny. On the one hand, I was attacked by the government, and on the other hand, by the "dissidents", who would never allow anyone to have a truly independent stance, one that was critical of what was going on.

What about the freedom of expression?
These groups have no concept of it, even though they talk about it incessantly. I broke that barrier. I did an investigative report on the so-called Cuban Council, where I unmasked all of the lies behind this group. I called my article, "Is the Cuban Council in its Death Throes?" That did it. I also denounced the corruption of people like Héctor Palacios.

What was the Cuban Council?
The joining together of numerous grouplets — 140 "opposition" organizations, they said — upon the instructions of the Cuban-American National Foundation. And it was connected, from the beginning, with Brothers to the Rescue and its head, José Basulto; with the Center for a Free Cuba, Freedom House, the Institute for Democracy in Cuba, and others. And also with Carlos Alberto Montaner and Hubert Matos. In reality, it was a council joining the inside and the outside, under the direction of the Interests Section, which organized a parallel event to the Ibero-American Summit held in Havana in 1999.

Another organization that gave major support to the Cuban Council was Reporters without Borders. And, of course, the U.S. government fundamentally. But in any event, it was a real madhouse.

How were relations among the "independent journalists"?
They had their ups and downs. It wasn't easy to maintain good relations, because everyone was after the dollars. There were people who only earned 20 dollars a month, and there was an underlying problem among the so-called "independent journalists". The majority didn't even fulfill the minimum requirements for exercising the profession. That was the case for Gilberto Figueredo, who averaged one spelling mistake per line. This led me to organize a meeting in Chinatown among the founding journalists. I spent a month getting the meeting together.

Where in Chinatown?
In the apartment of Estrella García, right on the main street of Chinatown, above a *paladar* (small privately run restaurant).

What was the primary objective?
There was a lot of anger towards Raúl Rivero. He hadn't adhered to the old saying, "The shark swims in the water, but it splashes the others." He became too greedy for his own good. He wanted everything for himself. He also hadn't properly channeled the concerns and problems put forward "to the group". He felt that he was

above everyone else, and was even convinced that he was un-touchable. He didn't have the guts to attend the meeting.

We took advantage of the meeting to draft a document that was signed by the majority of the participants, in which we described the enormous difficulties we had to face with the institu- tions that managed our resources abroad. When the news reached Miami, a scandal erupted. Then came the pressures, and people started backing off. They accused me at the Interests Section, where I was summoned to be interrogated by an official.

What happened?
I presented myself there, very calmly, and told the official dealing with me, "Look, here are the original and a copy of the document and the signatures, and here is a copy of the recording of the discussion." Before I left, I had to answer a questionnaire, apparently to test me. The matter was left there. The problem led to fighting among the different groups, it was a moment of crisis. From that point forward, the officials at the Interests Section stayed in closer contact with me. I was instructed by officers to avoid conflicts. The objective was to gain space.

Did you meet with any U.S. political figures?
One of the most important, in terms of interventionism, was Charles Shapiro, the head of the Cuba Desk of the State Department at that time. During his visit, he gave us instructions to organize a parallel summit to the Ibero-American Summit that was going to be held in Havana. I also met with members of Congress, economists and other personalities.

When was your first contact with the U.S. Interests Section?
In May of 1997.

With whom?
Judith Bryan, deputy officer. At that point I had already made a name for myself in the "independent" press. During our conversation she tested me to try to get to know me better. She even asked me if I wanted to leave the country. I told her that I didn't, because I wanted to be here to see my son grow up, and I was doing well economically.

José Basulto León

Sent to study in the United States by his father, he was recruited by the CIA between the years 1959 and 1960.

On May of 1960, he was trained by the CIA in the use of radio, cryptography and other techniques, on Useppa Island and in the training centers of Fort Peary, Virginia and Camp Trax, Guatemala. He ended his training in February of 1961 in Panama. He joined an infiltration team as a radio operator.

As a CIA agent, he traveled legally to Cuba under a false identity, using the name of Ernestino Martínez. He worked in Santiago de Cuba fostering and organizing counterrevolutionary groups in charge of backing the Bay of Pigs invasion. After the invasion failed, he left the country illegally through the U.S. naval base in Guantánamo, in June of 1961.

On August 24, 1962, he participated as a gunman on a boat that opened fire on the former Blanquita Theater (now the Karl Marx Theater) and on what was then the Rosita de Hornedo Hotel.

On November 21, 1963, he was part of an armed group that infiltrated Cuba through Santa Cruz del Norte. During the 70s, he had active ties with a Catholic university group in the United States, and was a member of the board of directors of the 2506 Brigade, which promoted counterrevolutionary activities in Miami.

He has masterminded numerous subversive plots against Cuba, encouraged illegal emigration from the country, and planned the sabotage of high voltage towers in San Nicolás de Bari and the smuggling of weapons to carry out the assassination of the Cuban president.

He is well-known for the material and financial support offered to counterrevolutionary groups working within Cuba, especially to the "dissidents" María Beatriz Roque and Diosdado González Marrero.

Did this contact take place on a regular basis?
Yes. I was given precise instructions and supplies to carry out my work. Just to give you an idea of how intense this relationship was:

between early 2002 and March 28, 2003, when my true identity was revealed, I went to the Interests Section 21 times.

Did you have any difficulty getting into the Interests Section offices?
Not at all. They gave me an open pass. I could go inside and use their computers to go on the Internet and send and receive e-mail.

What did the Interests Section officials ask you for?
Information on the economy, on the personal lives of our leaders, on the sociopolitical situation. We were given instructions to attack the government, indications as to the most vulnerable areas of the country in terms of news, and training for the exercise of the profession (journalism courses), as well as the means to carry out our missions (computers, printers, tape recorders, cameras, video cameras, etc.).

At around this time, at the end of the year 2000, the Interests Section had a greater interest in me, especially after another conflict erupted, when *Cubanet* expelled around 20 people with no explanation. Shortly before this happened, I had created the Federation of Cuban Journalists, and I used the group to try to unite people in the face of this problem. It was through this union of sorts that I was able to put up a good fight in the Interests Section.
This caught the attention of Vicky Huddleston, who visited me at my home. I eventually developed a very fluid relationship with her. I told her about what was happening: that people wanted money, that *Cubanet* had to change its payment system... That was in February or March of 2001. After that, she went to Miami, met with the people at *Cubanet*, and something happened that changed the payment system around May of that year. In other words, she gave instructions with regard to what I had asked for on behalf of the other "journalists". After that, I began to visit the Interests Section more regularly.

Could you tell me about some of those meetings?
For example, on the afternoon of February 12, 2002, there was a meeting that lasted about three hours at the residence of the head

of the Interests Section, Vicky Huddleston, where she instructed us to maintain contacts with the embassies of Belgium, Germany and Spain.

It was a luncheon meeting, and sitting at the table, among others, were Elsa Morejón Hernández, Magalys de Armas Chaviano, René Gómez Manzano, Isabel del Pino Sotolongo, Osvaldo Alfonso Valdés, Odilia Collazo Valdés, Luis Osvaldo Manzaneira Cucalo, Julio Luis Pitaluga, and myself. Vicky sat with us, and asked about obtaining a list of counterrevolutionary prisoners. She asked us if we agreed that there were around 200. Of course, everyone claimed that the number was higher, around 250.

At around three, when lunch was ending, she took a microphone and welcomed everyone present to her home. She said that we truly represented the Cuban people, and that our country would have to recognize the "dissidents", free the so-called political prisoners, allow freedom of the press, and make other democratic changes.

Jeffrey de Laurentis asked about repression of "dissidents", while Louis Nigro said he had visited a number of "independent libraries" in Camagüey, and noted a shortage of literature. At the end of the meeting, all of the participants were given small Tecsun brand radios as a gifts.

You have a good memory.
It's not that I have a good memory; I was able to take notes, because of being a journalist.

Did officials from the Interests Section visit your home?
Yes, of course. I remember that on April 11 of 2002, between 11:30 a.m. and 3:00 p.m., I was visited at my home by Maryann McKay, the deputy public affairs officer, who also asked me for information on the Cuban informal economy.

Before leaving, she told me that she was very pleased with her visit, and that on the next occasion Vicky might participate as well.

And did you visit the homes of Interests Section officials?
Yes. For example, on April 15 I visited the residence of Gonzalo Gallegos, public affairs officer at the Interests Section, accompanied by Raúl Rivero, Ricardo González Alfonso, Oscar Espinosa Chepe, Carmelo Díaz Fernández, Pedro Pablo Álvarez Ramos, Edel José García Díaz and Luis García.

On that occasion, Maryann McKay explained that there were two reasons for the meeting: to gather opinions on the possibilities of investment in Cuba and on whether these investments would help the process of transition towards a democracy. The "dissidents" voiced their disagreement with this.

Do you still have your notes from these visits?
On June 6, I attended a lunch hosted by Vicky, along with another seven officials from the Interests Section and 21 members of the so-called "independent press". It was a farewell lunch for Mary Ann Mackay, whose posting in Cuba was ending.

Sitting with the Interests Section head were Raúl Rivero, from Cuba Press; Mario Enrique Mayo, from the "Félix Varela" Press Agency, based in Camagüey; Luis García Vega, from the "Independent Journalists" Cooperative; Julio César Gálvez, from the Cuban "Civic Press" Agency; and Pedro Pablo Álvarez Ramos, from the United Council of Workers of Cuba.

Vicky read a message to the participants, where she spoke of the "importance that had to be given to the speeches made by U.S. President George W. Bush on May 20." She finished by expressing thanks for the work carried out during her term as principal officer of the Interests Section, and told us that all of us present there were very courageous people.

Gonzalo Gallegos, the Interests Section public affairs officer, announced that as part of his government's initiatives regarding Cuba there was a program for two years of schooling in the United States for Cubans between the ages of 17 to 25, aimed at academic upgrading in the United States in the fields of small business management and administration. He handed out application forms, but I don't know if this project was ever actually carried out.

As we were leaving, the Interests Section officials gave each of the participants a carrying case. These contained materials for our work as journalists, three Tecsun brand portable radios (they said we could have more, if we wanted), a waterproof solar-powered flashlight, and copies of the application forms for the scholarships offered by the Interests Section, stressing that the applicants must be individuals disaffected with the government.

I have more notes here. On July 1, I went to a working breakfast at Vicky's residence. I was accompanied by Manuel Vázquez Portales, Oscar Espinosa Chepe and his wife. On the U.S. side, in addition to the hostess, it was attended by diplomatic officials Louis Nigro, Gonzalo Gallegos and Ryan Dooley.

You were also invited for breakfast?
And really good breakfasts!

What did they want this time?
They were interested in our opinions on constitutional amendments. The participants voiced their concerns over the possible breaking of relations between Cuba and the United States, the immigration agreements, and the closure of the Interests Section in Havana.

The Interests Section officials commented on opinions regarding a possible mass exodus to the United States, and people looking for speedboats that would come to Cuba to help them emigrate. Vicky commented on the presence of large numbers of police officers on the beaches, at which point Vázquez Portal jokingly commented that "they had to be careful the police didn't leave Cuba as well."

Espinosa Chepe and Vázquez Portal maintained that the speech given by Carter at the University of Havana was the one that did the most damage to Fidel, and not the speech by President George W. Bush. Their argument was that the former president had been intelligent, moderate and courageous, while Bush was too aggressive.

Democracy Movement (Movimiento Democracia)

Founded at the beginning of 1995, and composed of members of the terrorist organization known as the Cuban National Commission (Comisión Nacional Cubana, CNC).

The top leader of the group is Ramón Saul Sánchez Rizo. He was born in Colón, Matanzas. He has a post-secondary degree in electronics. His address is 7105 SW 8th Street, Suite 101, Second Floor, Miami, FL 33144 (2000), Brickelave, Miami.

At an early age, he was already a renowned terrorist and a fierce anticommunist. In 1978, he was suspected of having participated in a terrorist attack against four Americans who were traveling to Cuba in an airplane that disappeared. He was the head of the organization known as Jóvenes de la Estrella.

In 1979, US authorities identified him as the second in command of the organization known as CORU, presided over by Cuban-born terrorist Orlando Bosch. That same year he was tied to the assassination of Carlos Muñiz Varela in Puerto Rico.

He participated in attacks on Cuban fishermen in the Bahamas and on the Mexican embassy. He has also taken part in plans for the kidnapping of important figures in Florida, New York, Venezuela, and Mexico, seeking to extort funds through the use of blackmail.

Since 2002, his organization has begun to give public support to counterrevolutionary groups in Cuba, and particularly to the so-called Varela Project, which it supported publicly during the recent visit to Miami by Oswaldo Payá.

Finally, we were invited to participate in the reception on July 4 to commemorate the anniversary of U.S. independence. And once again we were given supplies: in addition to documents with recipes for democracy, plastic bags with four radios each. The "opposition" members were driven home in an Interests Section car, except for me, because I had come on my bicycle and I rode it home again.

Did you attend the Fourth of July reception?
Of course.

What happened there?

The reception was held at Vicky's residence. There were around 35 of us "dissidents" in attendance. There were also diplomats from other countries, foreign correspondents, and a few guests from the Cuban cultural world.

They threw colored balloons from a balcony overlooking the grounds of the house, where the reception was held, and the participants were given U.S. flag pins and other similar souvenirs. Vicky dedicated a poem to us — specially dedicated to the "human rights activists", or something like that — and then went on almost immediately to read the speech given by U.S. President George W. Bush for Independence Day. It was all very patriotic.

On a more informal footing, Vicky's assistant, Peter Corsell, asked about the possible successors to Fidel and the consequences for Cuban society. During the conversation, he presented himself as an "enemy of the extreme right in Miami and Havana," and stressed the need to protect the immigration agreements between the two countries.

Ryan Dooley, who was responsible for attending to us, talked to a very small group of us about the desire to leave the country of many of the people present. He was clearly bothered by the harassment he was subjected to throughout the entire reception for these purposes, particularly by Jorge Olivera Castillo and his wife, and Magalys de Armas Chaviano's son. Entertainment was provided by a pianist from the United States and Fernando Sánchez López, from the Democratic Solidarity Party, who very "patriotically" accompanied him.

And there were gift bags, of course: a radio, a battery recharger, a booklet on various political and legal subjects and the Constitution of the United States, a Bacardi rum brochure, and two small leaflets, one with the speech made by former President James Carter in Havana — they had taken what was said at the last meeting very seriously — and another with statements by Bush on the policy towards Cuba.

A few weeks later, on August 14, I once again attended a lunch at the home of Gonzalo Gallegos.

They certainly seemed to keep you people well fed.
It's part of our payment.

What was the occasion this time?
To introduce Nicholas J. Giacobbe and Richard Cason, new dip-

lomats at the Interests Section.

What happened at the lunch?
Cason called on us to share our views and opinions on the current situation in the country. Manuel Vázquez Portal, Julio César Gálvez Rodríguez and Oscar Espinosa began. They commented on the pessimistic outlook following the signatures given by the Cuban people in support of the Constitutional Reform project. They claimed that all Fidel cared about was staying in power, and that the U.S. economic blockade was of no importance to our government, emphasizing that in the Central Committee of the Communist Party, all of the officials wore masks.

On addressing the issue of the "independent press", what became clear was the need for more resources in order for us to carry out "better quality work". This was a unanimous demand. There were various suggestions to improve our work. Vázquez Portal said that the press and Radio and Television "Martí" should focus on the values of the Cuban people: homeland, family, religion and freedom.

Less than two weeks later, on August 26, to be exact, I attended another function at the home of the Interests Section chief.

What was the occasion?
It was a farewell party for Vicky Huddleston. There were gifts for the hostess. I remember that Elsa Morejón Hernández, the wife of Oscar Elías Biscet, after falling over herself in praise for Vicky, recited a poem in her honor and then presented her with a painting of a Cuban country landscape. Marta Beatriz Roque emotionally spoke of the enormous help that Vicky had given to the "opposition". Others gave her a religious picture and a letter addressed to the State Department, praising her work. Vladimiro Roca, from

the Social Democratic Party, predicted that within two years we would have the democracy we yearned for and suggested that Vicky's replacement "follow the same line that she had, or an even harder one."

Later, we commented on the subjects that were addressed at the different tables.

Such as?
Louis Nigro asked about Alcibíades Hidalgo, who had occupied very important positions in the government. He asked Miriam Leyva Viamontes, from the Cuban Commission for Human Rights and National Reconciliation, about her opinion of this man, who had apparently gone to the United States illegally with considerable ease.

Oswaldo Payá Sardiñas, from the Christian Freedom Movement, spent his time trying to convince the people he spoke with of the need to step up pressure on the Cuban government to acknowledge the "Varela Project".

Baguer got into an argument with diplomat Ryan Dooley after saying that Payá was a failure and a loser, which drew an angry response from the U.S. official.

What kind of relationship did you have with Payá?
Distant. That of a journalist, a political observer, who also happens to be critical of his project. There was something very interesting about Payá: he didn't invite the "independent journalists" to his press conferences. Only the foreign press.

How did Vicky's farewell party end?
When lunch was finished, she called for everyone's attention by clinking her glass. She recalled how the beginning of her posting in Cuba coincided with the visit to our country by Governor George Ryan, and she declared that was a special pleasure to have us as guests at her farewell.

She noted that at that point in time, the "opposition" was divided into two sides, those on the left and those on the right. She said that this was not important, because it was all a question of fighting for democracy. As usual, on our way out we were given radios and copies of a book entitled *Outside Cuba,* published in collaboration with the University of New Jersey, with paintings by Cuban artists.

Did you have contact with James Cason?
From the moment he arrived.

When did you meet with him for the first time?
On September 17, at the home of Gonzalo Gallegos. We met in the library. The main reason behind the meeting was to introduce us as the principal "dissident" leaders.

Was there anything noteworthy?
No. It was more of the same. The people there asked for money — "support" — and once again we heard about the "independent libraries", and the press-related projects. With the exception of Carmelo Díaz from the "Independent" Trade Union Press Agency, who praised the station, the participants were very critical of *Radio "Martí".* They talked about the poor quality of programming, its lack of objectivity, describing it as simplistic, and therefore of little interest to the people. I myself commented that there had been a obvious "shift to the right of the station and programming problems," opinions that were generally backed by a number of those present.

Did you participate in the activities of the various groups?
My position as a journalist helped me get invited to their activities. On October 10, I was at Marta Beatriz Roque's house for the establishment of the Public Relations Committee for the so-called Assembly to Promote Civil Society in Cuba project.

At this meeting, they agreed, among other things: to distribute literature describing their work to the embassies of Italy, Germany and Sweden. To draft a request for international aid for the dissidents affected by Hurricanes Isidore and Lili. To congratulate Vladimiro Roca and Gustavo Arcos for their Civic Courage awards, equivalent to 50,000 and 5,000 dollars, respectively.

Did you accompany them on their visits to embassies?
At the Italian embassy, Marta Beatriz and other "dissidents" were received by Raffaela Pavani. We told her about the main lines of work to be undertaken to promote this project.

We also visited the British embassy, where we were received by the second secretary, Susannah Payne. After we had explained the reason for our visit, she asked about the motives for the disagreements between Marta Beatriz and Oswaldo Payá.

In response to her questions, Marta explained that these disagreements were the result of Payá's attitude of contempt towards the other opposition members, which he justified through accusations of supposed links between these groups and Cuban State Security Agencies.

Did you meet with Cason again?
On a regular basis. On October 30, we met at his home to work on the project headed up by Marta Beatriz, and he announced the upcoming visit, in December, by the head of the Cuba Desk at the U.S. State Department, Kevin Whitaker.

Did he come in the end?
Yes.

Did you get to meet him?
On December 18, between 1:00 and 3:00 p.m., along with another 12 dissident leaders, I met with Mr. Kevin Whitaker at the home of Gonzalo Gallegos.

For what purpose?
He congratulated us on the work we were doing and said that this kind of contact was very beneficial and should be repeated in the future.

Susan Archer, the second secretary for political and economic affairs at the Interests Section, took advantage of the occasion to introduce Whitaker to Aleida Godínez Soler, the leader of the independent unions, with whom the high U.S. official had an animated conversation.

Were your contacts with the Interests Section maintained in the new year?
In 2003 they were not just maintained, they were increased and reinforced. Sometimes we visited them, and other times we met in our homes.

Cason's activity became more active and much more provocative. He went so far as to tell us that we were not alone, and that we had the support of his government. I remember that when a foreign correspondent asked him about the possibility of the Cuban government interpreting his participation in these activities as an unfriendly act, he responded that "he was not afraid."

How did the idea come up of holding a workshop on journalistic ethics?
This was an idea we had had for a long time. We agreed to hold it on March 14 at Cason's residence.

Who informed the foreign correspondents?
I did. Giacobbe gave me the phone numbers.

How exactly was the workshop organized?
When I joined the Assembly led by Marta, she appointed me to the Press Committee, where I was immediately elected president. I met with Ricardo Zuniga two or three days later, because there were new conflicts brewing, and he practically begged me to work at ending this fighting.

There was a second meeting of the Press Committee, where we discussed the request for withdrawal from the Assembly from a group in Camagüey. The people there complained about conflicts of interest and excessive politicization, and said they did not want to be involved in all this.

Marta tried to have this group condemned for having left the Assembly, and she wanted the condemnation to come from the journalists themselves, but they refused to go along with it. I took advantage of this opportunity to propose to these people, who were pure Miami, the idea of reflecting on ethics, and holding a workshop. The result: Marta got up, went to the phone, and came back with the instructions from Gonzalo Gallegos to hold a meeting at his house, supposedly because they wouldn't be able to fit everyone into Marta's house. They talked about 60 "independent journalists", and then the Americans, who certainly knew from the very beginning that it would be impossible to gather 60 "opposition" members, came up with a brilliant plan: to hold the workshop at Cason's residence, which was big enough to also hold the foreign journalists accredited in Cuba.

How many "independent journalists" participated in the end?
There were 35 of us, plus five Americans.

What happened at the workshop?
We organized it in five commissions: photojournalists; interviews; analysis, conflicts and interests; relations between journalists and editors; and journalistic language. Once the discussions had concluded, the participants received a diploma certifying their attendance at this "event".

Whose signature was on the diploma?
The signature of dissident leader Manuel David Orrio del Rosario, who was actually Agent Miguel of the State Security agencies.

Why Miguel?
It's my son's name.

When was your last article published abroad?
In late March. It was an amusing report I entitled "Living on Fear". I described the fear felt by the "dissidents", I mean, the counter-revolutionaries.

Why the correction?
I still have the counterrevolutionary stuck inside me. I had to train myself to assimilate all of the language used in this setting, to the point where one day my officer was talking about the blockade, and I told him: "Listen, you have to say embargo when you talk to me, because if I get mixed up out there, I've had it."

Now you have to get the character you were playing out from under your skin...
Yes, now I have to rebuild my life, my family. I want to work as a journalist and write a book, maybe a novel.

In the beginning, did you have doubts, did you regret taking this step?

I never had any doubts, I was only worried that I wouldn't be able to take on a task like this in the midst of all my personal problems, but I managed to overcome these conflicts. I don't regret any of it. On the contrary. When I was informed that my true identity was going to be revealed, I was against it, because I felt that I had reached my peak: I was well-positioned, I had the full trust of the head of the Interests Section, and I was one of the leading "independent journalists". I thought that there was still a lot more I could do, but I am disciplined, and I understood the reasons. Of course, in personal terms, I feel a huge relief.

Why?

Can you imagine just how badly someone can want to be himself?

THE EVIDENCE WAS A BOMBSHELL

It was a difficult interview at first. We had trouble breaking the ice, and getting Agent Saúl to speak to us comfortably, without having to tear the words from his mouth.

Little by little, the conversation begins to flow and we discover a man with a prodigious memory, who can recount his past choosing the most essential details and most precise adjectives, in such a way that we can almost see the situations he speaks of.

Who is Pedro Serrano Urra? Why did he choose Saúl as his code-name? The answer lies in a book: "Saúl is the name of a character in a Cuban detective novel that was published in the 1980s. I liked the book, and I turned that character into the lawyer of the 'dissidents' in Pinar del Río". What follows is that new story.

AGENT SAÚL

When did you become an agent?
In 1999. I'm a lawyer, and at the time I had to quit my practice at the col-

lective law firm because of administrative issues. Some members of the "opposition", who were in need of legal aid, had gotten in touch with me. I met almost everyone in Pinar del Río that was involved in counterrevolutionary activities, including some people that left the country later on.

Exactly how did you begin to collaborate with them?
They came to my home to ask me to denounce my case abroad. I spoke with an official from State Security and he suggested I join the group. Almost immediately, the people who had come to see me introduced me to Víctor Rolando Arroyo Carmona, who was collaborating with the press agency known as the Union of "Independent" Cuban Journalists and Writers (Unión de Periodistas y Escritores Cubanos Independientes, UPECI), and was the top leader of these groups in Pinar del Río. He urgently needed a legal adviser he could trust. I went on to be "Víctor's lawyer".

They would introduce you like that, as a lawyer only?
No. My front was that of the director of the Center for Trade Union Studies, which was part of the United Council of Cuban Workers (Consejo Unitario de Trabajadores de Cuba). I had contact with René Laureano Díaz, Joel Brito and Víctor Manuel Domínguez, from the Trade Union Federation of Electrical Power Plants (Federación Sindical de Plantas Eléctricas), in Miami.

What tasks were you given as the lawyer of the counterrevolutionary movement?
I served as adviser in all legal proceedings, and in any situation that required taking a lawsuit to court. I would also present reports on judicial violations. I had to attend trials, see how the judicial processes were being carried out, to see if there were any violations.

I would give lectures to inform counterrevolutionaries on these issues. We studied what constituted an act of disobedience, assault, resisting arrest, defamation of President Fidel Castro and the officials of the National Assembly and the Council of Ministers, what constituted a breach of privacy and correspondence. The Center that I was running organized these lectures every Saturday.

Were you in contact with the U.S. Interests Section?
I never visited the Interests Section. We had planned some visits, but they were all cancelled for one reason or another. But I did attend meetings with representatives of the Interests Section.

Where?
At Víctor Rolando's home. I met there with two of the heads of the Interests Section, Vicky Huddleston and James Cason.

What were those meetings like?
They were quite blunt. They didn't beat around the bush. They were interested in all of the activities being organized by the "dissident" groups in Pinar del Río. They would ask for details, and they would tell us we needed to grow in numbers, that we had to organize ourselves, unite all of the "opposition" groups. They even borrowed some ideas from our Revolution: "Strength is in unity," "Everyone united," etc...

The part everyone was interested in was when they asked what resources we had and what we needed. They would always promise to help us.

When were you visited by James Cason?
In March of this year (2003), during the time that President Fidel Castro was doing a tour through a number of Asian countries. He was extremely interested in knowing what we felt about that visit, if it was going to have some repercussion in Cuba, if Fidel was going to return with new political ideas to apply to his country. He was obsessed with those details, which were far outside the scope of our knowledge and our interest.

He also asked us if we had ties to other members of the diplomatic corps...

Did he suggest anything in particular with respect to this?
In his opinion, it was very important for us to have them hear our denunciations. He was interested in knowing if any other diplomat had visited Pinar del Río, if we were getting aid from any other country. He told us other embassies were interested in offering aid to "dissident" groups. He spoke of Spain, Panama, the Czech Republic, Canada, Mexico... He mentioned five or six countries.

> **National Council of Cuban Political Prisoners (Consejo Nacional del Presidio Político Cubano)**
>
> Established in August of 2002. It calls itself the "highest representative of political prisoners at a national and international level."
>
> It is made up of: the International Coordinator of Cuban Ex-Political Prisoners (Coordinadora Internacional de Ex-Prisioneros Politicos Cubanos); Political Prisoners Patriotic Summit (Cumbre Patriotica Presidio Politico); the Association of Ex-Political Prisoners and Militants of Cuba (Asociación de ex Prisioneros y Combatientes Politicos Cubanos, Ex Club); Ex-Political Inmates of the Military Units in Aid of Production (Ex Confinados Politicos de las Unidades Militares de Apoyo a la Producción, UMAP); the National Front of Cuban Political Prisoners (Frente Nacional del Presidio Politico Cubano); Historical Center of Political Prisoners (Presidio Politico Historico); and the Independent Prisoners organization (Presos y Presas Independientes).
>
> Its leadership has included terrorists Roberto Martín Pérez Rodríguez and Sixto Reynaldo Aquit Manrique, advocates of violent action against our country.

And what else did he tell you?

He promised to make long-distance courses available to us, including graduate studies, Master's degrees and doctorates, aimed at "dissidents" who had some level of education. He was speaking to me and to another lawyer in the meeting when he mentioned this. He promised to send us a bibliography for us to prepare ourselves, and to send the exam later on, in coordination with Latin American universities. He had a very persuasive and conciliatory tone.

Why conciliatory?

He was speaking a lot about Cubans from here and there, that we were all one family, that Miami was not as terrible as they painted it. That the first thing we had to do, with the help of those Cubans in exile, was to obtain as much of a political space as we could, because only then would there be a transition in Cuba.

How long was the meeting?

About two hours.

What is the address of Víctor Rolando's home?
The meeting was in the Jacinto district, at Víctor's mother's house. Around ten of us met there, the bulk of the "opposition" in Pinar del Río. Víctor carried out most of his activities at his mom's place; he only did a bit of writing in his own home.

Did you have a selection process to choose the participants in the meeting, or were you ten in total, the members of the "opposition" in Pinar del Río?
There aren't many more members. In truth, the opposition groups are not even groups. Imagine, I was the municipal coordinator in the city of Pinar del Río for the United Council of Workers and, at the same time, the delegate for the province. There were five or six of us in the United Council. We would always say it was made up of 300 people from every municipality, but those people didn't exist.

And Cason accepted this illusion?
Luckily for the leaders of the "dissident" movement, Cason never thought to ask about the number of people in the groups. I always suspected he never asked because he knew perfectly well what the answer was, and he wasn't up to hearing more lies.

The other officials didn't ask either?
No. They had one theme: to grow and to unite. They were always pushing the same thing. They must know the "dissidents" better than we do, because they are constantly dealing with them. That story that two million out of the 11 million people in Cuba are dissidents, as Víctor loved to say, is something that only people ignorant of Cuban reality could believe, outside of Cuba. It's not something the Americans were going to buy, because they know the dissident movement well.

Was the head of the Interests Section defending one group in particular?
The "Varela" Project. He asked us to lend it support. He said that it had a lot of international backing and that it was going to continue having it. It was the step toward "democracy". He said something along those lines, without stopping to mention the huge legal stumbling blocks of the project.

What were the expectations of the ten dissidents for Cason's visit? Before Cason arrived, we discussed asking him if the remittances from Cuban families in the U.S. were going to continue coming, if the direct flights from Miami to Cuba were going to be maintained, and if the blockade was going to be lifted. We were especially interested in knowing how the money was being distributed, the famous 8,099,181 dollars from USAID in 2002, of which very little had reached our province.

Internal Dissidence Support Group (Grupo de Apoyo a la Disidencia Interna)

Appeared in the early 1990s. Forms part of the Institute for Democracy in Cuba (IDC), comprising 10 counterrevolutionary organizations based in Miami and beneficiaries of a million-dollar budget from Washington "to promote democracy in Cuba."

Its director, Frank Hernández Trujillo, has close links with U.S. politicians. The group's basic mission is to supply "dissidents" with money and materials, as a tool of the U.S. government in applying the so-called Track II of the Torricelli Act.

It currently heads the list of organizations supplying materials and money to the internal counterrevolution, with which it also has the most frequent contacts by telephone (to the point that it even allocates funds for telephone calls).

It will supply any internal faction, notably the families of former "political" prisoners, masons, followers of the Yoruba religion, etc., with the aim of inciting internal subversion.

Since 1997 the IDC has received a large operating budget, including fixed salaries for its leaders.

As a member of the IDC, it uses the latter's airtime on *Radio Miami International*.

It produces a bulletin printed by the IDC called *Somos uno* (We Are One), and uses various channels to attempt to circulate it in Cuba.

The members of the "opposition" were interested in maintaining the remittances and the direct flights?
Some of us were in favor, others were against them. Víctor was one of the members who wanted them to suspend the remittances and the direct flights. He was a hard-liner. Cason kept quiet about these issues.

Did he mention the money you would receive?
He made no comments about this. We were all very anxious waiting for him to address the economic issue. We thought that, following this visit, the dollars would start falling from the skies.

They also talked to us about the "independent libraries". There were three fundamental projects being carried out in Pinar del Río at the time, which were the hopes for a more robust "opposition". One of them was mine — the Center for Studies — which, incidentally, interested Cason immensely. Another was an art gallery, "Interior Space", where works by "dissident" painters were exhibited; most of the paintings made you want to run out of the place. They were of such poor quality that the gallery's promoter decided to give a few lessons to the "independent artists".

The third project, for independent clinics and pharmacies, was perhaps the most dangerous.

In what way?
Because it was aimed at subverting the Cuban health system, creating a parallel system. It was extremely aggressive and had a lot of support from abroad.

Do you know how it emerged?
Early in 2002, this project gained some notoriety in the Guane municipality. It was apparently the idea of Dr. Jesús Manuel Cruz Santovenia, from the Human Rights Party (Partido Pro Derechos Humanos), affiliated to the Andrei Sakharov Foundation. Since the doctor got his visa to leave the country, he convinced another doctor, Hanoi Hernández Pinero, to develop it further. This man was crazy to get a visa himself, so he jumped aboard. That's what was said; nevertheless, everyone knew that the inspiration had come from elsewhere.

Where?

In 2001, Marcelo Cano Rodríguez, a member of the Cuban Commission of Human Rights and National Reconciliation (Comisión Cubana de Derechos Humanos y Reconciliación Nacional), and a loyal collaborator of Elizardo Sánchez Santacruz, had been

sketching out this idea, at first to supply the "opposition" with its own, private clinic. They wanted to obtain equipment and a whole storage room full of supplies, which would also make it possible for them to provide "humanitarian" services to the population in general. In other words, there were signs of interest in the same project showing up here and there.

Did you find out about other similar projects?

Caridad Pérez Gainza, from the 24th of February Movement, also wanted to set up her own "independent" clinic. She wanted to start off using her asthma treatment equipment on her neighbors in Lawton, Diez de Octubre (in Havana). That's how it got started, until it became a project supported by counterrevolutionaries in Miami.

René Laureano Díaz González

Leader of the Federated Union of Electrical, Gas and Water Plants of Cuba in Exile (FSPEGA), based in Miami.

He began counterrevolutionary activities in 1959 and in the following year took part in a dynamite attack on the Tallapiedra thermoelectric power station. He sought asylum in the Brazilian embassy and left for the United States on March 6, 1961.

In the United States he joined the terrorist organizations December 9 Electrical Commandos (Comandos Eléctricos 9 de Diciembre) and Revolutionary Recovery Movement (Movimiento de Recuperación Revolucionaria, MRR).

He set up FSPEGA as an organization to support the union-based counterrevolutionary factions, voicing his total approval for their activities in the magazine published by his organization, *Lux*, and providing financial aid. He planned terrorist operations for execution by internal clandestine cells.

How do you know so many details?
They would write about this everyday in the "independent" press. This was a movement with a tremendous amount of international coverage. Of course, you could find everything I've told you about embellished with all of the adjectives you can think of: "Castro's hordes impede the humanitarian efforts of Caridad Pérez Gainza"; "violent reactions against Dr. Hanoi...", etc., etc. The truth is that all of them saw a great opportunity to demoralize and confuse the population.

Who was supporting this in Miami?
Frank Hernández Trujillo, from the Dissidence Support Group (Grupo de Apoyo a la Disidencia). He sent medicine to his employees in Cuba through every channel he could find. And they gave this a huge amount of publicity on the counterrevolutionary radio stations, of course.

Víctor Manuel Domínguez

He became involved in the cultural sector due to his interest in choreography.

He is a radio, film and television producer.

He began his counterrevolutionary activities in 1996 as member of the organizing committee of the so-called Alternative Cuban Art Project (Proyecto Alternativo de Arte Cubano), aimed at grouping together counterrevolutionary artists within the country.

He is currently a member of the Independent National Workers Confederation of Cuba (Confederación Obrera Nacional Independiente de Cuba, CONIC), serving as one of its top leaders.

He is the director of the project known as the National Trade Union Training Center (Centro Nacional de Capacitación Sindical), which is sponsored from abroad by the terrorist counterrevolutionary organization FESPEGA. He has ties with René Laureano Díaz and Joel Brito, counterrevolutionaries who send him supplies.

I remember that in February of this year, *Radio "Martí"* and *La Poderosa* announced the opening of the "Independent" Medical Clinic in Guane, run by Hanoi, in his own home. Some people showed up looking for medicine. Afterwards, we found out that this abomination had in fact been conceived in the United States. It was a "pilot project" coordinated by Dr. Manuel Alzugaray Pérez, from the Miami Medical Team Foundation, in collaboration with members of the "Independent" Medical Association of Cuba (Colegio Médico "Independiente" de Cuba).

Who is Manuel Alzugaray?
He is a friend of Otto Reich, the U.S. government special envoy for Latin America, who is working to have Alzugaray receive a U.S. government grant to finance counterrevolutionary activities both inside and outside of Cuba.

Were medicines sent to the provincial capital in Pinar del Río?
Víctor Rolando received medicines on many occasions through the Cubapacks International agency, and he shared these with a number of colleagues, who followed the same instructions given to other distributors of medicines.

Only medicine, or did they receive equipment as well?
Frank Hernández Trujillo sent Dr. Hanoi an electrocardiogram, equipment to measure blood pressure, clinical testing instruments, and asthma treatment equipment. This man almost built an entire hospital for himself.

You say that the "independent" clinics enjoyed a lot of international attention…
Yes, and not only through the Miami press. Jesús Melgar, who is a Cuban-American living in the United States, even tried to put together an international conference there, with representatives of all the "independent" clinics, along with doctors from Spain and Latin America.

Representatives from the clinics only?
No, also from the "independent" pharmacies, which they intended to supply with medicines that the state system was lacking or had in very small quantities. Lázaro Lemus González and Alberto Hernández Suárez, from the Union of Young Democrats of Cuba

(Unión de Jóvenes Democráticos) in Pinar del Río, tried to open up an "independent" pharmacy, with the support of Enrique Blanco and Frank Hernández Trujillo. Lázaro claimed that they would distribute the medicines by prescription and *Radio "Martí"* even announced that they had opened a pharmacy in Candelaria. It was all lies.

Maritza Lugo's dream was well known; she is the former president of the Frank País November 30 Democratic Party (Partido Democrático 30 de Noviembre Frank País), who now lives in the United States. She wanted to set up a pharmacy in every province, to wage a political campaign in favor of counterrevolutionary groups. In an e-mail, she mentioned that Frank Hernández Trujillo keeps an abundant stock of medicine in his home in Miami, to be sent to Cuba, and that he had commissioned a study of the zones most favorable to the project.

Víctor himself told me that he had been to a party at Dr. Hanoi's place, in Guane, on February 1, 2003, to celebrate the first anniversary of the "Independent" Medical Clinic.

Did you find out what had taken place there?
They spoke of opening two "independent" clinics in the Sandino municipality. Dr. Hanoi practically had a warehouse full of medicine in his home, and he gave out a package of medicine at the party.

Have these clinics ever offered services?
No. They're merely a place where they hand out medicine. As far as I know, the only pharmacy operating in Pinar del Río was in Candelaria, and it was run by Alberto Hernández Suárez, who's given out medicine to those who presented a medical prescription and their ID card. This man knows absolutely nothing about pharmacology.

Among the so-called sacred cows of the "dissident" movement, who lent direct support to this project?
Martha Beatriz Roque, and she was getting money from Miami for it. She herself has spoken about this. She mentioned having re-

ceived considerable funding to purchase the necessary equipment and that she had registered the pharmacies as a Commission for Health Assistance (Comisión de Asistencia a la Salud, COMAS).

Víctor is one of the individuals now in jail. Was he shown the evidence against him?

Yes. He was sentenced to 26 years in prison. The principal evidence was found in documents. Documents of every sort were taken from him: receipts for money he had received, some of which had been sent directly from the Cuban-American National Foundation (Fundación Nacional Cubanoamericana, FNCA).

He is man devoid of scruples, who was even looked down on by other counterrevolutionaries, because he was a very aggressive and egotistical man. He owed money to quite a few people, and he would brazenly sell the radios from the Interests Section, and whatever else he could get his hands on.

For instance, if they sent a camera for a member of the group, Víctor would decide to give it to someone else. The "dissidents" didn't like him one bit, but they tolerated him because he was the one who had ties to the Interests Section. He wasn't someone very good at giving recommendations.

Did he ever give you any money?
No, just a radio and a pair of jeans. He once gave me a 100 Cuban pesos and I gave it to State Security. I know that it came from funding sent by the United States, that someone here had changed it into Cuban money and given me only 100 pesos, but I don't know who it was. These things happened on a regular basis.

And your family?
I was an infiltrator from 1999 until April 3, 2003. I have two daughters from my first marriage, and both of them are members of the Union of Young Communists (Unión de Jóvenes Comunistas, UJC). One of them is in the third year of law, here at the University of Havana, and the other one is in the third year of music, at the School for Art Teachers in Pinar del Río.

From the time they were born, I've always been a role model

for them. We have always been so close that one day I sat down with them and I told them not to pay too much attention to what people were saying about me.

And your wife?
She didn't know anything. She teaches at a college, she has a degree in mathematics and is a member of the UJC. We have a two-year-old son. We live with my mother-in-law and her husband, who's an ardent revolutionary, and my ties to the counterrevolution led to all sorts of problems with my marriage and the relationship with her family. I was always putting up a front. I wasn't working and this was another problem. They were extremely happy to find out I was working for State Security. It was like a magic trick, where everything changes from one moment to the next.

The counterrevolutionaries never suspected you?
No. They didn't have an ounce of doubt about me. So much so that when they saw me at the trial, they thought I was going to be a counterrevolutionary witness. There were witnesses there from "dissident" groups, but, from the very beginning of my testimony, when the prosecutor asked me why I was going to testify, I said I was working with State Security.

Why is that?
They brought me in after presenting the evidence. When the prosecutor is presenting the case against someone, he generally presents the evidence that supports his claim. Of course, the defense lawyer is given the evidence beforehand, and he presents his own evidence based on the latter.

The Criminal Proceedings Law, in the first paragraph of article 340, allows for new and important evidence to be presented during a trial, evidence that has been obtained at the last moment, for instance. The court decides whether the evidence is relevant or not. I was brought in like that.

That's why, when the prosecutor asked me, "Why have you come forth to testify?", I answered him, "Because I am Agent Saúl, from State Security."

What happened with the accused?
They were so surprised and demoralized that Víctor Rolando Arroyo, someone who had been totally overbearing throughout the trial, didn't recover from the shock. He had been certain that they couldn't produce any evidence against him, until I showed up. From that moment on, he sat in his chair and kept his head down the whole time.

Did he make any statements to the court?
Not one. Not even when he was asked if he wanted to add anything to what had been declared. He knew that I knew. The evidence was a bombshell.

Manuel David Orrio del Rosario.

Pedro Serrano Urra.

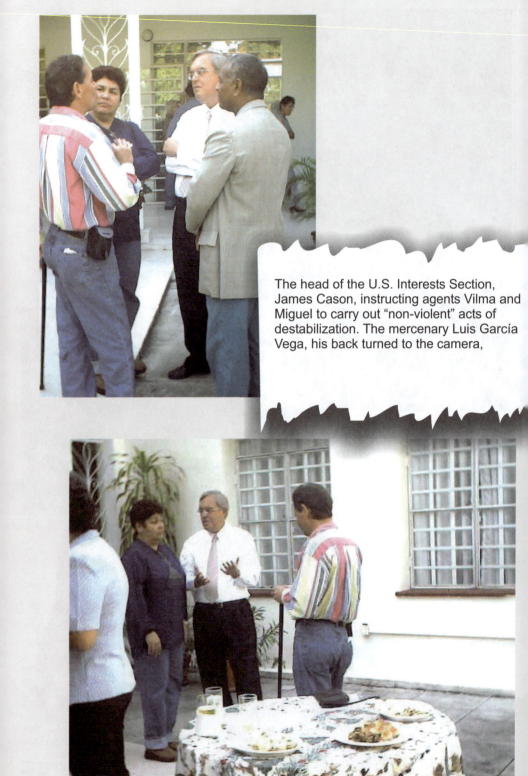

The head of the U.S. Interests Section, James Cason, instructing agents Vilma and Miguel to carry out "non-violent" acts of destabilization. The mercenary Luis García Vega, his back turned to the camera,

Héctor Palacios listens attentively — and somewhat uncomfortably — to James Cason, during the presentation of the book Ojos Abiertos (Open Eyes).

BASIC COURSE IN HUMAN RIGHTS

This is to certify that Héctor Palacios Ruiz has completed the basic training that qualifies him to work as a non-governmental Observer and Promoter in the area of HUMAN RIGHTS.

Havana, March 2, 2000

(Stamp of the Cuban Commission on Human Rights and National Reconciliation)

CERTIFICACIÓN NO.1

Por este medio certificamos que el ciudadano **Héctor Palacios Ruiz**, *ha recibido siete remesas de dinero por un valor de $1550.00USD (mil quinientos cincuenta dólares) a través de la Agencia AMERICAN INTERNATIONAL SERVICE S.A. en el período comprendido desde el 19 de octubre de 1995 hasta el 3 de febrero del 2000, las cuales detallamos a continuación:*

1. *Referencia 95010302*
   Fecha: 13/02/96
   Remitente: Sin remitente
   Importe: $200.00USD

2. *Referencia 95032602*
   Fecha: 09/11/95
   Remitente: Sin remitente
   Importe: $200.00USD

3. *Referencia 95081702*
   Fecha: 21/12/95
   Remitente: Sin remitente
   Importe: $250.00USD

4. *Referencia 9600500*
   Fecha: 08/01/96
   Remitente: Sin remitente
   Importe: $300.00

5. *Referencia 96044503*
   Fecha: 19/10/95
   Remitente: Sin remitente
   Importe: $200.00USD

6. *Referencia 96085301*
   Fecha: 15/03/96
   Remitente: Sin remitente
   Importe: $300.00USD

7. *Referencia 0004861*
   Fecha: 03/02/2000
   Remitente: Gladis Pérez
   Importe: $100.00USD

We hereby certify that the Cuban citizen Héctor Palacios Ruiz has received seven cash remittances adding up to a total value of USD 1550.00 (one thousand five hundred and fifty dollars) through the agency AMERICAN INTERNATIONAL SERVICE S.A., between the dates of October 19, 1995 and February 3, 2000, as detailed below:

Some of the monthly allowances received by mercenary Héctor Palacios.

Saying farewell to Vicky Huddleston: Caridad Gónzalez, Magalis de Armas, Elsa Morejón, Isabel del Pino, Reynaldo Cozano and Agents Vilma and Miguel.

me "independent" plications distributed the U.S. Interests ction.

Some of the equipment given to agents by the U.S. Interests Section.

Ciudad de La Habana, febrero 27 del 2003

Sr. Regis Bourgeat
Reporteros sin Fronteras, París, Francia.

Estimado Regis:

El día 22 la policía detuvo e impuso una multa a Juan Carlos Garcel, de la APLO, mientras trataba de dar cobertura informativa a un registro que practicaban los agentes en una casa en Puerto Padre, provincia de Las Tunas.

El día 24 los periodistas Ramón de Armas Guerrero y Omar Darío Hernández, de la agencia de prensa independiente El Mayor, de la cual el primero es el director, fueron detenidos por la Seguridad del Estado en la ciudad de Camagüey para evitar que informaran sobre los actos de la oposición local para conmemorar el séptimo aniversario del derribo de las dos avionetas de Hermanos al Rescate.

Con ese mismo propósito, en Santa Clara, también el 24 de febrero, la policía política impidió durante varias horas a la periodista de la agencia Cuba Press, Isabel Rey, abandonar la casa de un opositor, en donde pernotó esa noche para poder cubrir como reportera actos de la disidencia con relación a la misma esfeméride.

No deseo concluir este informe sin reiterar que Orlando Fondevila me envío el dinero. Está en el banco; pero por seguridad, no he extrído el efectivo debido a que no tengo la relación a cuales agencias o personas debo entregarlo las diferentes cantidades. No esa quiero tener en mi casa esa cantida de dinero por razones obvias. Por lo que me indispensable que me envíen esa relación. La última vez que pude hablar con su asistente me dijo que usted no se encontraba, y que llamaría al día siguiente para que yo les enviara los informes, y para que RSF me diera la relación, y entonces yo poder realizar las entregas correspondientes.

Deseo precisar que Fondevila me explicó que en el momento en que él realizó la transacción bancaria, el euro estaba por debajo del dólar, por lo que llegó algo menos. Si lo tiene a bien, comuníquese con Fondevila.

Por último, me complace comunicarle que hoy comenzamos a distribuir el segundo número de la Revista de Cuba, correspondiente al mes de febrero, pues, como anunciamos, la publicaremos cada dos meses. Espero que ya haya recibido el CD con el primer número.

Saludos,

Ricardo.

A special invitation to...

CNC Convention Fiesta & Cultural Evening

With performances by

Emilio (singer & guitar)
Pablo Terry & Sol de Cuba Band

sunday sept 5th, 2004
7pm - 11pm
GCDO Hall
290 Danforth Ave
(west of Chester Subway)

$10 cover charge
donations for beer & wine / empanadas / banana chips

The text of the letter reads as follows:

Dear Regis:

On the 22nd of the month, Juan Carlos Garcel, from the APLO, was detained and given a fine by the police, while he attempted to document a house search in Puerto Padre, Las Tunas that these officers were carrying out.

On the 24th of the month, the journalists Ramón de Armas Guerrero and Omar Darío Hernández, both from the independent press agency El Mayor (which is directed by the former), were detained in Camagüey by agents of State Security, to prevent them from documenting the activities of the local opposition party, which was commemorating the seventh anniversary of the downing of the two planes sent by the group Brothers to the Rescue.

With the same objective, also on the 24th of February, in Santa Clara, police officers forbade the Cuba Press journalist, Isabel Rey, from leaving the home of an opposition member, where she had spent the night in order to cover the activities of the opposition during the same commemorative event.

I don't want to end this report without reiterating that Orlando Fondevila has sent me the money. It is now in the bank; but, for safety reasons, I haven't withdrawn the money, as I have not been given a list of the people and the agencies that are to receive the various amounts. I don't want to keep such a large quantity of money in my own home, for obvious reasons. So, I urgently require you to send me that list. The last time I was able to speak with your assistant, he informed me that you were out, and that he would call me the following day to have me send the reports, and for RWB to send me the list that will allow me to deliver the corresponding amounts.

You should know that Fondevila informed me that, at the time of the transaction he carried out at the bank, the euro was below the dollar in value, so that a smaller amount was received. If you think it necessary, get in touch with Fondevila.

Lastly, I'm pleased to inform you that today we began to distribute the second issue of Revista de Cuba, which is the February issue, because, as we had announced, we shall be publishing it every two months. I hope you have already received the CD containing the first issue.

Sincerely,

Ricardo.

Ciudad de La Habana, 20 de diciembre del 2002.

Estimado Fondevila:

Ayer por la mañana cuando hablé con usted por discreción tuve que omitir una información importante. En la noche del 19, durante una recepción en la casa del Jefe de de la Oficina de Intereses de Estados Unidos en La Habana, presentamos la Revista de Cuba, de la Sociedad de Periodistas Manuel Márquez Sterling. Le envío por este medio el CD con el contenidos de esta publicación.

Le ruego que dentro de sus posibilidades la imprima y reproduzca, y que la envíe a Reporteros Sin Fronteras. Además, en Suecia a la revista Cuba Nuestra. Consideramos muy importante que los cubanos residentes en Europa la conozcan.

Sé que en estas festividades navideñas y de año nuevo esta labor se dificulta y que, además, usted se encuentra de vacaciones. Pero conozco también su dedicación a nuestra causa, y que por la misma haría un "trabajo voluntario". Naturalmente, es muy probable que reciba esta carta y el CD en enero; en este caso pienso que la urgencia del encargo que le pido sería mayor.

Sólo me queda desearle, a nombre de la Sociedad Márquez Sterling, y en el mío propio una feliz Navidad y un 2003 con la dicha que usted se merece.

Su amigo.

International money transfer card in the name of Ricardo González, who confirms in this letter that he has carried out the work commissioned by his bosses.

The text of the letter reads as follows:

Dear Fondevila:

When I spoke to you yesterday morning, I had to omit some rather important information out of discretion. On the evening of the 19th, during a reception held in the home of the head of the U.S. Interests Section in Havana, we formally launched Revista Cuba magazine, of the Manuel Márquez Sterling Journalists Society. I am enclosing a CD with the contents of the publication.

I would be much indebted to you if, at your earliest convenience, you could print out and make copies of our publication, and have it reach Reporters Without Borders and the magazine Cuba Nuestra in Sweden. We deem it very important that Cubans residing in Europe get to know our publication.

I am aware that this is much to ask for during the Christmas and New Year season, and that, aside from this, you are currently on vacation. But I am also aware of your devotion to our cause, and that you would be willing to take up this "volunteer work" for us. Quite probably, you will receive this letter in the month of January; should that be the case, please consider my request all the more urgent.

From all of us in the Márquez Sterling Society, allow me to wish you a Merry Christmas and the prosperous New Year that you deserve.

Your friend.

The mercenaries and their leader. Cason lends an attentive ear to Julio César Gálvez. Ricardo Gónzalez Alfonso stands in the background.

REPORTERS
SANS FRONTIERES

Secrétariat International - *International Secretariat*

CERTIFICADO

El abajo firmante, Robert Ménard, secretario general de Reporteros sin fronteras, certifica que nuestra asociación apoya financieramente a la agencia de prensa independiente *Cuba Press*. El pasado 30 de agosto, Reporteros sin fronteras entregó la suma de 900 dólares a Raúl Rivero, director de *Cuba Press*, para que dicha suma fuera repartida entre los periodistas de esa agencia.

Paris, el 2 de agosto de 1996

Robert Ménard
Secrétaire général

The text of the document reads as follows:

The undersigned, Robert Ménard, general secretary of Reporters Without Borders, certifies that our organization lends financial aid to the independent press agency Cuba Press. Last August 30, Reporters Without Borders delivered the sum of 900 dollars to Raúl Rivero, director of Cuba Press, so that said sum could be distributed among the journalists of this agency.

Comité Exécutif International - *International Executive Committee:*
Président: Fernando Castello (Espagne) - Vice-présidents: Karin Bojs (Suède), Renato Burgy (Suisse) et Noël Copin (France) - Trésorier: Michael Rediske (Allemagne)

comment.

La Habana, 25 de julio del 2002

Hago constar que se recibió la cantidad de 1750 dólares (US) de CUBANET, provenientes de Reporteros Sin Fronteras, a través de TRANSCARD a nombre de Oscar Espinosa Chepe.

Cubanet informó que hubo un descuento de 90 dólares (según lo recibido 83 dólares por concepto de pago de trámites).

De los 1750 dólares, 100 dolares quedaron en poder de Oscar Espinosa Chepe, de acuerdo con la orientación de Reporteros Sin Fronteras.

Se le entregó a Ricardo González Alfonso, corresponsal de RSF la cantidad de 1650 dólares.

Ricardo González Alfonso
Recibe

Oscar Espinosa Chepe
Entrega

More money sent to Oscar Espinosa Chepe and Ricardo González Alfonso.

The text of the letter reads as follows:

I hereby certify that 1750 US dollars from CUBANET, provided by Reporters Without Borders, was received through a TRANSCARD in the name of Oscar Espinosa Chepe.

Cubanet reports a 90 dollar service charge that was deducted from the total (according to the documents received, 83 dollars were deducted as a transaction fee).

Of the 1750 dollars, 100 dollars were kept by Oscar Espinosa Chepe, as instructed by Reporters Without Borders.

The sum of 1650 dollars was delivered to Ricardo González Alfonso, a Reporters Without Borders correspondent.

REVISTA
encuentro
DE LA CULTURA CUBANA

Miércoles, 17 de agosto del 2000

Estimado Oscar Espinosa Chepe;

ante todo queremos agradecerte, de parte de la dirección de la revista Encuentro de la Cultura Cubana, por la perseverancia con que has estado enviándonos tus artículos, los cuales nos parecen de una agudeza y calidad más que relevante.

La principal razón de esta carta es, sin embargo, la de comunicarte que en el mes de octubre vamos a comenzar una edición de Encuentro en la Red. Un periódico diario que saldrá exclusivamente a través de Internet, con un estilo más conciso y ágil que el de la revista en papel, un estilo en el que tus artículos encajarían de forma ideal. De más está decir que en el periódico intentaremos mantener el mismo rigor y la misma filosofía que hasta ahora hemos llevado a cabo en la revista en papel. Contamos con el apoyo de muchos colaboradores y nuestro norte seguirá siendo el mismo: crear un espacio de debate entre todos los cubanos, residan en el lugar donde residan.

Entre las diferentes secciones de las que contará el periódico habrá una titulada "La mirada" en la que no sólo nos gustaría publicar algunos de los trabajos que nos has enviado, sino también contar con tu colaboración para el futuro. Vamos a iniciar el número cero con tu artículo titulado Un perfeccionamiento singular.

Recibirás noticias nuestras en cuanto al pago. También estableceremos contacto contigo para ponernos de acuerdo sobre la forma más adecuada de hacerte llegar el dinero. Así, esperamos seguir recibiendo tus trabajos y te mantendremos al corriente de todo. Por ahora te enviamos un saludo cargado de agradecimiento y admiración. Hasta pronto,

Jesús Díaz
Encuentro de la Cultura Cubana.

Ps: Nuestra nueva dirección es...

The text of the letter reads as follows:

Dear Oscar Espinosa Chepe:

On behalf of the staff of the magazine Encuentro de la Cultura Cubana, I would like to extend my gratitude for the perseverance you've shown in sending us your articles, which we consider not only insightful but also extremely relevant.

My aim in writing you, however, is to inform you that we will be starting an Internet edition of Encuentro in the month of October. It will be a daily publication that will appear exclusively on the Internet, with a more concise and dynamic style than that of the magazine, making it ideally suited to your articles. Needless to say, we will be working to maintain the same rigor and the same philosophy that has guided our efforts in the magazine. We count on the collaboration of many individuals and our objective remains unchanged: to create a forum for discussion among all Cubans, no matter where in the world they live.

One of the various sections which will make up the publication will be entitled "The Gaze", for which we would like to publish some of the work you've sent us, and count on your future collaboration. We will start off the first issue with your article entitled: "A Singular Improvement".

You will be hearing from us with regards to payment. We will also get in touch with you to agree on the most reliable way to send you the money. That said, we hope to continue receiving your work and we will be keeping you posted on all developments. For the time being, please receive our most affectionate greetings. Looking forward to hearing from you,

Jesús Díaz
Encuentro de la Cultura Cubana

Vicky, Oscar Espinosa Chepe and Vladimiro Roca.

In the shadow of the imperial eagle, in the grounds of James Cason's home in Havana: Osvaldo Alfonso, Manuel Vázquez Portal, Héctor Palacios, María de los Ángeles Menéndez Villalta and Claudia Márquez Linares.

CARLOS ALBERTO MONTANER
AV. MENÉNDEZ PELAYO 83, BAJO DCHA. - 28007 MADRID
TEL: 91 - 434 0201 FAX: 91 - 501 1342
E-mail: camontaner@attglobal.net

11 de mayo del 2000

Sr. Osvaldo Alfonso Valdés
La Habana

Mi querido Osvaldo:

Aprovecho el viaje de este amigo para hacerte llegar algunos recortes. En el periódico polaco te mencionan, pero mi conocimiento de esa lengua se limita a reconocer el nombre de Chopin, aunque no su música, pues carezco totalmente de oído, algo que mi tía abuela Rita jamás me hubiera perdonado. Supongo que te tratan muy bien, pues mi amigo periodista quedó impresionado con la disidencia, pero muy triste con la situación general del país. Va también copia de la carta enviada a Canadá por medio de un courier. En un par de días llamaré a la persona para conocer su reacción.

En todo caso, me parece que la respuesta del gobierno cubano va a ser negativa. Creo que la condena en Ginebra y la creciente demencia senil de Fidel se conjugan para «apretar» más a la disidencia. Su reacción frente a los adversarios y frente a la adversidad es el desplante y el ataque. El reciente endurecimiento del tratamiento dado a los tres prisioneros de «la Patria es de todos» –al cuarto, a Vladimiro, no ha dejado de maltratarlo– es señal de su creciente falta de paciencia. Huye hacia adelante. Se dice que Fidel tiene un serio problema de irrigación sanguínea en la corteza cerebral, lo que en un plazo no muy lejano se traducirá en la muerte como complicación de esa dolencia, pero mientras eso llega aumentarán los signos externos de la decrepitud del Líder y seguramente de la represión policiaca.

Creo que el grado de control sobre la sociedad es de tal naturaleza que hace impensable cualquier tipo de resistencia convencional frente al gobierno, obligando a la oposición a aguardar a que el tiempo, la biología y el continuo desgaste del sistema abra una brecha por la que comience a surgir la democracia. Lo que observo es que la infinita mayoría de los cubanos comparte el criterio de que el sistema es despreciable, pero que nada se puede hacer por cambiarlo. Esto incluye a los comunistas de todos los niveles. He tenido la oportunidad de reunirme con algunos y la reacción es muy curiosa: si se les trata cordialmente (lo que siempre hago) inmediatamente cambian de *role*. Ni son ni se sienten parte del aparato. Por el contrario: se perciben como un tipo de víctimas secretas, atrapadas en una situación aún peor que la de los que no forman parte de la *nomenklatura*, pues cualquier desviación del discurso oficial los convierte en unos traidores. Tú eres un disidente, dueño de tus opiniones. Ellos están obligados a una peligrosa farsa.

¿Qué podemos hacer? Mi impresión es que estamos obligados a trabajar para el futuro. Fue lo que hicieron los socialistas españoles en los últimos tiempos del franquismo: se limitaron a formar cuadros y a esperar pacientemente a que la muerte del Caudillo despejara el camino. Pero la España de los años 73-75 era una sociedad considerablemente más abierta que Cuba. Es decir, lo que se haga tiene que ser con gran cautela y dentro de esa confusa zona de tolerancia dictada por el *Minint*, pues de lo contrario sólo se conseguirá asustar a la sociedad y llenar la cárcel de disidentes.

Instructions given to the "independent" liberals by Carlos Alberto Montaner.

The text of the letter reads as follows:

My dear Osvaldo:

I am taking advantage of this friend's visit to send you a number of press clippings. You're mentioned in the Polish newspaper, but all I can understand in this language is the name of Chopin - though nothing of his music, because I have a tin ear, something that my great-aunt Rita would never have forgiven. I assume you're being treated quite well, because my journalist friend was very impressed by the dissidents there, though very sad about the general situation of the country. I am also enclosing a copy of the letter that was sent to Canada by courier. I will be calling the person in a few days to find out about their reaction.

In any event, I am thinking that the response of the Cuban government will not be positive. I think that the condemnation in Geneva and Fidel's growing senile dementia are combining in detriment of the opposition. His reaction to any adversity is always insolent and aggressive. The recent mistreatment received by the three prisoners of "the Nation belongs to everyone" — they haven't stopped mistreating the fourth, Vladimiro — is a sign of his dwindling patience. He's moving forward at full speed. They say that Fidel has a serious circulatory problem in his cerebral cortex, that will result in his death in the not so distant future, but until that day comes, the signs of his decrepitude will go on increasing and, no doubt, so will the police repression.

I think that the sort of control being exercised over Cuban society is of such magnitude that it renders unthinkable any sort of conventional resistance before the government, forcing the opposition to wait until time, nature and the continuous wearing down of the system yield a space where democracy can begin to flourish. What I see is that the vast majority of Cubans are of the same idea, that the system is despicable, but that nothing can be done in order to change it. This includes the communists at every level of power. I've had the opportunity to meet with some of them and they all have a very curious reaction: if one treats them cordially (something I always do), they immediately switch roles. They neither feel nor show themselves to be a part of the apparatus. On the contrary, they see themselves as a sort of secret victim, trapped in a situation which is even worse than that of those who find themselves outside of the official *nomenklatura*, since any deviation from the official discourse immediately transforms them into traitors. You're a dissident, in charge of your opinions. They're forced to carry on with a precarious farce.

What can we do? My impression is that we're forced to work for the future. It was what the Spanish socialists did during the last days of the Franco regime: they limited their work to forming cadres and to waiting patiently for the death of the dictator to clear their path. But the Spain of 1973-75 was a considerably freer society than that of Cuba. Which means: whatever is done has to be carried out with great caution and within that nebulous zone of tolerance dictated by the Ministry of the Interior; otherwise, one will only manage to scare people and to overcrowd the jails with dissidents.

YAHOO! Correo ✉   <u>Cerrar ventana</u>

De: "Carlos A Montaner" <camontaner@attglobal.net>
A: "Claudia Marquez" <claudiadecuba2002@yahoo.com>
Asunto: respuesta tardia
Fecha: Wed, 30 Oct 2002 15:08:25 -0800

Queridos Osvaldo y Claudia:

Perdonen la demora en responder este e-mail. Tengo cientos de mensajes sin contestar y este se fue
quedando atras hasta casi perderlo de vista. Le mandare un articulo al amigo de ustedes. /// Para todos los
democratas dentro de Cuba es muy importante lo que acaba de suceder con el Premio Sajarov. Los dos
Oswaldos tienen razones para estar muy satisfechos. El gobierno cubano intento intrigar para que no se lo
dieran, pero actuaron muy torpemente. La insolente carta del embajador Rene Mujica a Cecilia Malstrom sirvio
para galvanizar a los liberales, sin los cuales hubiera sido imposible el triunfo de la candidatura de Paya. Este
episodio da otra medida de la "globalizacion". Es importante cultivar las relaciones internacionales e integrarse
en las familias politicas afines. Tu partido ha actuado muy bien en esa direccion. /// Espero que les haya llegado
mi ultimo libro. Se titula "Cuba: un siglo de doloroso aprendizaje". Esta dedicado a cuatro amigos: los dos
Oswaldos que luchan dentro de Cuba, y a Calzon y a Roberto Fontanillas, que no han dejado de hacerlo fuera
del pais. Un gran abrazo, Carlos Alberto.

----- Original Message -----
From: <u>Claudia Marquez</u>
To: <u>camontaner@attglobal.net</u>
Sent: Wednesday, October 09, 2002 7:09 AM
Subject: claudia y osvaldo de Cuba

Estimado Carlos, aqui le transcribo una carta de Osvaldo.

Querido Carlos Alberto:

Espero estes excelentemente bien de salud. Un amigo colaborador del Partido me ha dicho que te envio un e
mail pidiendote colaboracion para un proyecto que tienen. Se trata de un grupo de jovenes escritores,
identificados con nuestras ideas y que tienen muchos deseos de aportar a nuestra causa. Ellos son muy
talentosos, algunos, entre ellos el propio jorge, tiene libros publicados. Sin embargo, no quieren aceptar las
condiciones que impone el regimen para publicar y mucho menos la censura. Es asi que han decidido
publicar una revista, mas o menos algo asi como Vitral pero con un estilo mas literario. Nosotros, con la
computer que tenemos, gracias a nuestros amigos, vamos a ayudarlos a hacerla. Tambien quieren, si es
posible, tener un espacio para la publicacion en la pagina de internet de la Union Liberal. Pineso que es una
buena idea todo esto de la revista y con ello nos acercamos a la joven intelectualidad. Te recuerdeo que
quieren una colaboracion tuya, una resena de un libro u otra casa y que contactes con otros amigos
escritores cubanos en el exilio y tambien, incluso, con otros de cualquier nacionalidad, para que les envien
una colaboracion. Todo esto es complicado aqui en Cuba pero el futuro lo hacen aquellos que se atreven a
hacer lo que no se puede.

Espero ansioso tu ultimo libro, en una proxima carta te abordare otras cuestiones sobre como nos van las
cosas con el Partido. Un abrazo, Osvaldo.

CIA agent Carlos Alberto Montaner works to finance both the "liberal militants"
and the "independent journalists".

The texts of the e-mails read as follows:

Dear Osvaldo and Claudia:

Please forgive the delay in writing you this e-mail. I have a hundred unanswered messages in my mailbox and I almost lost yours from sight. I'll be sending the article to your friend. What has just happened with the Sakharov Prize is very important for all democrats in Cuba. Both Oswaldos have reasons to be very satisfied. The Cuban government tried to intervene to keep them from receiving the award, but they acted very stupidly. The insolent letter written to Cecilia Malstrom by the ambassador René Mujica served to galvanize the liberals, without whom Payá's triumph would have been impossible. This episode shows as another aspect of "globalization". It is important to foster international relations and to join those political groupings which are of similar thinking. Your party has moved quite well in this direction. I hope you've received my last book. It is entitled: "Cuba: A Century's Painful Lesson". It is dedicated to four of my friends: the two Osvaldos who fight within Cuba, and to Calzón and Roberto Fontanilas, who haven't stopped doing it from outside of Cuba. A warm hug to you, Carlos Alberto.

Dear Carlos, I am transcribing for you a letter from Osvaldo.

Dear Carlos Alberto:

I hope you are doing wonderfully well. A friend who is collaborating with the Party told me he sent you an e-mail asking for your assistance in a project they have. It consists of a group of young writers who sympathize with our ideas and who are very eager to contribute something to our cause. They are very talented; some of them, including Jorge, have published books. Nevertheless, they do not accept the conditions and the censorship that are imposed on them by the regime. That's why they've decided to publish their own magazine, something more or less like Vitral, but with a more literary style. With the computer we have, thanks to our friends, we're going to help them publish it. They've also said that, if possible, they would like to have the magazine published on the Internet page of the Liberal Union. I think that the magazine is a good idea, that can help us reach young intellectuals. Let me remind you that they are asking for your help, if you can do a book review for them or some such thing, and get in touch with other Cuban writers in exile and even with those of other nationalities, for them to contribute in some way. All of this is very complicated in Cuba but the future belongs to those who dare to do the impossible.

I anxiously await your last book. I'll be telling you more about how things are going in the party in my next letter. A hug, Osvaldo.

CARLOS ALBERTO MONTANER
AV. MENÉNDEZ PELAYO 83, BAJO DCHA. - 28007 MADRID
TEL: 91 - 434 0201 FAX: 91 - 501 1342
E-mail: camontaner@attglobal.net

¿Pueden tú y el PLDC desarrollar un plan para crear metódicamente *Grupos de Estudios Martianos* que difundan las «*Lecciones*» e ir generando núcleos de diez personas, que, a su vez, se vayan duplicando? La idea es poder tener en todo el territorio nacional, pero fundamentalmente en las ciudades grandes, unas personas persuadidas de las ideas básicas del pensamiento liberal, y que crean en que Cuba puede transitar hacia la democracia y la economía de mercado sin violencia, sin represalias contra nadie, con una «ley de punto final», en un esquema político en el que todos los que se sometan a las reglas del juego, incluidos los dogmáticos del estalinismo, tengan cabida.

Esta estructura primaria que se iría creando en la Isla a propósito de los *Grupos de Estudios Martianos* sería el embrión de una gran fuerza liberal, moderna, semejante a las que han traído la prosperidad y el sosiego a los veinte países más felices del planeta, en la que englobaríamos los distintos grupos que dentro y fuera del país comparte esta visión de los problemas de la sociedad. Nuestro trabajo desde el exterior consistiría en buscar fondos para sostener al equipo de operadores políticos dentro del país, de manera que puedan moverse libremente y dedicar todo su tiempo a estas labores pacíficas de organizar a los ciudadanos para estudiar, comprender y planear las acciones cívicas que habrá que llevar a cabo cuando llegue el inicio de la transición.

Nosotros disponemos de muy pocos recursos porque, contrario a la propaganda del gobierno cubano, nada recibimos, pedimos o aceptamos de ningún gobierno, y los pocos fondos de que disponemos son las aportaciones de algunos cubanos que se identifican con nuestra causa, y, en primer lugar, las nuestras. Mi pregunta concreta es: ¿es posible que el PLDC comprometa progresivamente a estos cabezas de núcleos, a los que se les puede hacer llegar por tu conducto unos veinte dólares mensuales (400 pesos al cambio actual) para que se dediquen diaria y sistemáticamente a multiplicar la organización? En caso de que eso sea posible es muy importante que ese «cuadro profesional» sea una persona honesta e idealista y no un simple cubano que desea ver aliviados un poco sus problemas económicos. Gentes con patriotismo, que crean en el futuro, y que cuando llegue el momento estén dispuestas a dar la batalla política. Podemos comenzar con cinco personas, al mes siguiente aumentar otros cinco, y así sucesivamente, en la medida en que tú compruebas que, efectivamente, se van extendiendo los GEM.

Creo que no hay que precipitarse, sino escoger muy bien a la gente, explicándoles con claridad los objetivos y los límites. Personas que no provoquen innecesariamente, y que con toda serenidad se dispongan a trabajar por el bien del país con generosidad y espíritu de sacrificio.

Por último, ya pasó por mi oficina el joven premiado por la Naumann. Está bien y provisionalmente trabaja como camarero. Al cura lo he llamado varias veces y nunca contestan el teléfono.

Van unas medicinas para tus padres. Quedo a la espera de tus noticias, un fuerte abrazo,

Carlos Alberto Montaner proposes a monthly salary of 20 dollars to Osvaldo Alfonso. The mercenary's response didn't keep anyone waiting…

The text of the letter reads as follows:

Can you and the PLDC develop a plan to methodically set up Martí Study Groups, which would take up the Lessons and gather groups of ten people who, at the same time, would go on multiplying themselves? The idea is to expose individuals throughout the country, and especially those in the large cities, to the basic ideas of liberal thinking, and to persuade them that Cuba can make the transition to democracy and to a market economy without violence, without reprisals taken against anyone, with a "clean slate law", within a political scheme where everyone who is willing to play by the rules of the game — and this includes the Stalinist dogmatists — can have his place.

This structure, which would begin to consolidate itself from the Martí Study Groups, would be the embryo for a modern and most powerful liberal spirit, not unlike the kind that has brought peace and prosperity to the twenty most fortunate countries on the planet, where we would gather the different groups that, both inside and outside of Cuba, share our vision about the problems faced by society. Our work from abroad will consist in securing the funding needed to sustain the work of political activists within the country, so that they may work unhindered and devote all of their time to the peaceful task of organizing and educating citizens, and urging them to study, understand and plan the actions that they will have to carry out at the time of the transition.

We don't have many resources at our disposal because, contrary to the propaganda of the Cuban government, we neither ask for nor accept any donations from any government, and the few resources we do have are contributions from a number of Cubans who identify themselves with our cause, and, above all, our own. My question is: is it possible for the PLDC to gradually enlist the leaders for these groups, who could receive, through you, some twenty dollars a month (400 pesos at the current exchange rate), so that they may devote themselves wholly to systematically expanding the organization? Should this be possible, it is very important to choose individuals who are honest and of conviction, and not Cubans hoping to alleviate their economic problems through this. People of patriotism, who believe in the future, and who'd be willing to put up the needed political struggle when the time comes. We can start off with five people, and add five more the following month, and so on, as you verify that, in fact, the Martí Study Groups are growing.

I don't think we should rush into this, we must choose the individuals carefully, and clearly explain to them our objectives and our limitations. We need people who won't resort to unnecessary provocations, and who'd be willing to work for the country's wellbeing with presence of mind, generosity, and a spirit of sacrifice.

Lastly, I want to tell you that the young man who received the Naumann award has already gone by my office. He's doing well, and working as a waiter for the time being. I've called the priest a number of times and no one picks up the phone.

I am sending you some medication for your parents. I am anxious to hear from you.

Mi querido Carlos.

Ya tengo en mis manos la laptop que me enviaste. Gracias a ... y a Frank Calson. Ahora ya podemos hacer muchas cosas que no podíamos por no tener este equipo. Comenzaremos de nuevo a edi... un boletín que nombramos 'El Liberal'. En él varios miembros de nue... tro partido escribimos artículos, ensayos, y reproducimos algunos text... de publicaciones que nos llegan. Luego de tener un original con ayu... da de varias embajadas sacamos unas 200 copias y las distribu... mos, esa cantidad puede ser mayor ya que algunos de nuestros activistas tienen posibilidades para que le saquen más copias.

En cuanto al estado del partido debo decirte que marcha bien. Calculamos que en estos momentos tendremos cerca de 500 activistas públicos en todas las delegaciones. Trabajamos por fortalecernos en las grandes ciudades del país. Ahora bien contamos además con más de 1000 colaboradores y simpatizantes. Estos son personas a las cuales atienden los activistas, se forman como liberales en las cuestiones básicas y que en la hora cero no tienen ningún inconveniente de afi... se públicamente al partido. Estas personas a su vez sirven de fortaleza para llegar a otras personas a las cuales no tenemos con... tabilizadas.

En la actualidad y gracias a que el ejecutivo nacional del P.L.D.C. cuen... ta con un buen equipo de personas instruidas estamos preparando un "Curso de formación de cuadros" en este curso impar... tiremos 6 asignaturas que son:

1. "Historia del Pensamiento Liberal (Universal y Cuba)
2. "Tendencias políticas actuales: demócristiana, socialdemócrata, comunismo, y fascismo.
3. Conceptos económicos básicos.
4. Historia socio-económica y política de Cuba.
5. Globalización y las diferentes posturas ante este fenómeno.
6. Estudio del Programa del P.L.D.C.

Alfonso answers: We have more than a thousand "sympathizers". He must have done his math: 20 dollars times a thousand. "Not bad," he'd think.

The document reads as follows:

My dear Carlos:

I am already using the laptop that you sent me. My thanks to you and to Frank Calzón. Now we can do many of the things we couldn't do before. We will begin to publish a bulletin once again, called "El Liberal". A number of party members will be writing articles and essays, and we will be reproducing some of the texts found in publications sent to us. Once we've put together the bulletin, we will be putting out and distributing some 200 copies with the help of a number of embassies in the country. The number of copies can be greater because a number of our activists have the opportunity to make more copies.

With respect to the present state of the party, I must tell you everything's going well. We estimate that, at the moment, we have close to 500 public activists in all of the delegations. We are working to grow stronger in the large cities of the country. As well, we count on the collaboration of more than a thousand sympathizers. These are people attended to by our activists, who are versed in the basic ideas of liberalism, and who — when the time comes — would have no qualms about publicly affiliating themselves to the party. At the same time, these people help us reach other people, whose numbers we have yet to calculate.

At the moment, thanks to the work of a great number of capable people in the PLDC, we are preparing a course on the "development of cadres". We will be giving six courses:

1. History of liberal thinking (in Cuba and abroad)
2. Current political trends: Christian democratic, social democratic, communist (?), neo-fascist.
3. Basic economic concepts
4. Socioeconomic and political history of Cuba
5. Globalization: the different stances adopted before this phenomenon
6. Analysis of the PLDC program.

Ciudad de La Habana, 23 de enero de 1998

Sr. Carlos Alberto Montaner
Presidente
Unión Liberal Cubana

Querido amigo Carlos Alberto:

Recibí con mucha alegría la llegada de tus cartas y los libros que enviastes, ya tenía impaciencia por recibirlos. Compartí ambas cartas
con Leonel Morejón como me lo pedistes, y también con los demás miembros de nuestro Ejecutivo, quienes la acogieron con mucho agrado.

Ya he leído más de una vez ambos documentos aprobados por la Internacional Liberal en el 48 Congreso, igualmente lo han hecho otros miembros del Partido, en uno de ellos la referencia a Cuba nos parece muy
objetiva y aprobamos totalmente lo que se plantea. En general nos pro-
ponemos reproducir éstos documentos para que puedan ser leídos por el
mayor número posible de personas y para los activistas y simpatizantes
del PLDC será un material de estudio muy provechoso.

Te puedo decir que aunque tenemos un programa económico-político y social, pensamos revisarlo y actualizarlo en los próximos días; esto lo
haremos el Lic. Leonel Morejón Almagro, el Ingeniero Héctor Fernando
Maseda Gutiérrez, Secretario de Relaciones Internacionales del Partido
y yo, luego me ocuparé de hacerte llegar una copia.

En cuanto al documento que te llegó por fax, realmente es false, cono-
cemos al Sr. Fernández Martínez como periodista independiente pero jamás ha tenido ningún vínculo de trabajo con nuestro partido, afortuna-
damente gracias a las relaciones que tenemos en la Embajada Británica
enseguida se nos comunicó de la solicitud hecha por este Señor para
viajar al Congreso y logramos neutralizar sus propósitos.

La propuesta de colaboración que nos haces me parece magnífica, en el
PLDC estamos también muy satisfechos de poder colaborar con ustedes,
pues nos une además del deseo de lograr la democracia y el fin del
castrismo en Cuba una identidad de ideales. Considero que los liberales tenemos un gran desafío en el futuro de Cuba y las mejores propues
tas, las más viables y los mejores métodos para alcanzar la sociedad
de libertad y prosperidad que queremos están en el Liberalismo.

Nosotros desde siempre hemos trabajado en la difusión de estos ideales
dentro de Cuba, está en nuestro plan de trabajo para nuestras delegaciones provinciales y municipales como tarea permanente. Ahora la propuesta tuya de organizar círculos de estudios martianos independientes
nos parece muy buena y la aprobamos, como me dices dejo en tus manos
la elaboración de las lecciones y de hacérmelas llegar.

De antemano te digo que llevaremos la propuesta al Secretariado de Con
cilio Cubano del que también formo parte, para así poder extender éste
trabajo, en un futuro dentro de los objetivos de Concilio para lograr
la unidad está el estudio de diferentes aspectos sociales, económicos

Dear Carlos Alberto:

I received your letter and the books you sent me with much joy, I was already growing anxious to get them. I shared both letters with Leonel Morejón as you asked me to, as well as with the other members of our executive, who were very pleased by what they read.

I've read both of the documents approved by the Liberal International at its 48th Congress more than once, as have other members of the party. The mention of Cuba in one of those documents strikes us as very objective and we agree entirely with what it proposes. We will be reproducing these documents so that they may reach the greatest possible number of people, and we think it will prove a most fruitful study material for the activists and sympathizers of the PLDC.

I should tell you that, though we have a political-economical and social program established for the party, we are thinking of updating and revising it in the following days: this will be done by Leonel Morejón Almagro, Héctor Fernando Maseda Gutiérrez, who is the Secretary for International Relations of the party, and myself; I will later send you a copy myself.

With respect to the document you got by fax, it is entirely false. We do know Mr. Fernández Martínez as an independent journalist, but he has never had any work relationship with the party. Fortunately, thanks to the good relations we keep with the British Embassy, we were immediately informed about his request to travel to participate in the Congress, and were able to intervene.

The proposal for collaboration you have made to us seems excellent to me. In the PDLC, we are also very pleased to be able to collaborate with you, as we are united not only in our desire to achieve democracy and an end to the Castro regime, but also by shared ideals. I believe that we as liberals will face tremendous challenges in the Cuba of the future, and the most viable proposals and most effective methods to attain the free and prosperous society we want are to be found in Liberalism.

We have always worked to divulge these ideals within Cuba; this is a permanent task of our provincial and municipal delegations. Your current proposal to organize independent Martí study circles strikes us as very good and we have approved it; as you've said, I'm leaving the elaboration of the classes in your hands, as well as the task of having these reach me.

At the moment, I can tell you we will be taking your proposal to the Secretariat of the Cuban Council, of which I am also a member, in order to extend the scope of the work. A future objective of the Council, which is aimed at achieving some measure of unity, is the study of different social, economic and political aspects of young people and other members of society. We have a modest little bulletin in the party which we circulate among members of the opposition, sympathizers and diplomatic personnel, where we have reproduced the documents of the Liberal International; I am pointing this out to you so you can see we are on the same wavelength with respect to divulging the ideals of Liberalism.

políticos de la juventud y otros. Tenemos en el Partido un modesto boletín que circulamos entre la oposición, los simpatizantes y el cuerpo diplomático, en el que hemos divulgado documentos de la Internacional Liberal, te señalo esto para que comprendas que estamos en sintonía en cuanto a los propósitos de divulgar los ideales del Liberalismo.

Quisiera saber qué se hizo con los documentos que enviamos al Congreso, sobre esto no he tenido noticias aún, todavía no he logrado hablar con Chumy Montaner; quisiera que me contaras más sobre las posibilidades que tiene el PLDC de ingresar como miembro observador en la Internacional Liberal, para nosotros es muy importante pues con ello no solamente nuestro partido, sino toda la oposición recibiría un gran apoyo político que como comprenderás necesitamos mucho, puedo asegurarte además que no pretendemos conseguir apoyo económico de la IL, recibimos muchos documentos que envió el Sr. Julius Maaten y sabemos que eso no es posible, te reitero que para nosotros lo más importante es contar con ese apoyo político, académico y las relaciones que pudiéramos alcanzar. Esperamos tu apoyo en este propósito.

Aquí seguimos trabajando mucho para fortalecernos, tenemos como ya sabes delegaciones en varias provincias, en algunas ya los miembros del PLDC son numerosos, como son: Las Tunas y Pinar del Río, además de la Ciudad de La Habana.

La situación política del país parece estable, pero en realidad el descontento entre la población crece y el descrédito del Gobierno es cada vez mayor, es cierto que la mayoría no quiere comprometerse contra el régimen, el pueblo sabe lo que eso cuesta y ve en gran medida la solución en emigrar, eso es un gran problema y necesitamos despertar valores cívicos en el pueblo, hacerle comprender que puede haber una alternativa y que es posible cambiar la realidad cubana.

Ahora cuando te escribo tenemos aquí como sabrás la visita del Papa, hay muchas expectativas en la población, muchos creen que el Papa influirá en el cambio político, pienso que sin duda políticamente ésta visita tendrá repercusión, pero creo será a mediano plazo. Quizá a partir de ahora el pueblo después de escuchar otro discurso diferente al del régimen crea en otros valores y sobre todo la juventud adquiera un compromiso con el futuro del país.

Con mucho gusto aceptamos el ofrecimiento de imprimir los documentos fundacionales del PLDC, como comprenderás los recursos con que contamos son muy modestos. Preferentemente puedes hacerlo con la "Síntesis Histórica" la "Síntesis de Programa" y el "Plan de Trabajo". Si te es posible identifícalos también en la parte superior con un logotipo, es suficiente que nos mandes una copia, aquí podemos reproducirlos.

Bueno, querido amigo, tal vez sea un tanto larga la carta pero deseé tratar todos los aspectos de la que me enviastes.

Puedes considerar que ya está abierta nuestra colaboración, todos los miembros de nuestro Ejecutivo te envían un saludo afectuoso y esperamos noticias tuyas.

Un abrazo,

Osvaldo Alfonso Valdés

The mercenary Osvaldo Alfonso reports to his boss in Spain, and asks for instructions that no doubt will coincide with those from Washington.

I'd like to know what happened with the documents we sent to the Congress, I haven't had any news about this yet, I have yet to speak with Chuny Montaner; I'd like you to tell me if it is possible for the PLDC to become an observing member of the Liberal International, this is very important for us, because not only our party but the entire opposition will receive great political backing, which we dearly need, as you should know. I can tell you we won't be asking for economic aid from the LI, we received many documents sent by Mr. Julius Maatem and we know this is not possible, I reiterate that the most important thing for us is getting political and academic support, and any relations we can establish. We hope to be able to count on your support, with this in mind.

We continue to work to grow stronger here, we already have delegations in a number of provinces, and we have many members of the PLDC in some of them, such as Las Tunas and Pinar del Río, as well as the City of Havana.

The political situation in the country seems stable, but the discontent among people is ever greater and the Government is discredited more and more every day. It is true that the majority is unwilling to fight against the regime, most people know what this entails and find the solution in emigrating; this is a great problem and we need to awaken civic values in people, have them understand that there are other alternatives and that it is possible to change Cuban reality.

As I write this, as you probably know, the Pope is visiting us, there are many expectations among the population, many believe that the Pope will influence a political change. I do believe that this visit will have political repercussions, but they will not take effect immediately. Perhaps, from this day on, after hearing a discourse different from that of the regime, people will start acquiring new values, and young people will perhaps grow interested in the future of the country.

We are pleased to accept your offer to print out the founding documents of the PLDC, you're probably aware that we have very modest resources. You can prioritize the "Historical Summary", the "Program Summary", and the "Work Plan". If it is possible for you to identify them with a logo at the top of the page, we'd appreciate it. It would be sufficient for you to send us one copy; we can make more copies on this end.

Well, my dear friend, this may be a long letter, but I wanted to respond to everything you spoke of in your last letter.

You can already count on our collaboration. On behalf of all the members of our executive, let me extend a most affectionate and warm greeting. We look forward to hearing from you.

A hug,

Osvaldo Alfonso Valdés.

Carlos Alberto Montaner
camontaner@attglobal.net

26 enero 2001

Mi querido Osvaldo:

Aquí van $200.— Lamentablemente no hay mucho que contar, salvo lo que todos sabemos: el régimen se endurece y todo el mundo tiene como horizonte la muerte de Fidel. Después, veremos. Todo es muy triste, pero así son las cosas. Un fuerte abrazo,

Cal Alberto.

Messages sent to Osvaldo Alfonso by Carlos Alberto Montaner: money, lots of money. Note that Montaner speaks of "Spanish friends in high places" that will soon be calling him.

My dear Osvaldo:

I am sending you $200. Unfortunately, there's not much to tell, save what we all know: the regime is toughening up and everyone is waiting for the death of Fidel. Afterwards, we'll see. It's all very sad, but that's the way things are. A hug, Carlos Alberto.

A. Osvaldo Alfonso   Carlos Alberto Montaner   22 Mayo 2001
                            camontaner@attglobal.net

Mi querido Osvaldo:
    Un amigo, a quien conoces, tiene la
bondad de hacerte llegar 30.000 pesetas.
Muy pronto te llamarán unos amigos
españoles de alto nivel para hablar
del Proyecto Varela. Sugerí cinco
hombres: Payá, Alfonso, Arcos, Raúl
Rivero y Tania Quintero.
        Va un fuerte abrazo y una revista
Encuentro.
                    CarlAlbM.

My dear Osvaldo:

A friend of mine, whom you know, has been kind enough to see that you get these 30,000 pesetas. Some Spanish friends in high places will be calling you soon to discuss the Varela Project. I've recommended five people: Payá, Alfonso, Arcos, Raúl Rivero and Tania Quintero.

A. Osvaldo Alfonso   Carlos Alberto Montaner   24 de mayo 2001
                            camontaner@attglobal.net

Mi querido Osvaldo,
    Un amigo común tiene la bondad
de hacerte llegar estos $200.— con
recado personal que te dará Raúl.
    Llámame a España cuando veas
esta nota. Un fuerte abrazo,
                    Carlos Alberto.

My dear Osvaldo:

A mutual friend of ours has been kind enough to bring you this $200. I'm sending a private message that Raúl will pass on to you. Call me in Spain as soon as you get this note. A warm hug, Carlos Alberto.

22 de febrero del 2003

Por la presente se le entrega al Sr. Osvaldo Alfonso Valdés
Miembro de la Comisión de Relatoría de TODOS UNIDOS de 40.00
U.S. (Dólares, que envian como ayuda humanitaria, los herma-
nos de A.C.D.)

Recibe Osvaldo Alfonso Valdés

The Cuban Democratic Association in Miami sends
the money. And the invitations pour in as well.

We hereby deliver the sum of USD 40.00 to Mr. Osvaldo Alfonso Valdés,
member of the Reporting Committee of EVERYONE UNITED (as
humanitarian aid on behalf of the brothers at the C.D.A.).

El Segundo Secretario (Político) de la Embajada de Canadá,
Christopher Burton,
tiene el honor de invitar al

Sr. Osvaldo Alfonso

a una cena

en honor de Kimberly Cowan, especialista de Cuba,
área de América Latina y el Caribe (LCR),
Ministerio de Astos. Exteriores y Comercio Int'l de Canadá.

Día: jueves 20 de junio de 2002
Lugar: Calle 220 #717 e/7ma-A y 9na,
Siboney
Hora: 19:30 hrs.

R.S.V.P.
204-2516 y 17

The Second Political Secretary of the Canadian Embassy,
Christopher Burton,
has the honor of inviting
Mr. Osvaldo Alfonso
to a dinner
in honor of Kimberly Cowan, Specialist on Cuba,
Latin American and Caribbean Region,
Department of Foreign Affairs and International Trade of Canada.

Ciudad de La Habana, 10-3-03

s de

... las ofensas que recibió por parte del presidente cubano.
... no es habitual de ser pagados por su gobierno.
... reiterarles nuestra gratitud por el apoyo moral que ustedes
... legítima y pacífica lucha por los derechos de los cubanos.
... estarán abiertas para acogerles siempre que lo deseen.
... usteza de nuestros propósitos y no tenemos motivos para
... nes con ustedes que no escondemos.

Osvaldo Alfonso Valdés

Presidente PLDC

Francisco Morales Aquino

Sec. de Rel. Internacionales JLC

A despicable letter: proof of how entirely the "independents" sell themselves.

Esteemed Mr. James Cason
Head of the U.S. Interests Section in Havana

Dear Mr. Ambassador,

In recent days, we have heard the insults directed at you by the Cuban
president. At the same time, he accused us, as is customary, of being
paid agents of your government.
 This is why we would like to reiterate our gratitude for the moral support
that you've shown us in our legitimate and peaceful struggle for the
rights of Cubans.
Our doors will always be open to welcome you whenever you wish.
We are convinced of the rightness of our cause and have no reason to
deny our ties to you, which we have never concealed.

James Cason founds the Cuban Young Liberal Party in the home of the mercenary Osvaldo Alfonso, president of the Liberal Party.

Leading the "activity": James Cason (1), Nicholas J. Giacobbe (2), and Ricardo Zuniga (3), representatives of the U.S. Interests Section in Cuba.

I WAS THE ONE WHO WROTE THE GENEVA REPORT

Liborio Noval tells them jokes to get the right photograph for this interview. "Relax, Doctor, don't get tense, you look like hell in the viewfinder," and Pedro Luis Véliz laughs, "I'm not tense, I swear."

When Ana Rosa Jorna joins him, the image that won everyone's vote appears by itself, without having to look for it. Liborio takes a number of photos and says, "You love each other more now than before, don't you?"

AGENTS ERNESTO AND GABRIELA

When did you begin your conspiratorial work?

Pedro: In the year 1996. Rafael Santiago Montes lived across the street from me. He was something of a big-shot in *Radio "Martí"*, denouncing human rights violations. He worked with me in the Comandante Piti Fajardo Hospital in Vedado (Havana).

He worked as a doctor?
Pedro: No, as an engineer. He was very qualified because he had studied in the Soviet Union. He would have a 24-hour work shift and then rest for three days in a row; this gave him ample time to carry out his counterrevolutionary activities, and he was a very aggressive man.

In what sense?
Pedro: Doing propaganda campaigns in favor of the Cuban Liberal Democratic Party (Partido Liberal Democrático Cubano), where he held a leading position. He had been detained for a few hours and he had tried to win over to his "side" a number of criminals who were being held in the police station at the same time. Since he was my neighbor and a colleague of mine at work, State Security came to talk to me.

What did they ask you to do?
Pedro: To approach him, to see if he'd swallow the bait, something he did the first time we met one another.

He immediately spoke to you about the Liberal Party?
Pedro: Not only that, he also told me that the leaders of this party would rotate as presidents to avoid detection by State Security. They didn't want them to identify a leader and take apart the group. He was very proud to tell me that at that moment he was the one in charge. He didn't give me a chance to say anything. He invited me to a meeting in his home, which was going to be held there the following night. So, practically overnight, I found myself with a number of tasks in a group that's fairly well compartmentalized.

What tasks did they give you?
Pedro: To create some counterrevolutionary cells in the hospital, to provide medical treatment to leaders of the "opposition" — I actually had a number of counterrevolutionary group leaders admitted to the hospital — and to try to convince people in administrative positions to join my cell. If I managed to attract other people, I would stop being just another member and become a leader of that group.

I also got instructions to write denunciations about the Cuban public health system, to be broadcast by *Radio "Martí"*.

What sort of denunciations?
Pedro: Epidemiological problems, for instance. There was an outbreak of hemorrhagic conjunctivitis at the time, and they set their sights on that. We were always looking for some critical element around us to exaggerate.

You would go on Radio "Martí"*, and speak on their programs?*
Pedro: No. I would write them and Santiago Montes or another director would read them as their own. Afterwards, they agreed to come up with a pseudonym for me, so as not to give me away, and my various "noms de guerre" emerged: Arturo Pérez, Pedro Arturo, Arturo Pérez Medina, Pedro Arturo Véliz Pérez.

It was one of these denunciations that allowed me to get to know the man who called himself president of the Cuban Medical Association.

Who was he?
Pedro: His name is Augusto Madrigal Izaguirre, a doctor who was tried and sentenced for corruption. When he came out of jail, he got in touch with counterrevolutionary groups. He knew Rafael Santiago, Héctor Maceda Gutiérrez and Osvaldo Alfonso Valdés, the other "presidents" of the Liberal Party.

What was the objective of the Liberal Party?
Pedro: These people were not even half the patriots they claimed to be. Their true political line was getting out of the country and leading the show to obtain money from the United States, which they would later pocket. That's why all hell broke lose in the Liberal Party. Money was what distanced Maceda and Osvaldo Alfonso from Rafael Santiago.

And what did you do?
Pedro: I followed Rafael Santiago, who left for the Liberal Current (Corriente Liberal). You can't imagine how much I had to study at the time to be up-to-date on European liberalism, social democracy and other matters of the sort.

Hispano-Cuban Foundation (Fundación Hispano Cubana, FHC)

Established in November of 1996 through the joint initiatives of Guillermo Gortázar Recheverrua, a representative of the People's Party (PP), Jorge Mas Canosa and Carlos Alberto Montaner. It presents itself officially as an organization devoted to the promotion of Hispano-Cuban culture, but in truth, it serves the policies of Aznar, the PP and the Cuban-American National Foundation by promoting and organizing cultural events and activities which count with the participation of intellectuals and artists who are hostile toward the Cuban Revolution.

It has worked to gather information about Spanish businessmen and their dealings with Cuba, about alleged violations of human rights, and to discourage potential foreign investment.

It has received financial aid from the Spanish government and it employs the Casa América, a government organization, to promote and foster anti-Cuban stances in Latin America.

The organization has handed out awards to some of the leaders of counterrevolutionary groups and has attempted to broadcast anti-Cuban radio programs.

Gortazar Recheverrua is currently working as a university professor. He is the promoter of the project known as the Committee to Aid the Establishment of Democracy in Cuba (Comité de Ayuda a la Instauración de la Democracia en Cuba, PDC). He has served as the director of the magazine *Hispano Cubana*. On numerous occasions, he has procured political asylum for groups of Cubans traveling to Russia on flights that have stopovers in Madrid. With the support of Wilfredo Pérez Quevedo, he has been promoting the creation of a branch of the FHC in Russia.

Afterwards, Liberal Current also split up because of quarrels within the group, and I left for another organization once again: to join Dr. Madrigal, this time. That's how I became the national coordinator of the "Independent" Medical Association of Cuba.

Who were the directors of this Medical Association?
Ana Rosa: The neurosurgeon Hilda Molina had been president for

some time, but she wasn't up to the job because she is paranoid in the extreme: she thought everyone who looked at her was an agent working for State Security. She was replaced by Dr. Iraida de León, who was a very provocative person, like Oscar Elías Biscet. Then came Augusto Madrigal, who was somewhat more moderate. And, finally, there was Pedro, who was even more moderate than Augusto.

When did they make you president of the Medical Association?
Pedro: Madrigal was sent to Chile by Timothy Brown, a confessed CIA agent, pretending to be a diplomat working at the U.S. Interests Section. Brown set it up for the president of the Association to get in touch with Brown's brother, who was a diplomat in Chile. The idea was to meet with Chilean professionals to get them to support Cuban "dissident" doctors, and to demand free elections in Cuba and respect for human rights.

When Madrigal got the chance to leave for Chile, he had already gotten most of his family out of the country. He left me — provisionally, he said — as president of the Medical Association. This counterrevolutionary organization had a president, a national coordinator and a three vice-presidents.

When did you take up the leadership of the Association?
Pedro: When he left, it created a power vacuum. I was the second in command and I spent close to a year saying that Madrigal was the president and I was the coordinator, until they said to me, "Listen, that man's not coming back, you take charge."

Who told you this?
Pedro: Everyone, State Security and the other members of the national council of the organization. In January of 1998, I was officially made president and at that time Manuel Alzugaray Pérez, from the Miami Medical Team Foundation, presented me with the project called "Awakening Smiles" (Despertando Sonrisas).

Which was…?
Ana Rosa: Perhaps one of the most sinister plans of recent years.

Who was behind it?
Pedro: It's a long story.

Leopoldo Francisco Fernández Pujals

On July 18, 1960 he emigrated to the United States with his family and settled in Miami. He worked for Johnson & Johnson as a sales manager for Latin America, while simultaneously carrying out operations in the region for the CIA.

In 1981 he moved to Spain. In 1987 he created Telepizzas, an extremely lucrative business that became a major source of funding for numerous counterrevolutionary projects.

In 1981 he contributed money for the founding of the counterrevolutionary organization known as the Cuban Aid Society (Sociedad de Ayuda a los Cubanos, SAC), in Madrid. He was made a member of the board of directors, but stepped down several months later.

On September 4, 1999 he founded the Elena Mederos Foundation, named for his great-aunt, for the purpose of promoting an international movement to condemn Cuba.

He has provided funding for numerous declared counterrevolutionaries based in Miami, including René Cruz Cruz and Eusebio Peñalver Mazorra, both of whom have collaborated with Luis Posada Carriles in aggressive anti-Cuban plots.

He has contributed significant financial resources to the counterrevolutionary organization called the Cuban Center (Centro Cubano), to cover the expenses of Cubans who defect in Spain.

He has also provided funds to the counterrevolutionary NGO Reporters Without Borders as a means of supporting alleged "independent journalists".

Can you summarize?
Ana Rosa: Do you remember the man who went over to Spain and got rich delivering pizzas?

Telepizzas!
Ana Rosa: His name is Leopoldo Fernández Pujals. He was born in Cuba and emigrated to the United States when he was 13 years old. He lived there for something close to 20 years and had ties to the Cuban-American National Foundation. He later went to Spain,

but he remained beneath the shadow of the Foundation, which explains the success of his "pizzas".

When things started going well for him, he sold all of his shares for millions of dollars and directed a good part of his earnings toward "fighting for human rights and divulging the evils of the Cuban regime."

He founded the Elena Mederos Foundation, named after a former minister of Social Welfare, at the time of the triumph of the Revolution. The star project of this "humanitarian" organization was Awakening Smiles.

Manuel Alzugaray called you from Miami to propose this project to you?
Pedro: Yes, and Leopoldo's wife called me immediately after that.

What did it consist of?
Pedro: The idea was to take sick children out of the country, along with a guardian, a mother or father, for them to undergo surgical procedures abroad.

What was bad about it?
Ana Rosa: Just look at how "humanitarian" the idea is. It says here: "Principal aim of the project: to carry out surgical procedures on Cuban children, between the ages of 0 and 15 years, that can't be carried out in their own country and that do not require subsequent treatment or, should this be necessary, that require treatment that may be offered by Cuban institutions." And, later on: "We will not take on chronic cases. Oncological cases or organ transplants will not be accepted." Do you see? They were going to administer a few band-aids and make an big publicity stunt out of it. On the other hand, not only was it far from being a "humanitarian" project, it also concealed some monetary interests and a very obvious political maneuver.

Why do you say this?
Ana Rosa: A number of things interact in this project. In the first place, it is quite obviously a political strategy. Leopoldo sold his Telepizza shares and he made no secret of the fact that this foundation was principally concerned with overthrowing the Cuban Revolution.

But, besides this, one of the explicit aims of the Elena Mederos Foundation is to finance itself. Here we have the conferences they promoted, the number of participants, the costs of travel, the cost of materials, the aims to be outlined, the websites they were going to set up.

Look at the list of conferences: "Human Rights. What we defend: Basic documents of international laws on human and workers' rights. What we abhor: Cuban laws, the Penal Code, the Constitution, Law # 88, Law # 77, and Fidel's speeches. Human Rights reference documents on Cuba. Amnesty International. Human Rights Watch, Reporters Without Borders, the UN."

All of this costs money. Do we need to say more to show that Leopoldo is neither patriotic nor altruistic?

What other organizations surround the Elena Mederos Foundation?
Pedro: The Hispano-Cuban Foundation, the Cuban-American National Foundation, the Miami Medical Team Foundation (MMTF), Physicians' Association of Clinics, Hospitals and Annexes, which is also based in Miami. I had contact with directors from all of these organizations and I participated with many of them in a number of programs for *Radio "Martí"*, where Lincoln Díaz-Balart, the priest Francisco Santana, Manuel Alzugaray and others also participated. The whole gang sitting together at the same table.

How did the Awakening Smiles project get to Cuba?
Pedro: They sent emissaries on two occasions. The original idea was to set up a phone line inside a church, with someone to answer it 24 hours a day, so that the person who called could also receive spiritual advice. They left some money behind for a phone connection to Spain or the United States to be established, every so often.

Could this be carried out?
Pedro: Not like that, and when they showed me the plan to put it into effect, as a project of the "Independent" Medical Association, I also tried to hold them off.

What did you do?
Pedro: We told them that we didn't understand it all that well, that we were the ones here in Cuba, and not them, and, for instance, I didn't agree with opening offices in the 14 provinces, but rather felt it should be done by regions. I argued about the salary I was going to be paid, and when we reached an agreement, we started asking for office equipment and for all of the utensils that we could think of and that we felt would be useful to set up the office.

Did they buy them?
Ana Rosa: Immediately: we asked for a fax machine and they bought three of them, as well as typewriters, paper, stamps, everything.

Did someone come around to check up on you?
Pedro: Two Spanish men. We visited a number of provinces.

How much did they pay you?
Ana Rosa: The Elena Mederos Foundation paid 100 dollars a month to each of us working on the project.

What exactly did your work consist of?
Pedro: We made several trips across the country to get in touch with some children. Afterwards, we went to the embassy to get their visas and those of their relatives. They would ask for details of everything we did both in Miami and Spain.

Who was in charge of all this at the Spanish embassy?
Pedro: Most recently it was Pedro Martínez-Avial Martín, an embassy advisor. He told us we would have no problem whatsoever with the paperwork, and even offered us use of the diplomatic pouch, if we ever needed to send documents that could not be sent by fax. We never used it, never.

Why not?
Pedro: We were duty-bound to discourage that insane scheme. Can you imagine another Peter Pan operation, but with sick children! During the time we worked on the Awakening Smiles project, we would do the tours and draft the clinical histories — using real

cases — but choosing ones with characteristics we knew they were going to turn down, those that required post-operative care.

Where were the cases found?
Ana Rosa: *Radio "Martí"* waged a heavy-duty campaign, and there were people who wrote to the program or directly to the Foundation. They would send us the letters and demand a follow-up. We had to look for the children, verify that they really had the medical problem they claimed to have, submit them to a medical examination, get them to fill out a request form to be admitted into the treatment program abroad, and send it to the San Rafael Hospital and to a non-governmental organization belonging to Opus Dei, all of this in Spain. They would say, "But, you're sending us cases that are not eligible," and we would tell them, "They're the ones we have."

Pedro: So then they would say, "Look for other cases." And I would answer, "Look, I can't put up a sign outside my house saying: Headquarters of the Independent Medical Association of Cuba, running a project known as Awakening Smiles that takes children out of the country."

And how did it all end?
Pedro: We got kicked out and we were quite happy about it: the "Independent" Medical Association of Cuba did not send a single child abroad.

What happened with the cases whose families had written to Spain or the United States?
Ana Rosa: They were given medical attention in Cuba. I remember a little girl from Santiago de Cuba, very pretty, who had gone deaf and who was very smart. She was in the fifth or sixth grade, in a regular school. She was extremely bright. She would read the teacher's lips, and when he turned around, a girl who sat next to her would tell her what he was saying.

Pedro: I showed my official the girl's clinical history, and she was treated at the Hermanos Ameijeiras Hospital in Havana. She was given a cochlear implant — the nerve used for hearing — and recovered very well. She's doing wonderfully.

Francisco José Hernández Calvo

Born in Havana, and an engineer by profession. He was a member of the U.S. Marines, where he obtained the rank of Captain.

In 1981, along with Jorge Mas Canosa, he founded the Cuban-American National Foundation (Fundación Nacional Cubana American, FNCA).

In 1984, he was the president of the Caribbean Basin Investments Corporation (CBI).

He became a member of a paramilitary arm of the FNCA at the time it was founded and has acted as its director on more than one occasion.

He is personally responsible for administering the millions of dollars in financial resources which the FNCA has devoted to funding assassination attempts against President Fidel Castro.

He was implicated in the public scandal that linked the FNCA to the plot to assassinate Fidel Castro during the 7th Ibero-American Summit held at Margarita Island. One of the Barret semi-automatic assault rifles seized from the terrorist group meant to carry out the plot, detained in Puerto Rico on October of 1997, was registered in his name.

He had close ties to Luis Posada Carriles and the Central American group under his command. In a communication with the counterrevolutionary leader Victor Rolando Arroyo Carmona, he proposed inserting counterrevolutionary groups into the United Nations system, requesting international recognition, and participating in events as a means of exerting pressure on the Cuban government.

When did Ana Rosa begin to work by your side as an agent?
Pedro: When our relationship was going down the drain, I spoke with my official and I asked him for help. They carried out an investigation and decided they could trust us. Agent Gabriela was born. From that point on, the work became more firmly grounded and my marriage was saved. I felt much calmer with by her side.

Did she know about everything?
Pedro: The essential details, yes. For her own security, we had to omit some details.

How many children do you two have?

Ana Rosa: We have two: Luis Ernesto and Ana Laura.

Why do you say that your marriage was saved?
Pedro: I would get home at 11 at night and I didn't know what story to tell her. Ana was already working at the Héroes de la Moncada Clinic, treating patients just like me, and she would get home early. She couldn't understand my absences, and she was convinced I was having an affair.

When they told her what was actually happening, I was sure that when I got home that night, I wasn't going to have to cook my own dinner …Because she had applying all of those "cold war" tactics up until then.

How long did you work together?
Ana Rosa: For five years. I joined in the work with the Elena Mederos Foundation.

When did you establish ties to the U.S. Interests Section?
Pedro: When I began to collaborate with Dr. Augusto Madrigal. In June of 1998, the Interests Section summoned us for interviews with three journalists from the *Dallas Morning News* who were interested in Cuban reality. Timothy Brown was the one who gave them our names, and the meeting was held during a work breakfast at the Hotel Nacional.

On December 5 of that same year, we were invited to the home of the head of the Interests Section, Michael Kozak, where a meeting was held with Senator Christopher Dodd to discuss the issue of the U.S. "embargo." Dodd had met with Fidel, and the diplomats had ambushed him and forced him to meet with the "dissidents", in the name of the political "balance" that the United States so fervently defends whenever it finds it convenient.

How did that meeting go?
Pedro: The majority of "dissidents" recommended that the em-

bargo be maintained. Others asked for it to be lifted, but on the condition of supposed democratic and political reforms, and a third group suggested that only the blockade on food and medicines be lifted.

In the midst of that whole controversy, I asked for the block- ade to be lifted altogether. And I added, "It breaks my heart every time I have to treat a seriously ill patient and the medicine to save him is not available. Or when I find someone suffering from malnutrition because of a lack of food. Besides, everyone present here lives in Cuba and the idea that the embargo is aimed against the government is a myth. We're the ones who suffer."

Things got a bit ugly, and Christopher Dodd came over and hugged me. Of course, to keep up appearances, I told him, "I was invited here and I'm not sure whether I'll still have a job on Monday." And he answered, "If something happens to you, call me up."

Were you fired?
Pedro: No, of course not. Let me explain something to you. Working with children took up a lot of my time, and I wasn't able to cultivate more intense relations with the Interests Section.

At one point or other, my comrades in State Security proposed that I leave the hospital to lighten the load somewhat. Bear in mind that I also had a lot of problems at work, because I had to keep up my façade as a counterrevolutionary among revolutionaries. That was plain hell.

But I asked them to let me continue practicing. My officials respected my wishes, but that meant simultaneously attending patients and making long trips, either on bicycle or foot, to prepare the documentation, to receive and send faxes.

Nevertheless, I kept up my ties with the U.S. Interests Section, particularly with Nicholas J. Giacobbe.

Did they visit you at home?
Pedro: Yes, and not only my home, but also that of Odilia Collazo, that of María de los Ángeles Menéndez, that of Moisés Rodríguez…I have a funny anecdote about that.

On December 10 of 2001, a meeting had been called in the home of Odilia, the president of the Human Rights Party. She invited the entire world — I didn't know how she could do this when her home was so small.

State Security had installed a device which prevented people from parking cars in front of her home and somewhat impeded their arrival. When I was about to leave, I got a call from a counter-revolutionary and he told me, "Arturo, State Security is in front of Odilia's place and they're not letting anyone in." I called my official and asked him, "What should I do?" "You have to go over there." And I said: "Hey, and what about the operation?" "Try to get in there anyway you can. Let me handle it." I called him once again, and he told me, "Arturo, I couldn't get a hold of anyone. Everyone's working in the operation. Sneak inside, you have to be there."

I got into my car, I filled it up with people and I left for Odilia's place. I turned in at another street and I went in reverse at full speed. I slammed on the brakes and I yelled at the other people to get out fast. I left the car in the middle of the street, with the doors open. The people inside the house all applauded and yelled, "Another one!"

Shortly afterwards, Victor Vockerodt got there and passed on a message for me: "Tell that crazy doctor to park his car properly; he left the car with the doors open. I'll protect him." He approached me and said, "Look, when I leave, follow me in your car, so you don't get into any trouble." Isn't that wild? Agent Ernesto left under the escort of a car with diplomatic plates from the Interests Section of the United States of America!

Which member of the U.S. diplomatic corps visited your home?
Pedro: Ricardo Zuniga. He came over and told me a series of anecdotes about the tour he and James Cason had done through the country's provinces. He told me, for instance, that he had met with a doctor living in the middle of a mountain, in a remote place in eastern Cuba. When they asked him what medicine he had there, if he needed any money, trying to cozy up to him, he told them in a rather rude tone that he had all of the medicine and all of the equip-

ment he needed to get by. That the only thing he had problems with was transportation, because of the remoteness of the place. But that no one was dying on him, because he would see to it that his patients got the care they needed, be it through mules or carts.

Ricardo Bofill

A former counterrevolutionary convict, he took asylum in the French Embassy for a period of six months. He left the embassy of his own will in January of 1987.

At the beginning of the 1960s, he was a member of the counter-revolutionary group known as the Christian People's Association (Asociación Cristiana Popular), and later, at the close of the decade, he was sanctioned for his activities in this mini-faction.

In 1983, he began a campaign to attract international attention. He presented himself to various international organizations and diplomatic missions as an alleged "prisoner of conscience".

The French journalists Renaud Delourme and Dominique Louis Nasplezes contacted him on the instructions of Armando Valladares and other former counterrevolutionary convicts, to carry out international defamations of Cuba.

In prison, he showed himself to be recalcitrant in his conduct and created the counterrevolutionary organization known as the Cuban Committee for Human Rights (Comité Cubano Pro Derechos Humanos). He subsequently drafted a letter where he expressed his repentance and requested that his confine-ment be changed to house arrest or parole, on account of his hypertension. He asked the revolutionary government to allow him to begin again "with a clean slate."

In 1985 he was set free, after serving only two years of his prison term. He turned down every job that was offered to him and be-gan to conspire against the country once again.

In March of 1988, an article published in Cuba by journalist Félix Pita Astudillo provided proof of Bofill's relations with the U.S. In-terests Section. He appeared on national television receiving money from U.S. diplomats and betraying other counterrevolu-tionaries. He left Cuba in October of the same year.

He met up with revolutionary doctors. Zuniga asked me if they were telling the truth, and what I thought. I looked him in the eye, trying to hide how moved I was by the words of my colleague, and I said to him, "Look, don't put a lot of stock in it. The government sends revolutionaries, the best of the graduates, to the worst places. What do you expect them to tell you?"

Did the Americans ask you for information about the public health system?
Pedro: They wanted to know everything, such as the situation in the hospitals, the clinics, the emergency rooms. They were obsessed with the health of the Comandante, what afflictions he suffered, if I knew what medicine he needed, what foods didn't agree with him.

Giacobbe even told me — I said this during the trial of the mercenaries — that he was hoping to witness the President's death in the years he had been assigned to work here.

I wrote down all of the things they wanted to know about in a notebook.

What other things did they want to know?
Pedro: The consequences of the visit of John Paul II and that of James Carter; the attitude of the people and of the opposition toward the U.S. blockade; the economic and social repercussions for the public health system; the attitude of the people towards the possibility of hard-line capitalism, like in the former socialist countries; the possibility of social upheavals.

In the public health sector: medical students and the potential lack of incentive to continue their studies; the program of study at the Latin American School of Medicine; if the models followed are American, French, or Russian; if the programs there are devoted only to the training of family doctors or if they can be trained for other tasks. Everything concerning the intensive training schools for nurses; the effects on the population of public health projects and programs; the family doctor program; results and degree of satisfaction among the doctors as well as the population; if people could seek treatment from other doctors or other institutions; the situation of the public health care centers, including hospitals, clinics, family doctor's offices, equipment, laboratory material, re-agents, imaging technology, and so on.

Anything else?
Pedro: The people's level of satisfaction with the pharmacies and the lack of medicines; the national epidemiological situation, es-pecially with regard to cholera, dengue, malaria, tuberculosis, AIDS; the information provided by the Cuban government and health authorities on outbreaks or massive epidemics; if the media dis-seminated measures to take against outbreaks; the situation of children's health, pregnant women, concern over low birth weight. The infant mortality rate, life expectancy and parameters used to measure the social wellbeing of the population.

Did they ask for this information all at once, or little by little?
Pedro: They asked for it on different occasions, though they would sometimes repeat the same questions. The issue of public health in Cuba was primary, then came everything else. They also wanted to know if the statistics presented by the government were true. I answered that there were representatives of very serious interna-tional organizations, like the WHO and PAHO, in Havana, and that if they couldn't say that those indicators and rates were untrue, I was in no position to doubt them.

I suggested they direct their questions to them. Nevertheless, I told them: "I have many doubts about those numbers." In brief, I always tried to put them against the wall.

What relationship did they have with the Medical Association you directed?
Pedro: They often asked how many members we had. They wanted to use that number as an index of the situation in Cuba. We would assure them we had 800 members and that we had not only doc-tors but also paramedical personnel.

You actually had that many members?
Pedro: Of course not. We barely had 20 members, and even the positions on the national board of directors were invented — in fact, my wife and I acted as directors.

Were you given instructions to create an "independent library"?
Ana Rosa: The instructions came through different channels: the U.S. Interests Section, the Miami Medical Team Foundation and Cuban Democratic Action (Acción Democrática Cubana). They came almost simultaneously from the three of them.

Manuel Alzugaray has been a close friend of Otto Reich for many years. Alzugaray met with Reich in Venezuela, when Reich was the U.S. ambassador there, and he met with him also in Nicaragua, at the time of the Contras. They even did television shows together. Alzugaray said that they had dinner together in restaurants in Miami.

Pedro: Otto Reich, who was in charge of Western Hemisphere Affairs at the State Department and was one of the people who authorized licenses to import medicines to counterrevolutionary groups in Cuba, wanted to know how to do this without coming into contact with the government. One day, when I was conversing with Alzugaray, he told me that he was receiving instructions for us to carry out and that the most important thing was to put together the "independent" clinics and pharmacies. They would be responsible for supplying us with everything we needed. All we had to do was take a list to Giacobbe detailing the medicines and other things we were receiving for him to pass on to the State Department. Meaning that Democratic Action had to justify to its true bosses how the money given out by USAID was being used.

Did he tell you how they were hoping to use that money to destroy the Cuban Revolution?
Pedro: I have a recording of a conversation with Manuel Alzugaray from 2002, where he tells me that the creation of the "independent" pharmacies and clinics follows the same principle employed in Nicaragua, Poland and Russia to put an end to communism. He told me that, when I was handing out the medicines, not to discriminate against Party members. "You have to set your sights on winning people over to the cause at the time of the transition in Cuba. After that, we'll see what happens..."

Can we listen to it?
Pedro: Yes, here it is. This is Alzugaray speaking: "You give it out to anyone who shows up, it doesn't matter if it's a communist, or if they were ever a member of the party or some such thing. Don't worry about it. That's going to be beneficial to you in the long run. We can't be too partisan here, because we have to say we're doc- tors, a humanitarian organization. We don't discriminate because of color, religion or anything. You have no idea what sorts of benefits this is going to bring to that group of yours, and to the members personally. It was what we did in Nicaragua, in Poland, in Russia, in all of those countries that have left the communist sphere, and that's how we've managed it…"

Here, he also admits that Otto Reich was the person who approved the Pilot Program, and the one who drafted the proposal for the U.S. government to approve money that was going to be sent to counterrevolutionary organizations.

What is the Pilot Program?
Ana Rosa: A multilateral project for sending medicines and medical equipment, aimed at exercising a negative influence over the population and medical sector. These materials would be delivered, for the most part, to old age homes and marginal neighborhoods by counterrevolutionaries working in the health care sector independently and parallel to the work of the Ministry of Public Health (MINSAP).

Did Alzugaray send you money?
Pedro: A hundred dollars a month, in the name of the Miami Medical Team Foundation, which is registered as part of the Institute for Democracy, which is financed by USAID. The money would be directed to my wife. It came regularly, until they stopped sending it altogether, when we started working with Democratic Action and put together the National Office for the Reception of Human Rights Violations.

You said before that you also had contacts in PACHA…
Pedro: The Physicians' Association of Clinics, Hospitals and Annexes, yes, through its president Vicente Lago. This man supported

the Medical Association, especially the members working in the eastern provinces. It was the same idea: information, posters, magazines, medicine. We also had contact with Dr. Marcelo Cano Rodríguez, who was president of the Medical Association of Cuba, a group working parallel to the Independent Medical Association of Cuba, which later joined Democratic Action in Miami.

Ana Rosa: Just look at the terrorist nature of these organizations:

On August 9, 1998, two of the members of the Miami Medical Team Foundation, Enrique Basas and Luis Orlando Rodríguez, participated with Luis Posada Carriles in the plans to assassinate Fidel Castro during his visit to the Dominican Republic.

Counting the Free Cuban Medical Association in Exile, another group made up of "health care professionals", that makes three organizations of this sort that "aided" us these past years.

What happened with the other Medical Association?
Pedro: Elizardo Sánchez Santacruz, who is the head of the Cuban Commission for Human Rights and National Reconciliation, has been the one who has directed and guided all of the activities of Marcelo Cano Rodríguez, the president of the Medical Association, which was put together following the decision of the Miami-based groups to establish another, more aggressive front parallel to the one I was directing, in order to take apart the Cuban public health system.

These people have recruited doctors with the material and financial aid of Frank Hernández Trujillo, from the Dissidence Support Group.

They had a very clear line of action, which consisted of getting in touch with health care professionals interested in emigrating to the United States. They incite them to sign a counterrevolutionary document opposing the Ministry of Public Health regulations for travel abroad. They tell them to carry out acts of provocation.

In exchange for what, you ask? A visa to travel to the United States and the support of the U.S. Interests Section to obtain the permission to leave the country.

Who is Alzugaray?
Ana Rosa: A man who left at the beginning of the Revolution and who has put together a very impressive curriculum vitae as a terrorist since then. He provided medical attention to deserters from former socialist countries, he was in the U.S. Naval Base in Guantánamo during the rafters crisis. There are magazines and posters he sent us over there somewhere.

What sorts of medicines were sent from Miami? How did they get them into the country?
Ana Rosa: They would send medicines that didn't require a medical prescription, because that complicated matters. They weren't urgently needed. They didn't save anyone's life, although there's always a need for them, especially analgesics that reduce fever, anti-inflammatory medicines, vitamins, minerals…Now, drugs such as anticoagulants, or medicines used intravenously, those were never sent.

They would be brought by "mules", and we met with a very special one.

Who?
Pedro: A state senator from North Carolina, Henry William Barker, who was supposedly bringing a humanitarian donation from the Love Valley Presbyterian Church. In fact, he had come here following instructions from Lincoln Díaz-Balart and the Miami Medical Team Foundation. We have photocopies of all of the documents that he brought.

What do they say?
Ana Rosa: For example, this is a letter written by Ana Carbonell, head of Lincoln Díaz-Balart's office, explaining how he can get in touch with Pedro, giving him our phone number, and telling him that Alzgugaray can give him the names of "opposition" doctors who live in rural areas of the country. Also, a letter he had sent to the Office of Foreign Assets Control of the Treasury Department, explaining that he was bringing medicine to the island, donated by the people of North Carolina, by its churches in particular, and that

the names of doctors he would be visiting had been recommended by Congressman Díaz-Balart, something that his assistant, Ana Carbonell, can verify.

Does he mention who he is?
Ana Rosa: He introduces himself as a 56-year-old attorney, honorably discharged from the U.S. Navy, who has served as an Assistant District Attorney for eight years and in the North Carolina Senate for two terms. In reality, this man behaved like a classic CIA agent.

Why do you say that?
Pedro: There are many elements, everything from his behavior to the documents he was carrying. For example, the letter where he lists the medicines he had to deliver to us reads, in Spanish:

"Operation USA is pleased to donate the products listed below to the Cuban people, to be used in pediatric hospitals in the attention given to children and the poor..." The words Operation USA have been crossed out, and, above, an arrow indicates that it is in fact the Love Valley Presbyterian Church that is making the donation, a letterhead superimposed on the official letter. Something put together rather shabbily and hastily.

This man returned to Cuba with more medicines, gifts and money. He would always stay at our place. When he trusted us a bit more, the last time he came, he brought with him a weapons catalogue, and asked us which guns we would prefer. I remember it was kind of a fold-out catalogue. We were horrified; we told him that our opposition to the government was peaceful, that we were against the shedding of blood, and asked him how he could forget that we were doctors.

Were you already working at the time for the National Office for Gathering and Reporting Human Rights Violations, along with Odilia Collazo?
Pedro: That was afterwards. I started to work with her there developing the reports she would later present to the government of the United States, as proof of the violation of human rights in Cuba.

Did they make phony reports?
Pedro: We would exaggerate the facts, and many cases came to us from people whose only aim was to leave the country — they had family in the United States or wanted to get ahead economically — and who had been turned down again and again by the U.S. Interests Section. Don't forget that the granting of visas began to go down dramatically, to the point that this year they've given out just a handful.

How would you carry out this work?
Pedro: I was in charge of reworking everything that was put in my hands, as well as everything that came from our own imaginations. Everything related to the issue of public health was written by Ana Rosa and me.

What would you do with this report?
Pedro: It was sent to the U.S. Interests Section and they would pass it on unchanged to the State Department. In reality, as you know, the touching up of the contents was done in advance.

You submitted the report for 2002 this year?
Pedro: Yes, before the discussion at the Commission on Human Rights in Geneva.

The document you put together was the one used for the political maneuvers against Cuba in Geneva?
Pedro: The same one, without omitting a single point. It is also the one that's been circulating in all the recent slander campaigns against Cuba. If you read it carefully, you realize that the essential points are very clearly stated: "In Cuba, no one is tortured in prisons, there have been no reports of political assassinations, nor reports of people having been disappeared for political reasons" — something which is entirely true.

Of course, what the U.S. government wanted to hear is there also, everything they've worked so hard for these past years — we have to grant them that, Cason in particular.

Just look at how ironic this is: I saw the representative of Costa Rica on television, reading an amendment in English with the information that we had put together for that report. And to top it off, the representative of the United States had no qualms about stating publicly that what that despicable man had read there had been submitted by the United States. He was right about that, except for one detail.

Which was?

Pedro: That I was the author. I was the one who wrote that report, Agent Ernesto from Cuban State Security.

FROM MAMEY TO THE MAYOR'S OFFICE OF GÜINES

YAMILA PÉREZ REYES AND NOEL ASCANIO MONTERO

They are two very different people, an ideal couple to take on the pressures of working within the "dissident" groups. Yamila is someone visceral, emotional, she can hardly sit still. Noel is someone with a sharp and thoughtful wit, who has a quiet and ironic manner to him. They've known each other since they were children, playing together in Mamey, the neighborhood in Güines that saw them grow up, fall in love, and bring a child into the world.

Their relationship was on the verge of ending. Yamila never mentioned she was an agent of State Security, and Noel was suspicious of his wife's friends and meetings, until he was secretly summoned and the truth was made known to him. This other life they shared, that began quietly in Mamey, came to an end the day the delirious members of the "dissident" movement in the province of Havana decided to establish the Mayor's Office of Güines.

AGENTS CELIA AND ABEL

One of you is an agent and the other an assistant?
Yamila: No, both of us are agents.

When did you begin to work as an agent and why?

Yamila: I begin to work for State Security in the year 1993. They gave me this assignment because they believed I was in a position to get inside the counterrevolutionary groups working in Güines.

What were you working as at the time?
Yamila: I was a laboratory technician.

For which laboratory?
Yamila: In the Piti Fajardo Hospital, in the Güines Municipality, in the province of Havana. That's where I started with this whole hustle and bustle.

What organizations did you become involved with?
Yamila: With the Human Rights Party (Partido Pro Derechos Humanos), as a municipal delegate. The president was Odilia Collazo. By the middle of 1996, I went on to the "Independent" Press Agency (Buró de Prensa Independiente). I also took part in the Cuban Liberal Current (Corriente Liberal Cubana), in the Party for Human Rights (Partido por los Derechos Humanos), run by Tania Díaz Castro, in the "Independent" Medical Federation (Federación Médica Independiente), the National Center for Independent Agricultural Studies (Centro Nacional de Estudios Agrícolas Independientes, CENAIC); I was also a provincial delegate for the Latin American Federation of Rural Women (Federación Latinoamericana de Mujeres Rurales, FLAMUR) and secretary of the Francisco Riverón Hernández "Independent Libarary".

Weren't they far too many responsibilities for just one person?
Yamila: Not for a "dissident".

You two were the ones who wrote a letter to the director of the National Library, Eliades Acosta, when he published an article in Juventud Rebelde *about the "independent libraries"?*
Yamila: That was in March of 2002. It was written by Jadir Hernán-

dez, and Noel, my husband, was one of the people who signed it. The only library that was operating in the Güines Municipality at the time was the one in my house.

How was it sustained?
Yamila: That library was equipped, from the beginning, with what the U.S. Interests Sections gave us. We would pick up books there and they would send us others. They would bring all sorts of things, from *Disidente* and *Hispano-Cubana* magazines to samples of universal literature.

Who was your first counterrevolutionary superior?
Yamila: Rolando González Yánez, who was the provincial delegate for the Human Rights Party.

Where would you go? What things would you do?
Yamila: I would travel with him to San José de las Lajas, where Odilia Collazo's right hand man lived, José Manuel de la Paz. I would also visit Odilia Collazo at her place every two weeks, to submit reports on violations and to get instructions from her. We visited prisons, and picked up medicines and food from the counterrevolutionary groups, to take them to the so-called political prisoners.

You were allowed to visit the prisoners?
Yamila: Yes, of course.

What year did this take place?
Yamila: What I'm talking about took place during my first years in this work. Afterwards, in mid-1996, I started at the Independent Press Agency, with Luis López Prendes.

What happened to López Prendes?
Yamila: He left the country. I went to see him off at the airport before he left for the United States.

And what happened afterwards?
Yamila: We continued working with Gilberto Figueredo, from the "Independent" Press Agency, with whom I spent entire nights going around the entire city of Havana, through different municipalities. Through Vedado and Centro Habana, for the most part. He

said that's where you could find the most problems, but, in fact, we'd make up the problems. For instance, he would say that at such and such a time, a patrol car had come by — this was true — and that the police officers had gotten out of the car and beaten up a citizen. That last part was a lie.

Noel: All of those little trips at night almost cost us our marriage...

Yamila: True, but you bought all of the excuses I gave you...

Ángel Cuadra Landrove

Resident of Miami, of Cuban origins. He is the head of the counterrevolutionary organization known as the Ex Club, short for the Association of Ex-Political Prisoners and Militants of Cuba (Asociación de Exprisioneros y Combatientes Politicos Cubanos).

In 1967, he was sentenced to a prison term of 15 years for the crime of conspiring against Cuban state security. He was released on parole in 1976, to be put in jail once again in 1977.

He was adopted as a "prisoner of conscience" by Amnesty International and named prisoner of the month by this organization in 1981. He left Cuba in 1985.

In his absence, he was named president of the Second Congress of Intellectuals for the Liberation of Cuba. He attended the Third Congress and enjoyed much publicity in the counterrevolutionary press.

In 1986, he took part in the Third Congress of Alpha 66, where he spoke of the literary aspects of so-called political imprisonment. He also has links to the Cuban-American National Foundation, although he is not officially a member of either of these organizations.

In 1992, he was elected vice-president of the Ex Club and in mid-2001 he was named president, following the death of Rolando F. Borges Paz.

He has sent pamphlets to the Commission on Human Rights Committee in Geneva, criticizing Cuba for alleged violations of human rights.

He has ties with mercenaries in Cuba, particularly with Raúl Rivero Castañeda, whom he supplies with funding, medicine and clothing.

Where would those reports be sent?
Yamila: To *Radio "Martí".*

Where did Figueredo come from?
Yamila: He told me he was a journalist, but he never showed me his diploma, and he never even mentioned where he had worked in the media. After that, I spent some quiet time at home, until Jadir Hernández showed up.

Explain...
Yamila: He's in the United States now. He was one of the people who became a "dissident" to get a U.S. visa. Actually, it was Noel he approached, because some people in Havana had told him we were human rights activists. He proposed that we join Tania Díaz Castro. This took place in August of the year 2000.

Who was this person?
Yamila: He's a lawyer. He came with Miguel Galván.

And who is Miguel Galván?
Yamila: He's an engineer, who has a Master's degree thanks to the Revolution. He wasn't working by the time we met him, because he was getting some 80 dollars every month for writing false reports about Cuba.

How were they getting that money?
Yamila: Through some of the groups in Miami. They would use "mules", people who came from the United States. The money was sent to us by Diosmel Hernández.

Where did he come from?
Yamila: He's the sponsor of the CENAIC. This Diosmel will probably come up at other points in this conversation.

Let's talk about Miguel...
Yamila: Miguel Galván was from Jadir and Noel's group; they later created the Cuban Civic Alliance (Alianza Cívica Cubana). The name of this organization was originally the South Havana Civic Coordinator (Coordinadora Cívica Habana Sur), and we founded it on September 12, 2002. I was the secretary for Social Issues and Noel was the secretary for International Relations.

Noel: We made up the members of that alliance, with a pen and paper, quite literally... It was made up of 35 ghost organizations.

Tell us about it.

Noel: We were sitting at a table, in a library...Some groups had names, but no members. The truth was that all of us in total added up to 18 people, and we would claim there were 600 of us.

Jadir would say, for instance, "We're weak in the list of trade unions. Let's make up a name related to that first..." That's what happened with the youth group, the women's group...We would sign ourselves up in many groups, but sometimes, when it was time to vote, one of us would change their mind and we had to start from scratch. It was a circus.

And after the organization had been established?

Yamila: That information was sent abroad.

Noel: The Cuban Civic Alliance was established with the aim of demonstrating that Güines had a solid "opposition", and that it was united. What sort of an opposition was that, with three or four tiny groups fighting among themselves? Give me a break. Even the name "Alliance" had its catch – it made you think that it involved a huge load of people, that collective decisions were made and, consequently, you had to consult with it for any decision to be adopted by the "opposition" leaders in the City of Havana. It's not the same thing for Oswaldo Payá to say that something was signed by so-and-so, as compared to saying, "This was signed by the Alliance." This was Jadir Hernández´s idea, and it's even set down in the statutes of the organization. We were painting Güines as the home of a strong counterrevolutionary movement with many groups.

Yamila: Let me give you another example: I was the leader of the group FLAMUR, and I would claim there were 30 people on the executive. Nothing but lies! It was me, myself and I. Things got to the point where Miguel Galván and Jadir were not satisfied with the 35 groups and wanted more. They wanted to put together a children's group and they set their sights on our little boy. That's when we put our foot down: "Hey, give it a rest, will you! Aren't you ashamed?" The last thing we needed was to turn the poor boy into the leader of the "dissident" pioneers.

Noel: They wanted to attract children to start inculcating them with ideas against the Revolution, in exchange for gifts. They had already held Christmas parties and they had spent some money, but not much, because the gifts weren't worth a dollar each: a little doll, a toy car, that sort of thing.

When did you first visit the U.S. Interests Section?
Noel: When Miguel Galván approached me and told me he needed a secretary for the Association of "Independent" Engineers and Agronomists of Cuba (Colegio de Ingenieros y Agrónomos Independientes de Cuba, CIAIC) — just take a look at the name! What he was really after was an interview with someone from the Interests Section, to get himself known. We went to the Interests Section on March 12, 2001.

Who did you have the interview with?
Noel: With an official named Patricia French, from the Human Rights Office there. She asked about the plans for the Association of Engineers, its membership, and its potential for economic profit. She gave us a few magazines — *Cubanet* and *Disidente* — and made an appointment with us for another meeting there.

Miguel was extremely nervous and kept dropping things. His idea had been to take something to them that would really impress them. And it worked; she arranged another meeting at the Interests Section, for July of 2001.

You were received by the same official?
Noel: We went there, but to deal with another issue, the "independent" libraries. We were received by Maryann McKay, who was responsible for the press and culture. She asked about our "independent library" and its activities, its public acceptance and its plans for the future. She asked about the people of Güines and their reading habits. I wrote everything down. She also gave us books, pamphlets and counterrevolutionary magazines. There were nearly 40 publications. It was too much for us.

Cuban Democratic Directorate (Directorio Democrático Cubano, DDC)

Founded at the beginning of the 1990s following the collapse of Socialist bloc in Europe. The chief objective of the organization is to exercise international influence and persuade countries in Europe and Latin America to lend their support to counterrevolutionary movements within Cuba.

It is the counterrevolutionary organization that enjoys the most substantial funding from the government of the United States, in its unfaltering mission to destroy the Cuban Revolution.

Its present political agenda is centered on obtaining international support for the "Varela" Project.

As such, it was the publically acknowledged organizer of Oswaldo Payá's visit to Miami in January of 2003.

The delegations of the DDC in third countries call themselves Solidarity Committees, and are comprised of Cuban immigrants and nationals of those countries who back these anti-Cuban projects.

The DDC has close ties to universities in Russia, Prague and Warsaw, as well as to political figures such as Lech Walesa, Vaclav Havel and Mark Laar of Lithuania.

In Latin America, they run the so-called Support Committees which have representatives in Mexico, the Dominican Republic, Argentina, Chile, El Salvador and Nicaragua.

In Mexico, the Committee is known as the International Promoter of Human Rights (Promotora Internacional de Derechos Humanos, PIDH).

They run a center of ideological subversion known as the Center of Studies for a National Option (Centro de Estudios para una Opción Nacional, CEON), which administers copious resources aimed at the production of subversive materials directed against Cuba in every forum that presents itself.

This center receives funding from the U.S. government to finance trips to other member countries of the DDC, and to pay the salaries of counterrevolutionary leaders who devote themselves to analyzing the experiences of the transitional processes that took place in Eastern Europe, in order to apply them to Cuba.

Yamila began working as an agent first, and Noel came later...Tell us about how you started to work together...

Yamila: At first, when I started out, we had a lot of problems at home. Noel would notice I was traveling to Havana and to different provinces a lot, and he thought I was cheating on him with another man.

Noel: I decided to ask for a divorce...

Yamila: He said to me, "Either you tell me what's going on or this is over." It was natural, but I wasn't prepared to tell him anything, unless I was instructed to do so by my official. He knows it very well: the Revolution comes first, then comes everything else, including my own marriage. I sat down to talk with my officials, and they wanted to know my opinion. Just imagine: I've known him since we were kids, and we even lived on the same block. He's a revolutionary, from a decent family, and, at the time, a member of the Union of Young Communists... They did the necessary research, and here he is.

Noel: We complement each other because we have very different personalities. Her façade was useful to me, and I started to work on my own.

Yamila: He would carry me and I would carry him, and it was very beautiful working together. Do you understand?

Noel: Because of our personalities, there were times when things got a bit ugly.

Why is that?

Yamila: We had very intense arguments.

Noel: At one point or another, someone even got slapped.

Why?

Yamila: Tania Díaz Castro kicked Miguel Galván out of the vice-presidency of the Human Rights Party, and she decided to give me his post to keep me under control. I have a very strong character, similar to hers, and to avoid having problems with me, she promoted me. Galván was so furious when he found out that he showed up at my place and told me I had been kicked out of the Cuban Civic Alliance, in Güines, where I was vice-president. We had a big argument and I said to him, "You didn't put me there and you're not kicking me out; I'll leave when I want to leave, not when you want me to."

Noel: There was a lot friction around because of jealousy and power struggles. Yamila was getting more and more recognition and he tried to discredit us, to distance us from everything.

Yamila: Galván circulated an e-mail saying that Noel and I were agents working for State Security, along with other gossip. I found this out from other "opposition" members. They came to my place to bring me the message. I asked for permission to give him what he was asking for.

And Noel?
Yamila: He understood. He wanted to go after him. We kept going over the problem in our heads and on the morning of January 28, the group known as 10th of December tried to place a floral wreath in José Martí Park, in Güines. I went to the park and found him there. It was a Sunday, they were dispensing beer and the place was packed. He was with another counterrevolutionary, Virgilio Marante Guelmes.

I waited for him to get close to me and I punched him in the nose and kicked him in the testicles as hard as I could. I didn't give him a chance to react. He shrank back, got on his bicycle and rode off, and I went after him, yelling everything that crossed my mind, from the Park to Mamey, where Noel and I live. I yelled at him for four or five blocks, things I can't exactly repeat here, and that he wasn't really a man, that he had no dignity, no morals, nothing.

What happened after that?
Yamila: He left Güines for a while. After that, if we ran into one another on the street, he would cross over to the other side. He was completely demoralized and alone. He's a sinister figure in the history of the counterrevolution in Havana, with ties to every single conspiracy in existence, capable of cheating his own mother if the situation called for it.

Did you participate in the hunger strike at 34 Tamarindo?
Yamila: As a journalist, yes. That was in June of 1999. I went there twice, with Gilberto Figueredo. On the first and last days of the strike. The home of Migdalia Rosado is at 34 Tamarindo Street, in the (Havana) neighborhood of Luyanó.

But you didn't take part in the strike?
Yamila: Gilberto took me there because he wanted me to learn

how to make a denunciation to send to the Miami media. I went as part of my apprenticeship as an "independent" journalist.

Noel: Figueredo gave you a pseudonym, Gretel, for you to avoid detection by State Security.

Yamila: Yes, but I actually used it on very few occasions.

Frank Hernández Trujillo

Top leader of the counterrevolutionary organization known as the Dissidence Support Group (Grupo de Apoyo a la Disidencia). Between the years 1962 and 1963, he was an active member of the U.S. army, specifically of the so-called Cuban Special Units. Hernández Trujillo is one of the most active members of the Institute for Democracy in Cuba (IDC), a group composed of 10 counterrevolutionary organizations which have received more than one million dollars from the U.S. Agency for International Development (USAID) in recent years. In 1995, he became the principal leader of the Dissidence Support Group, an organization which carries out subversive activities against Cuba and receives funding from USAID. The organization claims to have established either direct or indirect contact with more than 400 members of counterrevolutionary groups and to have sent material and financial aid to more than 100 of them.

He has played a leading role in providing material aid to counterrevolutionary groups within Cuba, sending food, medicine, subversive literature, electronic agendas, ink pads, radios and tape recorders, among other goods.

The main recipients of this aid in Cuba are Martha Beatriz Roque, Victor Rolando Arroyo Carmona, Raúl Rivero Castañeda and Osvaldo Alfonso Valdés.

What did you see in the house on Tamarindo Street?
Yamila: A farce. You went into the living room, then continued on to the bedroom, and there were a number of beds set up, side by side. Lying there, pretending to be fasting, there were a number of people trying to look like they were suffering, especially if you told them that you were a reporter. They fed the press this whole propaganda horror story: that they were living in subhuman conditions, that there was a sewer water leakage, and so on. And everyone knew that no one ever went on a fast there.

Someone told you this?
Yamila: Figueredo himself told me that when all the other people left, in the evenings, they would prepare themselves snacks and eat them. Also, when they had no visitors, in the afternoon. They themselves admitted that they ate when no one else was around. And they had plenty of condensed milk, plenty of sweetened malt drinks to keep them going, jars of baby food, soup mixes… People even said they had put a roasted pig through the blender to have a strictly liquid diet. It was an insult to our intelligence. And in front of the foreign correspondents, they played victims.

I remember that Oscar Elías Biscet walked into the living room with Figueredo — I was walking ahead of them — and, in a loud tone of voice, he called on the journalists to take photographs and yelled: "Now we are free, now we have democracy, long live human rights." Biscet put on a big show in front of the cameras.

Afterwards, the details about what actually went on there became well known, and there was no way they could deny them.

Noel: Tell them, Yamila, tell them what flag you saw there.

Yamila: The American flag.

Where exactly was it?
Yamila: It was in the living room, next to a photograph of some prisoners.

Noel: And a photograph of Jorge Mas Canosa, no?

Yamila: Yes, it was next to the photograph of a prisoner, one of the people that had just been put in jail around the time and there was a huge international campaign in support of him. You saw it as soon as you went in, practically facing the door. They were putting on a show, you know what I mean? A big show.

What were your principal tasks most recently?
Yamila: My work with FLAMUR.

How did FLAMUR get started?
Yamila: It was group put together in the United States, headed by Magda Edilia Hidalgo. She used to live in eastern Cuba. She left for the United States and founded this group. The first president here in Cuba was Leticia Martínez, who was Magda's sister-in-law.

They were hoping to organize women from the countryside to

have them receive medicine, food and materials for making baskets to send to hospitals, with propaganda in them. The "gifts" were delivered by an "independent journalist" who would carry a tape recorder and a video camera with him, to tape or to record the mother receiving the diapers, the medical gauze, the bottles of milk, and the pins from the basket. In exchange for all this, the mothers had to say that they were truly grateful to FLAMUR.

The recording would be sent to Magda and she would put it out on *Radio "Martí"*, in a program she had at four thirty in the afternoon.

José Cohen Valdés

Linked to the counterrevolutionary organizations known as the Cuban-American National Foundation (Fundación Nacional Cubano Americana, FNCA) and New Generation Cuba (Nueva Generacion Cuba).

A deserter, formerly a captain in the Ministry of the Interior, he left the country illegally on August 18, 1994.

From the moment of his arrival in the United States, he has expressed himself publicly against the Cuban Revolution.

Sponsored by the FNCA, he traveled to Washington on January 6, 2000 to carry out the so-called Mission Elián, as part of the campaign against the return of Elián Gonzalez to Cuba. He presented a compilation of information on Cuban families that have been separated.

On January 9, 2000, in the office of Congresswoman Ileana Ros-Lethinen, he founded the counterrevolutionary organization New Generation Cuba, which grouped together young Cuban-Americans of the extreme right.

On March 2, 2000 he submitted a report to the Commission on Human Rights on alleged cases of divided families, in order to promote a campaign against Cuba within this international organization.

From March 16 to 18, during a LASA event held in Miami, he took part in acts of provocation and aggression against Cuban scholars. He repeated these some days later during a Cuban solidarity event held at Hunter College, New York.

He has taken part in aggressive actions and declarations directed at Cuban diplomatic personnel at the Cuban mission to the UN and in Washington.

Were there other gifts?

Yamila: The strategy was to organize the women around small businesses that allowed them to have an income in the name of FLAMUR. The raw material would come from Miami. There were different projects: sewing clothes, manicures, hairdressing. The important thing was to compete with the government.

In what way?

Yamila: If the government was selling a new dress for 20 pesos, we had to sell ours for 15 or 12 pesos. We made diapers, and we had to deliver them to single mothers, with low incomes, with two or three children. We would give these things away to them, for them to spread the word about how good FLAMUR was.

Noel: They also sent medicines, and asked for photographs.

Yamila: People would bring me the medicines and then tell me to spread them over the top of the bed and have my picture taken with them, for them to be able to verify that I had indeed gotten the delivery.

Who would bring the medicines?

Yamila: Émigrés who were sent by them. Speaking of which, not so long ago, around seven months ago approximately, we got a shipment of fabrics that had been "cannibalized" on the way over. Magda told me over the phone that they had sent 10 meters of each kind of fabric: a yellow one with blue dots, a leopard skin one, and a white one, for us to make dress shirts. We only got the white one, about three and a half meters of it. We got a meter and a half of the leopard skin fabric, and cut across the bias, so we couldn't even use it to make pot holders. There were two and a half meters of the yellow fabric, and half a big spool of brown thread.

What had happened?

Yamila: The intermediaries in Havana had stolen the rest.

How many women became members of FLAMUR?

Noel: In Güines, there was never a branch of FLAMUR in operation. There were supposed members there, but it never actually did anything, no sewing group, nothing.

And the pictures they asked for?

Yamila: I'd gather together my sister, my mom, all the women in my family, who didn't have the slightest idea what the whole charade was about.

Noel, what was your role in this?
Noel: In 1995, I began to collaborate with Yamila. I was the man who stamped the documents, who took down the minutes and drafted some reports. They chose me because I had a university degree — I'm an agrarian engineer. Afterwards, when my wife started to work for the Independent Press Agency, with López Prendes, they asked me to do some commentaries for the Miami media. I would write them, but I didn't directly participate on Radio Martí. I kept my distance from that. Until the year 2000, when Jamil and Miguel got me involved with Tania Díaz Castro's party. From that point on, I had a more active participation. They made me provincial delegate of the CENAIC — which had its headquarters in Santiago de las Vegas — and then the FLAMUR sprang up.

Who would you meet with in Santiago de las Vegas?
Noel: With Adoración Tulipa Amores. We would hold the CENAIC meetings at her place.

What did you do there?
Noel: Initially, we designed the structure of the group, the code of ethics, a whole apparatus to justify the organization. The delegations were named and the responsibilities were distributed, by province, in order to compile economic information on the situation of the country, in the agricultural sector in particular. We put together reports, also.

Who was commissioning the studies?
Noel: Diosmel and his team in Miami. They had a kind of nongovernmental organization, which created the "Independent" Cooperatives project.

What was their significance?
Noel: Noel himself told us that it was an initiative of the Orthodox Renovation Party (Partido de Renovación Ortodoxo). The project was created between July and August of 1997. It was divided from the start. There was one group, talking about "transition", which sprang up in the province of Santiago de Cuba, headed by Diosmel

— who left the country in 1997 and left Jorge Vejar in charge — and another group, calling itself Progress 1, in Guantánamo, headed by Reynaldo Hernández Pérez. This man was also the president of the National Association of "Independent" Farmers of Cuba (Associación Nacional de Agricultores Independientes de Cuba). The division of these two groups took place in 1997, a few months after the project had been founded.

New Generation Cuba (Nueva Generación Cuba)

NG Cuba appeared on January 6, 2000, during the legal battle over the custody of Elián González. The group made its first public appearance during an Elián-related protest held in front of the Tower of Liberty in downtown Miami.

The group is composed of people under the age of 40 and is designed to carry out anti-Cuban campaigns, related for the most part to migratory issues and aimed at countering some of the negative effects brought about by the extreme right of the Cuban-American community in Florida.

It is run by the traitor José Cohen Valdés and the counterrevolutionary Bettina Rodríguez, a human rights activist.

Its first project was the so-called Mission Elián, whose aim was to study the issue of current Cuban emigration to the United States and other countries of the world, and particularly the alleged irregularities in the migratory laws of Cuba and the restricted freedom of Cuban citizens to travel abroad. They present this as the responsibility of the Cuban government, as part of an international campaign of denunciations made before different forums that address the issue of human rights.

Their chief collaborators have been U.S. Congresswoman Ileana Ross Lehtinen and the Cuban-American National Foundation. The latter has been a source of funding.

NG Cuba has sent money to counterrevolutionaries, including, for example, Martha Beatriz Roque Cabello, the participants in the hunger strike held at 34 Tamarindo in the year 1999, and Vladimiro Roca Antúnez.

How did they sustain themselves?
Yamila: They tried to get publicity. Scandal was a means to get money.

Noel: As I remember it, they started doing things to get attention. For instance, the National Association of "Independent" Farmers wrote letters to the government, inviting a number of leaders to participate in the first meeting of "Independent Cooperatives", which would supposedly take place on May 5, 1998, in Loma del Gato, Santiago de Cuba. This was published in the Miami press, stirring up a lot of fuss around it.

And the U.S. Interests Section?
Yamila: They were extremely interested and paying close attention to everything we did. Every time we had an interview with an official of the Interests Section, we had to give them a report about what we were doing. They helped publicize these activities abroad and suggested contacting non-governmental organizations with representatives in Cuba, such as Agro-Action of Germany.

Noel: In August of 1998, Diosmel sent a document to the FAO representative in Cuba, Fernando Robayo Rodríguez, asking for financial aid for the "Independent Cooperatives" project in Santiago de Cuba, Guantánamo and Havana.

Yamila: Which, altogether, didn't have more than 10 members.

Noel: The interesting thing is that, before we went to see the FAO representative in Havana, Diosmel paid a visit to the offices of the organization in Washington. He said he was the director of the National Alliance of "Independent" Farmers of Cuba, and advised them that the members of this project would pay a visit to the branch of their organization in Cuba to ask for financial aid, and when this took place, a wave of repression would likely be unleashed.

Did Diosmel explain to you why he was doing this?
Yamila: He wanted to provoke the government, making requests he knew would never be approved. A simple strategy of provocation.

Noel: Diosmel came to Cuba in November of 2002, and he was arrested…

What did he say?
Noel: He answered all of the questions they put to him. He said he wanted to build up his "Independent Cooperatives", with very few members, almost all of them in urban areas of cities in the eastern region of the country. His intention was to present a bill to the National Assembly of People's Power, something along the lines of the "Varela" Project.

Yamila: And the Swiss? Remember them?

Noel: He said the Alliance was run from abroad by the International Association of Cooperatives, based in Switzerland, of which he was a consultant in Miami.

What does this organization do?
Noel: They wanted to develop the "Independent" Farmers Cooperatives project in Cuba, subordinated in Miami to engineer Bernardo Pestano. From 1999 onwards, they received a total of 184,000 dollars in the course of four years from the National Endowment for Democracy (NED), through monthly bank transactions.

Did this money ever reach you?
Yamila: Diosmel sent us some money, medicines and other things. His plan was to send between 150 to 200 dollars a month to the "independent" cooperative members. He himself told us that if he didn't hand over the money, the NED would not continue giving him money the following year.

Noel: This money had made it possible for him to travel to Geneva, to the sessions of the UN Commission on Human Rights. Of course, he presented his list of human rights violations on the island. He had asked for money from a number of organizations to do this, including USAID. Someone from this agency — David Mutchler — turned him down, saying that his project lacked political objectives. Almost like divine intervention, he received the "gift" from the NED shortly afterwards.

Unwavering for Freedom and Democracy in Cuba (Plantados hasta la Libertad y la Democracia en Cuba)

Set up in 1998; never joined the so-called Cuban Political Prisoners Bloc (Bloque del Presidio Político Cubano) or the recently established National Council of Cuban Political Prisoners (Consejo Nacional del Presidio Político Cubano). Its headquarters are at 149 SW 57th Ave., Miami FL 33144.

Its top leaders are Mario Chanes de Armas, Ernesto Díaz Rodríguez, Eusebio Peñalver Mazorra, Angel D'Fana and José Mederos. They regularly travel abroad to pursue their defamatory campaigns against Cuba, in which they allege violations of human rights, in interviews with the press and with political leaders. They support the activities of the counterrevolutionary groups, providing them with funding on a regular basis and promoting the establishment of internal clandestine cells for carrying out acts of sabotage against the economy.

Peñalver has kept up close links with Posada Carriles and has participated with the latter in plotting acts of violence against Cuba and its leaders.

What other organization was supporting him in Miami?
Yamila: It sounds like a joke, but Diosmel told us that he was considered by many in Miami — the hard-liners, mostly — as a "leftie".

Noel: In reality, this was a project of Frank Hernández Trujillo from the Dissidence Support Group, who has a good feel for the business of "dissidence". He knows that the more organizations he puts together, the more money he gets.

Who did you have to deal with here, in Cuba?
Yamila: Miguel Arcángel Camejo Planes, the "president" of the CENAIC in Havana.

How did this organization come to approach you?
Noel: Diosmel came into contact with someone in Miami who had studied agronomy with me in Cuba. That helped my façade a lot. His friend assured him that I was a born "dissident", as well as my wife.

Diosmel started little by little. He started by asking for trifles, then he started giving me written instructions, that were delivered by the directors of the CENAIC.

Do you still have the messages?

Noel: Yes, take a look, this one says: "Hello, my friend, I'm glad we can communicate this way, and go about perfecting it little by little. I'm working on the last report again. I want it to be on the website tomorrow. I may not be able to set up the graphics for the time being, but the report is very good. Speaking of other things, because of the work you've done, I think you should be the one taking center-stage […] A good friend of mine will be there in November, and he may have the time to pay you a visit. His name is Juan Alonso and I'll be giving him the information for him to write you this way. A hug, Diosmel."

We would check our e-mail, which was the principal means of communication, every time we went to the Interests Section.

When was the last time you set foot in the U.S. Interests Section?
Noel: Around six months ago, more or less.

Yamila: I was there on March 28, that was the last time I went to the Interests Section.

What sort of a relationship did you have with the U.S. Interests Section?
Yamila: It was very close, so much so that they gave us a survey about *Radio "Martí"* with the letterhead of the Cuban Commission, from Güines, to make it look like our own initiative. Maryann McKay asked us about everything, to the last detail.

What were they interested in knowing about Radio "Martí"?
Noel: Everything, if it had transmission problems, in what areas, which was the most popular program, suggestions...

Yamila: Opinions…

Noel: Do you see? That title up there, Cuba Commission, that's the group in Güines, the one headed by Miguel Galván Gutiérrez. Supposedly, it had just been established, and the U.S. Interests Section was so well informed about it that they had a survey form printed up with the letterhead of the group, to do surveys in support of *Radio "Martí"*.

Yamila: Everything was connected. The U.S. Interests Section knew everything we were up to, in detail, thanks to Diosmel and company. The official from the Interests Section would then show up and they would take it for granted that we were about to carry something out, because they themselves had commissioned it. That's the way it was, as shameless as that.

Noel: The Cuban-American National Foundation was involved in this, quite deeply. And they made no secret of it. I have an e-mail from Diosmel that reads: "Allow me to congratulate you first for the great work you've been doing despite all the obstacles. The people at the Foundation were very much impressed with the quality of the work you've sent and with the relevance of the information…" This is from 2003. There, they give me the good news that I have to found the Cuban Civic University, and they suggest that if I behave and do everything they order me to do, I can aspire to an important position in the Ministry of Agriculture. They were the ones who invented this ridiculous thing, the project to create the Mayor's Office of Güines.

What Mayor's Office was that?
Yamila: In the home of Miguel Galván, on January 28 of this year, the Mayor's Office of Güines was founded. A very elderly man, José Orta Acosta, was proposed for the position of Mayor. This man is 87 years old, I think, and they use him like a rag doll.

Noel: It all happened like that comedy show on television, "San Nicolás del Peladero". Do you remember the Mayor's Office of San Nicolás and that character, Cheo Malanga? The same thing was happening here.

Yamila: It seemed like a joke, they were going to pay the Mayor 10 dollars and five dollars to every councilor. The monthly budget for the office would be 40 or 50 dollars.

Who was behind this?
Yamila: Diosmel, who even admitted that things had gone too far this time. Everyone who found out about the "Mayor's Office of Güines" killed themselves laughing..

Why is that?
Noel: They were desperate. They didn't even have five people and they expected to have less in the future. Miguel and Orta had the support of a couple that were waiting for their visa to leave the country. I think there was one more person.

Yamila: They didn't want to get into too much trouble, only to create something to keep the counterrevolutionaries in Miami happy, and above all, to get money. They were forever thinking up schemes, "We're going to go on a march, we're going to draft a denunciation, we're going to organize a vigil, a hunger strike..." And they looked at the old man and changed their minds.

Was the Mayor's Office ever founded?
Noel: Yes, of course. Diosmel even sent a declaration on behalf of the Cuban-American National Foundation. They would grab onto anything. They said it was a brilliant idea. Eight Mayor's Offices were going to be created around the country, as well as publishing houses, newspapers...

Yamila: Even a strategic team, no doubt...

Noel: And just when they were most enthused about this, Galván wrote an e-mail to Diosmel, saying, "We have serious problems."

What did he say? That they were the victims of "repression"?
Noel: Not a chance. Didn't I tell you that this was "San Nicolás del Peladero"? They made Orta sign a piece of paper that said, "The elected Mayor informs your excellencies abroad" — Diosmel and his bosses — "that we are unable to maintain this Mayor's Office for the common good of the City of Güines, in desperate need of a good patriot. The circumstances impede it." Something along those ridiculous lines.

So what was the excuse?
Noel: That with 40 or 50 dollars they could pay the elected representatives, but — and you had the see the angelic face that Miguel Galván would put on — "What if a citizen comes along with a problem and asks us for money?" And there was Orta saying, "No one's going to touch my 10 dollars!" The Mayor's Office lasted an hour.

Yamila: They consoled the poor Mayor, "Don't worry, old man, when we form the national government, we'll find you a job..."

Luis Véliz Martínez and Ana Rosa Jorna Calixto.

Yamila Pérez Reyes and Noel Ascanio Montero.

DOSSIER DEL PROYECTO

DESPERTANDO

SONRISAS

Cover page for the dossier of the Awakening Smiles Project, of the Elena Mederos Foundation. It proposed taking sick children out of the country so that they could receive surgery in Spain. The objective: to attack the Cuban health system.

Dr. Pedro Luis Véliz, AKA Agent Ernesto, and Bill Barker, during one of his visits to Havana.

Some of the items brought by Bill Barker. This man went so far as to ask Drs. Pedro Luis Véliz and Ana Rosa Jorna to choose from a weapons catalogue the sort of guns they would want to use in the event of an upheaval in Cuba.

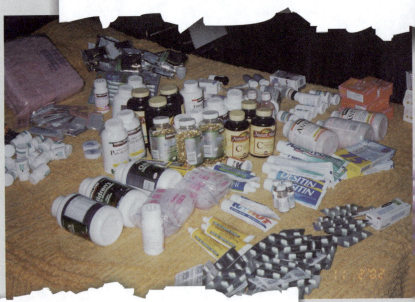

The medicine brought by Bill Barker to "save the people of Cuba".

Love Valley Presbyterian Church

239 Mitchell Trail
Love Valley, NC 28625

CARTA DE DONACIONES

~~Operation USA~~ está satisfecha por donar los productos enumerados abajo a la gente Cubano para el uso en los hospitales pediátricos para el cuidado de niños y los pobres a través de los recursos de la salud pública del país. Estos productos no tienen ningún comercial valor.

Consignatario

Dr. Noemi Gorrin Castellanos
Consejo De Iglesias De Cuba
Comision Medica

Lista de carga # 2

Bandages	18 packs	Antacid Tablets	1 bottle of 96
Latex Gloves	1 box (100)	Rolaids	3 bottles of 12
Liquid Soap	7 bottles	Acid Reducer	1 box of 10
Bufferin	26 bottles of 39	Stress Tablets	2 boxes of 30
Excedrin	11 bottles of 100	Vitamins	21 bottles of 2410
Ibuprofen	3 bottles of 100	Niocin	2 bottles of 100
Motrin	2 bottles of 50	Calcium	2 bottles of 100
Asprin	36 bottles - 3252	Folic Acid	3 bottles of 250
Acetaminophen	11 bottles - 1811	Dental Floss	18 boxes

Authorization

Bill Barker   _3/23/01_
Bill Barker, Director of Cuban Missions   Date
Love Valley Presbyterian Church

Received in Havana by: _____   _____
                                                                    Date

_____
Print

The text of the document reads as follows:
Love Valley Presbyterian Church is pleased to donate the products listed below to the Cuban people, to be used in pediatric hospitals in the attention given to children and the poor through the country's public health system. These products have no commercial value.

Bill Barker, P.A.

Attorney At Law
225-A Broad Street
Post Office Box 1339
New Bern, North Carolina 28563

BILL BARKER

February 12, 2001

Mr. Steve Pinter
Chief of Licensing
Office of Foreign Assets Control
U.S. Department of Treasury
1500 Penn Ave., NW
Washington, D.C. 20220

Dear Mr. Pinter:

I wish to travel to Cuba to deliver non-narcotic medicines and medical supplies to physicians to be dispersed by them to their patients. These items have been donated by the people of North Carolina primarily thru their churches. I am sponsored by my church, as you can see by the letter enclosed.

The doctors involved have been recommended to me by U.S. Congressman Lincoln Diaz-Balart. You may contact his assistant Ms. Anna Carbonell at 305-477-8359 to confirm this or for any added information you need. My Congressman, Walter Jones is also aware of this project and may have information that would help you.

For your information, I am a 56 year old attorney, born and raised in North Carolina. I have an honorable discharge from the U.S. Navy, served as Assistant District Attorney for 8 years and in the North Carolina Senate for 2 terms. Other than helping the children of Cuba, I have no agenda in this endeavor.

I would like to travel in late March and would like to make 3 to 4 trips per year. Each visit would last 3 to 5 days during which time I would be staying with doctors and therefore would not spend much money on hotels, etc. My purpose is not to help the Cuban economy, but only to relieve suffering by the children.

Please grant me the necessary permit or license for this humanitarian travel.

Sincerely,

Bill Barker

Bill Barker

Letter written by Bill Barker to the Office of Foreign Assets Control of the U.S. Treasury Department. He mentions that he will visit doctors recommended by Congressman Lincoln Díaz-Balart.

Fax sent to Bill Barker from the office of Lincoln Diaz-Balart,
telling him who to contact in Havana, and to state that he is there
on the behalf of Manuel Alzugaray, from the Miami Medical Team
Foundation, who has known ties to counterrevolutionaries in
Cuba.

MEMO

Via Fax: 1-252-638-1114

To: Bill Barker

From: Ana Carbonell

Re: List of Cuban Doctors

****

fax

Please contact Dr. Arturo Perez at either 011-537-3029-57 or 011-537-61-7551, he will
be expecting your call. He will guide you to the physicians in the rural areas of Cuba. Once you
contact him, mention that you are there on behalf of Dr. Manuel Alzugary. If you have any
questions please contact me at 305-710-3625.

OOS3 -7-30-29-57
OOS3 7-61-75-51 fax

HPER TEVL

MT PARCI   CALLE 25 804

WBIOTICA   APPARTEMANT I
IMANINS
INERALS)   ENTRC B Y C   FAR

                       PMUNICIPIO PLAZA

U.S. Cong. Lincoln Díaz-Balart 305-477-8359
Anna Carbonell

U.S. Cong. Walter Jones 202-225-3415
Thomas Bilbos

Glaxo - Vicki Buster 919-483-3259

Commerce - John Bolstiers 202-482-3283
Treasury Jackie Hillion · 202-622-2480, 1657 Fx

Operation USA - Cathy Schutzer 323-658-8876
Cuba Travel Service - Lisa 310-772-2822

Ministry of Health Dr Hose Portilla 537553368, 62
Nancy Acosta 553399 42,57

Council of Churches Dr. Noemi Gorin 241792 (O)
234942 (H)
Elina Caballos 328452

Father Fernando de la Vega 631889
Ms. Ondina Menocal 305-551-6641, 510-5984 (M)

Dr Arturo Perez 302957

The phone numbers of Bill Barker's principal contacts for his trip to Cuba. He was carrying this document with him.

EMBAJADA DE SUIZA
SECCION DE INTERESES
DE LOS ESTADOS UNIDOS DE AMERICA

P A S E *ABIERTO*

UNIDAD: I.V. UNIT

NOMBRE: *Oscar Elias Biscet*

CANTIDAD DE PERSONAS *1*

FECHA: ABIERTA

HORA: *8:30*

FIRMA: _____

EMBASSY OF SWITZERLAND
U.S. INTERESTS SECTION
OPEN PASS
UNIT: I.V. UNIT
NAME: Oscar Elias Biscet
NUMBER OF PERSONS: 1
DATE: OPEN
TIME: 8:30
SIGNATURE:

La Habana 7 de julio del 2001

Por la presente se le hace entrega a la Sra. Magalis de
Armas, esposa del destacado disidente Vladimiro Rocas, de
un paquete de medicamentos y veinte dólares (20.00) US
que desde Puerto Rico a través de la Operación Liborio, envía el destacado patriota Sr. Enrique Blancos.

Para Constancia.

Magalis de Armas.   _____
                                   Firma

La Habana 7 de julio del 2001.

Por la presente se le hace entrega al Sr.
Blas Giraldo Reyes Rodriguez, Vecino Ave.
26 de Julio #30, entre tercera del Este
y ferrocarril, Reparto Colón, Santi Spíritus
de una caja de medicamentos para que preferentemente se le de a los presos políticos y sus familiares. Además se le entrega
diez dólares para que sufrage gastos en
relación a esta gestión.
Blas Giraldo es el Delegado del grupo --
Ex Club cautivos de la provincia de Santi
Spíritus.
Este patriota se encargará en lo sucesivo de
recibir y distribuir los medicamentos que
envie el Proyecto Humanitario Liborio que
redica en Puerto Rico, y su maximo gestor
es el patriota cubano Enrique Blanco.

Recibe

Blas Giraldo Reyes

              Firma_____

Operation Liborio: money and medicines to create
a parallel system to the Cuban Public Health Care
System.

The text of the documents read as follow:

We hereby certify that a package containing medicines and the sum of USD 20.00 has been delivered to Mrs. Magalis de Armas, wife of the renowned dissident Vladimiro Roca, sent from Puerto Rico through Operation Liborio, by the renowned patriot Mr. Enrique Blancos.

Received by Magalis de Armas

We hereby certify that a box of medicines, as well as a total of USD 10.00 needed to cover related expenses, has been delivered to Mr. Blas Giraldo Reyes Rodríguez, residing at # 30 Vecino Ave. 25 de Julio, between 3ra del Este and Ferrocarril, Reparto Colón, Sancti Spiritus, so that he may deliver these medicines to political prisoners and their families.
Blas Giraldo is the delegate for the group Ex Club in Sancti Spiritus.
This patriot will be in charge of receiving and distributing all medicines to be sent by the Liborio

Humanitarian Project, based in Puerto Rico and directed by the Cuban patriot Enrique Blanco.

Received by Blas Giraldo Reyes

- 2 -

ayudar con estipendios a presos y los miembros de la Operación en Cuba; más o menos habían unos 100,000 dólares para enviar a Cuba; quizás esa haya sido la razón principal para negarnos su aprobación.

Ahora analizaremos lo relacionado con nuestro amigo Frank, cuando tú conversastes con él yo le llamé y me aprobó 1,500 dólares para enviar cada mes, eso duró 3 meses, parece por su carta que tiene dificultad con la familia del tío, esperemos tenga suerte y pueda resolver. Operación Liborio va a someter de nuevo los documentos solicitando la ayuda pero en este caso solicitaremos para el envío y compra de medicamentos; a un tío se los someteremos por $125,000 y al otro tío por $60,000, a c\ver si tenemos suerte y nos aprueban nuestra solicitud. Es necesario que hagas una buena carta con toda la información posible de lo que significa la Operación para que ustedes puedan subsistir en su tragedia; tienes que proporcionarles los nombres y direcciones de la mayor parte de las personas que se beneficiarían con los medicamentos. También resalta la situación de nuestro amigo Frank, que lo está solicitando en su carta. Esperamos tener éxito en esta situación ya que cada día se complica más.

Héctor, cuando llegó la administración anterior a Radio Martí, o sea, Herminio San Román y Roberto Rodríguez Tejera, surgió un conflicto interno y el resultado fué que Angélica Mora tuvo que irse a Washington obligada por las presiones que la llevaron a esa realidad. Es de todos conocido el beneficio que produjo para la oposición en Cuba Angélica Mora y siempre ha sido el deseo de la oposición que esta compatriota regrese a Radio Martí. No tuvimos éxito en esa gestión con la administración anterior pero ahora entró a dirigir las transmisiones a Cuba Salvador Lew y su número de teléfono es (305) 437-7010. Sería justo y razonable que la mayor cantidad de personas en Cuba hagan una petición solicitando el regreso de Angélica Mora a Radio Martí.

Recibe mis saludos,

ENRIQUE

Fragments of a fax sent to the mercenary Héctor Palacios by Enrique Blanco.

The text of the document reads as follows:

…to help prisoners and members of the Operation in Cuba with stipends; there was something close to 100,000 dollars to send to Cuba, which is probably the principal reason they denied us their approval.

Let's talk now about the matter concerning our friend Frank. When you spoke with him, I called him up and he approved the idea of sending 1,500 dollars every month; this went on for three months. By the looks of it, he has problems with his uncle's family, let's wish him luck and see if he gets out of that bind. Operation Liborio...(Ilegible)…for sending and buying medicine, we'll request USD 125,000 from one guy and USD 60,000 from the other, let's see if we're lucky and they approve our request. You have to write a convincing letter with as much information as possible about the Operation, for you to be able to endure these tough times. You have to send them a list of names and addresses of the majority of the people who will be getting the medicines. Also, emphasize the situation of our friend Frank, who's asking us to do it in his letter. We're hoping to have some success in this situation, because things are getting worse and worse every day.

Héctor, when the previous administration took over Radio Martí, that is, Herminio San Román and Roberto Rodríguez Tejera, there was an internal conflict of sorts and it ended up with Angelica Mora having to leave for Washington, forced to leave by these pressures. Everyone knows the benefits that Angelica Mora brought to the opposition in Cuba, and the opposition has always wanted her to return to Radio Martí. We had no luck with the former administration in trying to get her back but now Salvador Lew has taken over the broadcasts to Cuba and his phone number is (305) 4637 7010. It would be right and reasonable for as many people as possible in Cuba to sign a petition requesting the return of Angelica Mora to Radio Martí.

Regards,

Enrique

* Grupo de Apoyo a la Disidencia
  * Support Group to the Dissidence
    * Gruppo di Appoggio alla Dissidenza
      * Groupe de Soutien à la Dissidence

2 de septiembre, 2001

Sr. Enrique Blanco
Operacion Liborio
Puerto Rico

Estimado amigo:

Aqui te mando el cheque para el ultimo envio. Debido a las complicaciones que hemos tenido con el senador Christopher Dodd, te pido por favor que suspendas los envios hasta que te avise, ya que los fondos que esperabamos estan congelados hasta que el Sr. Dodd dedica levantar la suspension de estos. Creo que seria conveniente le avisaras a la gente de Cuba lo que esta pasando y que lleven cartas a la Seccion de Intereses dirigidas a:

Senador Christopher Dodd
448 Russell Building
Washington, D.C. 20510

Ya nosotros hemos movilizado a mucha gente a traves de la Isla, pero siempre hay algunos que no hemos podido contactar.
Creo que una carta de Operacion Liborio explicando la importancia de nuestras operaciones tambien no vendria mal.

Saludos

Frank

1000 Ponce de Leon Blvd., Suite 312, Coral Gables, FL 33134
Phone: (305) 447-2713 • Fax (305) 285-0311 • E-mail: gadcuba94@aol.com

Letter from Frank Hernández Trujillo to Enrique Blanco, who sends a copy to the counterrevolutionary Héctor Palacios.

The text of the letter reads as follows:

My dear friend:

I am sending you the check for the last shipment. Due to the problems that we've had with Senator Christopher Dodd, I'm asking you to kindly discontinue the shipments until further notice, since the funds we had put aside for this have been frozen until Mr. Dodd decides to reactivate them. I think it advisable to notify the people in Cuba about what is going on, and for them to take letters to the U.S. Interests Section, addressed to:

Senator Christopher Dodd
448 Russell Building
Washington, D.C. 20510

We've already mobilized a lot of people throughout the Island, but there are some we've been unable to contact.
I think a letter from Operation Liborio, explaining the importance of our activities, would also be a good idea.

Regards,

Educación, Capacitación e Información

The text on the t-shirt reads:

The cooperatives offer education and training to their members, elected representatives, administrators and employees so that they may effectively contribute to the development of those cooperatives. They inform the community, especially young people and leaders of public opinion, about the nature and the benefits of cooperation.

Las cooperativas proporcionan educación y capacitación a los asociados, representantes elegidos, administradores y empleados para que puedan contribuir de forma eficaz al desarrollo de las mismas. Informan a la comunidad, especialmente a los jóvenes y líderes de opinión, sobre la naturaleza y beneficios de la cooperación.

T-shirt sent for distribution among the "independent" cooperative members. In the agrarian model of the counterrevolution, the farmers wear suits and ties.

CUP - Cuba packs
Ant - Antillas

Período: 28/12/2000 - 20/09/2002

Código de Cliente: **FR68319U**
Nombre: **FRANK HERNANDEZ TRUJILLO**
Dirección: **1000 PONCE DE LEON BLV. #312**
CORAL GABLES FL 33134

Estado de su cuenta: 0.00

RESUMEN DE ENVIOS REALIZADOS

Página No.: 1

Fecha	Envio No.:	Destinatario:		Código:	Carné de Id.:	Dinero:	Pqte(Lbs):	Compra:	CR/DB:
2/02/2001	102770	SENIA BLANCA RIGA	*Cubapacks*	SE89518	Conf. Pendiente			2 LAMPARAS — *CUP*	
2/02/2001	102771	ARGELIO RICARDO	*Cubapacks*	AR89517	Conf. Pendiente			LAMPARA — *CUP*	
8/02/2001	22594	FERNANDO SANCHEZ	} *Antillas*	FE89361	42030322136			VIDEO — *Ant*	
8/02/2001	22595	GERARDO SANCHEZ		GE89362	47101308724			VIDEO — *Ant*	
3/03/2001	102898	HUMBERTO MELO ARIAS	*Cubapacks*	HU90246	Conf. Pendiente			2 LAMPARA — *CUP*	
3/03/2001	22925	PEDRO CRESPO	} *Antillas*	PE90249	64021001560			VIDEO — *Ant*	
3/03/2001	22926	HECTOR PALACIOS		HE90245	41062215507			VIDEO — *Ant*	
1/04/2001	103155	SANTIAGO ALONSO PEREZ	*Cubapacks*	SA63048	Conf. Pendiente			LAMPARA — *CUP*	
1/04/2001	23344	HECTOR PALACIOS	} *Antillas*	HE90245	65042325952			VIDEO — *Ant*	
1/04/2001	23345	ROBERTO DE MIRANDA		RO91610	46033027508			VIDEO — *Ant*	
7/04/2001	103217	ARMANDO VILLAR PENA		AR91875	48011502522			PAQUETE ESPECIAL — *CUP*	
7/04/2001	103218	ANGEL GIMENEZ	} *Cubapacks*	AN91872	44100207164			PAQUETE DE *Alim* — *CUP*	
7/04/2001	103219	GERARDO SANCHEZ		GE89362	47101308724			PAQUETE DE *Alim* — *CUP*	
8/04/2001	23464	ANGEL GIMENEZ		AN91872	44100207164			COCINA ELECTRICA — *Ant*	
8/04/2001	23465	ARMANDO VILLAR PENA	} *Antillas*	AR91875	48011502522			TELEFONO — *Ant*	
8/04/2001	23466	GERARDO SANCHEZ		GE89362	pas 0057247-1			TELEFONO — *Ant*	
0/04/2001	103221	ANA MARIA ESPINOSA ESCABILLO	— *Cubap*	AN91993	49072607295			PAQUETE DE — *CUP*	
0/04/2001	23499	MARTHA ROQUE		MA91997	45051602056			MODULO # 1 — *Good Ant*	
0/04/2001	23500	ANA MARIA ESPINOSA ESCABILLO	} *Ant*	AN91993	49072607295			JUEGO DE CAZUELAS — *Ant*	
0/04/2001	23501	ANA MARIA ESPINOSA ESCABILLO		AN91993	49072607295			JUEGO 21 POTES — *Ant*	
7/04/2001	103286	ROBERTO DE MIRANDA	} *Cubapacks*	RO91610	51041512772			PAQUETE DE — *CUP*	
2/05/2001	103352	GLADYS LINARES		GL92458	Conf. Pendiente			LAMPARA — *CUP*	
2/05/2001	103353	GLADYS LINARES	} *Antillas*	GL92458	Conf. Pendiente			TELEVISOR — *CUP*	
2/05/2001	23765	GLADYS LINARES	— *Antillas*	GL92458	42092301171			VIDEO — *Ant*	
0/05/2001	103688	LIBRADO LINARES	} *Cubapacks*	LI93901	60060914924			PAQUETE DE *Aliment.* — *CUP*	
0/05/2001	103689	GLADYS LINARES		GL92458	47092615778			PAQUETE DE *Aliment.* — *CUP*	
0/05/2001	24479	LIBRADO LINARES	— *Antillas*	LI93901	60060914924			TELEFONO — *Ant*	
1/05/2001	103694	FERNANDO SANCHEZ		FE89361	42030307554			PAQUETE DE *Aliment.* — *CUP*	
1/05/2001	103695	MANUEL INFANTE	} *Cubapacks*	MA93972	68041309455			LAMPARA — *CUP*	
1/05/2001	103696	MANUEL INFANTE		MA93972	3301091445			PAQUETE DE *Aliment.* *CUP*	
1/05/2001	24508	YANIT VALDES		YA93975	73083001119			2 TELEFONO — *Ant.*	
2/06/2001	24684	GISELA DELGADO SABLON	} *Antillas*	GI50188	65042325952			VIDEO — *Ant*	
2/06/2001	24685	ROBERTO DE MIRANDA		RO91610	46033027508			VIDEO — *Ant*	
3/06/2001	103797	ROBERTO DE MIRANDA	} *Cuba packs*	RO91610	51041512772			PAQUETE DE *Alim.* — *CUP*	
3/06/2001	103798	GISELA DELGADO SABLON		GI50188	65042325952			PAQUETE DE *Alim.* — *CUP*	
6/07/2001	8010700216	ANGEL GIMENEZ	} *Antillas*	AN91872	44100207164	300.00		Dinero — *Ant*	
7/07/2001	6010700271	MANUEL INFANTE		MA93972	43121808550	300.00		Dinero — *Ant*	
0/07/2001	25202	LIBRADO LINARES	— *Antillas*	LI93901	Conf. Pendiente			TELEFONO — *Ant.*	

A list of items sent from Miami, care of Frank Hernández Trujillo. Lamps, pots and pans, television sets…and all to "fight for the freedom of Cuba."

Federación Sindical de las Plantas Eléctricas, Gas y Agua de Cuba (exilio)

Instructions sent to Aleida Godínez by René
Laureano Díaz: he proposes the founding of CONIC

11 de febrero de 2001

Estimada Aleida:

La información que te solicitamos investigaras sobre los despidos a los trabajadores por
cuestiones políticas o vinculadas a ellas, debe recoger los siguientes aspectos:

Nombre y dos apellidos
Dirección
Centro Laboral donde trabajaba, sector y de ser posible la dirección del centro
Sindicato al cual pertenecía el trabajador
Edad
Breve explicación de las causas que motivaron el despido.
De ser posible obtener copia de la resolución de separación o sanción

Seria muy valioso para este trabajo que te apoyaras en otras organizaciones en aras de
lograr un inventario lo mas completo posible de los afectados.

Te reitero nuestro agradecimiento a ti y al resto de los ejecutivos de la Federación por la
excelente labor que vienen desarrollando en defensa de los derechos de los trabajadores
cubanos, en este proceso de lucha no violenta en el que nos enfrentamos al régimen.

Fraternalmente

René L Díaz

Aleida: El Proyecto de convertir la Federación
en CONFEDERACION es sumamente importante
para todos, ustedes y nosotros. Con este cambio
se producirá un reconocimiento de organismos Inter
nacionales del movimiento Laboral y su ayuda tanto,
material, económica y de otra índole no se hará
esperar. Saludos, René.

7175 S.W. 8 STREET, SUITE 213, MIAMI, FLORIDA 33144 • PHONE: (305) 262-9770   FAX: (305) 262-6050

Pudiera tazarse el siguiente nombre:

"CONIC"   CONFEDERACIÓN
OBRERA
NACIONAL.
INDEPENDIENTE DE
CUBA. Reunanse y Pienselo

The text of the document reads as follows:

Dear Aleida:

The information we asked you to gather on workers who have been laid off due to political issues or related matters must include the following things:

Complete name of the person.
Address
His/her place of work, the sector, and, if possible, the address of the workplace
The worker's union
Age
A brief explanation detailing the reason(s) behind being laid off
If possible, a copy the resolution to lay off or sanction the worker

It would be most valuable to your work to seek the collaboration of other organizations, in order to put together a more complete inventory of those affected by this.

Let me reiterate our gratitude to you and to the rest of the executive of the Federation for the excellent work you've been doing in defense of Cuban workers' rights, in this non-violent struggle that we wage against the regime.

Fraternally yours,

Rene L. Díaz.

Aleida: The proposal to transform the Federation into a Confederation is extremely important for everyone, both you and us. This change would lead to recognition by international labor movement organizations, and material, economic and other kinds of aid will certainly follow. Regards.
The following name might work:
CONIC: Confederación Obrera Nacional Independiente de Cuba (Independent National Workers Confederation of Cuba).

Miami FL.
Junio 11- 2001

Estimada Aleida: Saludos para ti y
los compañeros en esa.

Te estamos enviando los disquetes
con el contenido del reporte de violaciones
que circula en la OIT en la 89 asamblea
para que los hagas llegar a todos
los que estimes necesario; sería muy
conveniente que Pedro Pablo tuviera una
copia de este documento.

Averigua que pasa con la UNIÓN SINDICAL
de azucareros de Amancio en Tunas, hace tiempo
no sabemos de ellos.

Aquí te envío lo de este mes de Junio,
incluyendo a MARCOS. Pepsicola me prometió
que te vería ahora, él ya te conoce por
fotografía. -- Saludos ¡René! Joel te manda un
abrazo. --

Es necesario que
le entregues a Rosario
el sobre que le
manda ROSA. --

Aleida	$200.00	ALICIA	40.00
VICTOR	80.00	Piñato	40.00
ARROYO	50.00	MARCOS	20.00
Lozano	25.00		
Candod	50.00	TOTAL	570.00
Sergio C.	40.00		
Montecello	25.00		

The text of the document reads as follows:

Dear Aleida:

My greetings to you and our colleagues.

We're sending you two floppy disks with the report on human rights violations that was circulated at the ILO during the 89th Congress, for you to pass it on to everyone, as you deem necessary. It would be very convenient for us if Pedro Pablo got a copy of this document.

Please find out what is going on with the Sugar Workers Union of Amancio, in Las Tunas; we haven't heard from them for a long time.

I am sending you the money for this month, including the money for Marcos. Pepsicola promised me he would see you soon, he already knows you from a photograph.

Regards, René.ll

Aleida	$200.00
Victor	80.00
Arroyo	50.00
Lazaro	25.00
Caridad	25.00
Sergio G.	40.00
Montecillo	25.00
Alicia	40.00
Pimentel	40.00
Marcos	20.00
Total	570.00

COMISIÓN CUBA
C.N.C.

C.N.C.

Florida # 171 e/ Vives y Puerta Cerrada, H. Vieja, Ciudad Habana, Cuba.
Calle 52 # 9914 e/ 99 y 103 Guines, La Habana, Cuba.

Comisión Cuba

RADIO MARTÍ (ENCUESTA)

Municipio de residencia: _____ Provincia: _____

Edad: Menos de 18 años ___ De 19 a 35 años ___ De 36 a 55 años ___ De 56 o más ___ **Sexo:** F ___   M ___

Usted es: Estudiante: ___ Obrero ___ Profesional ___ Técnico Medio ___ Ama de casa ___ Jubilado ___

Escucha Radio Martí: Sí ___ No ___   ¿Qué horarios?: Mañana ___ Tarde ___ Noche ___ Madrugada

Por la interferencia ¿en cuáles horarios se escucha mejor?: Mañana ___ Tarde ___ Noche ___ Madrugada

Posee radio de onda corta: Sí ___ No ___ **Sus vecinos, familiares y amigos ¿escuchan RM?:** Sí ___ No ___ Algunos ___

En su opinión ¿cuáles son los cinco programas mejores? (lunes a viernes): 1. _____ 2. _____

3. _____ 4. _____ 5. _____

¿Cuáles son los programas que NO le gustan? (Lunes a viernes): 1. _____
2. _____

3. _____ 4. _____ 5. _____

En su opinión ¿cuáles son los cinco programas mejores? (Fin de semana): 1. _____ 2. _____

3. _____ 4. _____ 5. _____

Survey form given to Yamila Pérez (Agent Celia) at the U.S. Interests Section, to be filled out by the members of her groups and passed off as an initiative of the Cuban Commission, in Güines.

The survey goes as follows:

Municipality of residence:
Province:
Age:
Gender:
You are a: Student / Laborer / Professional / Junior college graduate / Homemaker / Pensioner

Do you listen to Radio Martí?: Yes / No   When?: Morning / Afternoon / Night / Early Morning

Due to interference, what are the best times for reception?: Morning / Afternoon / Night / Early Morning

Do you own a short-wave radio? Yes / No

Do your neighbors, relatives and friends listen to Radio Martí? Yes / No / Some

In your opinion, what are the five best programs? (from Monday to Friday):

What are the programs you do NOT like? (from Monday to Friday):

In your opinion, what are the five best programs? (Weekends:

VA CUBA INC

MIAMI
285 N.W. 27 AVENUE #18
MIAMI, FL 33125

Phone 305/649-3491   Toll Free 1-877-882-2822   Fax (305)649-4631

Medicina-Alimentos

Pg. 1

Inv.# 179294

Date: **MAR 25, 2003**

Cliente: RENE SOTOLONGO
3281 DAY AVE.

Destinatario: NOEL ALFONSO MONTERO
CALLE 74 # 9909 E/ 99 Y 103, GUINES

MIAMI   FL 33134
(305) 302-9058

HABANA CAMPO   CUBA

QTY.	DESCRIPTION	VALOR	TOTAL
2	CAJAS SAZON GOYA 180 gramos	3.00	6.00
4	GOYA CALDO POLLO 80 GRAMOS	1.19	4.76
1	PASTA DENTAL CON CEPILLO	2.00	2.00
1	IBUPROFEN 4 ONZAS	6.00	6.00
1	SALONPAS 120 SHEETS	5.00	5.00
1	ANTIDIARRHEAL 96 CAPLETS	8.00	8.00
1	ANTIDIARRHEAL DE 16 ONZAS	8.00	8.00
1	ALELRGY MEDICINE 400 MINITAB	8.00	8.00
1	HYDROCORTISONE 2 ONZAS	3.00	3.00
1	OMEGA III 150 TAB	10.00	10.00
1	MITRUM 250 TAB	12.00	12.00
2	BICOMPLEX 250 TAB	12.00	24.00
1	CALCIUM 250 TAB	12.00	12.00
1	GLUCOSAMINE 250 CAP	12.00	12.00
1	VIT C 250 TAB	10.00	10.00
1	VIT E 250 TAB	12.00	12.00
1	ASPIRINA 500 TAB	5.00	5.00

VALOR DECL.:	147.76
PESO (10 lbs 0 oz)	10.0
ENVIO:	80.00
DESC.:	0.00
ADJUST:	0.00
TOTAL:	$ 80.00
PAYMENTS:	80.00
BALANCE	0.00

Empleado: Haydee

A list of products (mostly food and medicines) sent from Miami to Counterrevolutionary organizations in Güines.

VA CUBA INC
MIAMI
285 N.W. 27 AVENUE ·18
MIAMI, FL 33125

Medicine -Food

Inv. # 179249
Client: Rene Sotolongo
3281 Day Ave.
Miami Fl 33134
(305) 302 - 9058

Date: Mar. 25, 2003
To: Noel Alfonso Montero
Calle 74 #9909 e/ 99 y 103
Habana Campo, Cuba

QTY	DESCRIPTION	COST	TOTAL
2	Boxes Goya Seasoning 180 gm	3.00	6.00
4	Goya Chicken Bouillon 80 gm	1.19	4.76
1	Toothpaste with toothbrush	2.00	2.00
1	Ibuprofen 4 oz.	6.00	6.00
1	Salonpas 120 shees	5.00	5.00
1	Diarrhea remedy 96 caplets	8.00	8.00
1	Diarrhea remedy 16 oz.	8.00	8.00
1	Allergy medicine 400 minitabs	8.00	8.00
1	Hydrocortisone 2 oz.	3.00	3.00
1	Omega III 150 tab	10.00	10.00
1	Mitrum 250 tab	12.00	12.00
2	Encomplex 250 tab	12.00	24.00
1	Calcium 250 tab	12.00	12.00
1	Glucosamine 250 cap.	12.00	12.00
1	Vit C 250 tab	10.00	10.00
1	Vit E 250 tab	12.00	12.00
1	Aspirin 500 tab	5.00	5.00

OFICINA NACIONAL

DE

RECEPCIÓN E INFORMACIÓN

DE

VIOLACIONES DE

DERECHOS HUMANOS DE CUBA

INFORME ANUAL

2002.

INDEPENDENT FROM WHAT?

The Dean is writing a book. He asks us to hasten the interview, for he has written a mere 50 pages and, at his age, has very little time to spare. In August he will turn 82 and hopes to tell, in his own words, everything he experienced within the world of Cuban "political dissidence", a world he got to know as well as the palm of his hand, and of which he can doubtless furnish us with astonishing anecdotes.

Néstor Baguer Sánchez Galarraga, perhaps the oldest active agent of Cuba's State Security, wants to avoid an introduction in an interview where time promises to fly. Here it goes, then, without much further ado.

AGENT OCTAVIO

Why did you choose the name of Octavio?
I chose it after Octavio Sánchez Galarraga, an uncle of mine who would have loved doing that sort of work.

What did your uncle do?
Octavio Sánchez Galarraga was a lawyer; he defended people of modest means. Another renowned Sánchez Galarraga was my uncle Gustavo, who was a poet and a journalist, one of the few that stood up against Machado's dictatorship. He gave a speech at the Vedado Tennis Club (now the José Antonio Echevarría Social Club), speaking against Machado, on a December 31, and the dictator called my aunt María, the mother of the Galarraga family. "Listen, see what you can do with that boy, because Crespo — the thug — is after him, and I can't always protect him."

There's something interesting. The Sánchez Galarraga family is of Basque origins. That's why we've preserved the beret, like the one I have on.

Luis Ortega and Max Lesnik, two Cuban-American journalists who live in Miami, were friends of your father and told us that the last time they saw him was in Mexico.
Yes, my father went into exile because his second wife — my mother had divorced him when I was two years old — had a hysterical fit and decided to leave Cuba. My father went after her. My brother emigrated along with him

Your father was also a journalist…
He wrote a column for *El Crisol*, which was a newspaper put out at noon. The press was on the corner of Manrique and Virtudes, in Centro Habana. He wrote reviews of shows. His name was Francois Baguer.

When did you start out as a journalist?
I wrote my first article when I was 14 years old. A number of students and I founded the magazine *Siboney*. Of course, I was in charge of the entertainment section.

During your interview with the prosecutor that was held before the trial and was aired on television, you said that you owed your anti-imperialist views to your family.
If there's someone who taught me to be that way it was my father. He used to quarrel with my uncle Gustavo Sánchez Galarraga, who

wrote for the society pages. During the days of the Spanish Republic, Gustavo would say that if they wanted to kick him around, that they do it with 50-dollar boots. My father would answer that he preferred being kicked around with sneakers, because they would hurt far less.

My father was the first Cuban journalist to be given a cultural award by the Soviet Union.

Before the triumph of the Revolution?
Yes. When the first Soviet movies were brought over, my father wrote excellent reviews. When everyone was saying that they were garbage, he was saying that they were works of art and that people should see them. The embassy gave him a cultural award.

What happened to your father?
Just think of it: the man, at his age, he had to work as a reporter in the Mexico City airport in order to survive. He would go to the airport at around three or four in the morning to meet with people. Nevertheless, he had been an extremely renowned professional in Cuba, a master journalist. I wrote him a letter, but my brother returned the sealed envelope to me, so I know that my father never found out what I wrote him. He died in 1986 and I got the news a year later.

He had no need to leave Cuba. He had two pensions, one as an officer in the Navy and another as a journalist. He lived alone with his wife. He had both of us to help him, and that would have been more than enough to lead a perfectly comfortable life, but that woman's ambitions were something terrible.

What were you doing at the time of the triumph of the Revolution?
I lived in the Mulgoba district, in Santiago de Las Vegas, which was a rich people's neighborhood at the time. They put me in charge of organizing the Committees for the Defense of the Revolution (CDRs). Then came the Bay of Pigs invasion, and when I reported to the Militias, the officer in charge told me that I was needed here, that I should stay behind and carry out political functions, founding more CDRs and helping wherever help was needed. They needed someone trustworthy at the José Martí Airport, so they put me to work there, to guard it as a militia member.

Afterwards, I was transferred to the Ministry of Foreign Trade, where they needed a journalist. The Ministry put out a daily bulletin that had a list of prices, financial analyses, economic plans.

You have a degree in journalism?

Yes. When I started out as a journalist, there were no schools of journalism here. I worked at *El Crisol* and I wrote. That was my school. Then the Marquez Sterling School was founded, and my father was a teacher there, but I had already gotten a taste of journalism and no one could tear me away from the presses. Writing was my thing.

When the Revolution came to power, I got a call from Elio Constantín, who was an extraordinary sports journalist and the secretary of the commission established to validate the degrees of journalists. He asked me if I wanted to go to school or take an exam. I told him to give me a full examination. No mercy. I took the exam the following day and they gave me the degree.

Nonetheless, in a Reuters dispatch that was published in The New York Times *this past April 10, they refer to you as an "alleged journalist." "Alleged journalist Néstor Baguer" were the exact words…*

How strange! When I was a "dissident", the American press never thought of calling me an "alleged" journalist or an "alleged" dissident…No one would have thought of it. I'm going to give you a copy of my degree, so you can publish it in the book and dispel all doubts.

When did you start working for Cuban State Security?

At the time when I started working for the Ministry of Foreign Trade.

How did it happen?

It was an institution that was much sought after by the enemy, as you can well imagine. I had done a number of articles on Cuban products. For example, a study aimed at managing the export of Cuban bee honey. I studied the markets, the cost. In Cuba, honey can be produced year-round; the finest honey in the world can be made here.

I was all caught up with my work on bee honey, when one fine day they started talking about the need to dredge Cienfuegos Bay and Havana Bay, and to buy the necessary equipment. It wasn't easy to get our hands on it, after the U.S. had declared the blockade against Cuba. But I had an English neighbor who facilitated the purchase.

Armando Pérez Roura

Born in Ceiba Mocha, Matanzas, and currently residing in Miami. He was a spokesman of the Presidential Palace during the Prío government, and kept this post during the Fulgencio Batista dictatorship. He was also a newscaster for *Radio Reloj Nacional*.

During that same period, he was Dean of the School of Newscasters until 1961.

In 1969, he sought asylum and took up permanent residence in the United States.

He was a member of the terrorist-linked counterrevolutionary organization Alpha 66, and a correspondent of CORU. He was also one of the main directors of radio station WRYZ, or *Radio Centro*, which was bought by the CIA to broadcast anti-Cuban programs.

He traveled to Venezuela on a number of occasions to interview the terrorists Orlando Bosch Ávila and Luis Posada Carriles, who were in prison for their participation in the blowing up of a Cubana Airlines plane over Barbados in 1976. He was involved in Posada's first prison escape plan of 1982.

He also had ties with dictator Anastasio Somoza.

In 1984, he joined the counterrevolutionary organization known as the Cuban Liberation Movement (Movimiento Libertador Cubano).

Currently, he is the director in chief of the station *Radio Mambi* in Miami, accused of using "laundered" money, due to his son's known involvement in drug trafficking. The latter was caught attempting to enter a shipment containing millions of dollars worth of cocaine into the state of Florida in the early 1980s.

He is the head of the terrorist organization known as Cuban Unity (Unidad Cubana), which has close ties to the Council for Cuba's Freedom (Consejo por la Libertad de Cuba), composed of terrorists from the paramilitary arm of the Cuban-American National Foundation (Fundación Nacional Cubano Americana, FNCA).

Who was he?

The manager, in Cuba, of the Lloyds Company, from London. He was a very English Englishman. Every afternoon, when I got home from work, he would say to me: "Baguer, your whiskey." It was an unfaltering ritual. It couldn't be at a quarter after five, nor at a quarter to five, but at five o'clock.

When he heard me say that a dredger was needed, and that both Holland and Japan had refused to sell us one due to pressures from the United States, he proposed that we buy it in England. "That sort of dredger is built in Scotland," he said, and he gave me a card and even paid for my trip. He asked me for a commission. And that's how it happened.

I took off for London with a fellow who worked for State Security. When we got there, we met a very friendly gentleman staying at the same hotel. He sat beside me. It was customary for regular visitors to be introduced to one another at the bar, and since I always sat in the same spot and he would always choose the same seat, they introduced us.

He was an American; without much preamble he started to ask me about my business there. His insistence caught my attention, and I started to ask around. I found out he had gone there precisely because of my visit.

That English company is the one that sets the prices for export?

It is one of the largest companies in the country. I managed to get them to accept a seven rather than a five-year payment period for the Cuban government. I left for Scotland, to the shipyard, but they informed me that they could sell absolutely nothing to Cuba, for they would be placed on a blacklist. We proposed opening a London-based company with my English neighbor as head, and me as secretary. They agreed to that.

The following evening I ran into the American. He introduced himself as a CIA agent, shook my hand and said, "You won, I lost. I respect you for that." That's how the famous dredger found its way to Cuba.

Of course, when I got here I reported the incident to State

Security, and ever since that time — the year was 1969 — I've been collaborating with them. I haven't stopped doing it since then.

You continued working for the Ministry of Foreign Trade?
No, I transferred over to the radio station *COCO*, as head journalist. Afterwards, I worked for *Radio Metropolitana*. When I began work in defense of the Spanish language, they called me up from the newspaper *Juventud Rebelde* to write a column, to which I gave that very title: "In Defense of our Language." After this I worked at the newspaper *Trabajadores* and at *Radio Habana Cuba* and the *Cadena Habana* radio network, and led a very active life in journalism, until I declared myself a "dissident".

Why did you declare yourself a "dissident"?
State Security asked me to establish contact with the mercenaries and I went to see Elizardo Sánchez Santacruz, who was the window into that world.

How were you received?
I got to his house and when I asked for him his wife asked, "Are you referring to the President?" "Well," I said, "if he's the President of Cuba, all the more reason to talk to him. Tell him that Néstor Baguer is here."

Their Minister of Information…
Who was just starting out, don't forget that… I went into the living room while they went to get the "President", and they brought me a glass of whiskey and a tray of seasoned olives. "Damn, they sure live well in the Palace!", I thought.

That was the year 1993…
The worst time of the Special Period, with terrible shortages everywhere. Elizardo came into the living room, he hugged me and told me: "Welcome! We really need you here, because my brother-in-law, Yndamiro Restano, doesn't know how to write, and I need a good journalist to take charge of the Independent Press in Cuba." I accepted on the spot.

Right there and then…
He was desperate. He suggested that I go on a scholarship to

Costa Rica first, to a certain institute of journalism there, I don't recall the name. "You can go there for two or three months, and we'll cover all of your expenses." I answered: "Look, Elizardo, after so many years of work for the Cuban press, I can't accept being sent to Costa Rica to learn journalism. Costa Rica is a piece of shit, I know the place. Send someone else there." That's what he did, and the man he sent there didn't come back.

He then told me that he would find someone to buy my articles first. He spoke of a magazine that was published in Puerto Rico, *Disidente*, where he had invested some money. He is a partner in that business. Afterwards, when we were closer, he asked me to go there everyday, whenever I wanted to, to read the latest news and get suggestions from him.

Did you do it?
No. I wasn't going to let them do with me what they did to the other poor bastards…

What did they do?
They used them for serving coffee more than writing.
I told Elizardo that I couldn't take a bus to his house everyday, that I would write the articles and that he should tell me who to send them to. That they could pay me afterwards and everyone would be happy. Do you know what he answered me? "We can't work it that way, because I need to have everything under control." "Well, Elizardo, then I think we can't go on working together."

Elizardo is a sharp guy.
Yes. He was a philosophy professor at the university. He has a speech which he hasn't changed in 20 odd years. He doesn't touch it. He's a real snake; he declares in public that he doesn't take money from the Americans, forgetting to mention: "unless they send it from Europe." The people who send him the most money are the Swedes, the French and the Spanish, and he's never been short of money. He has an ego that's out of control, he's someone who flies in and out of the country as he pleases. He's a very special case.

He had a public "falling out" with the Americans over issues of funding. You have to hear him and his buddies go on about that. It's circus, my friends, with puppets and all.

You lost touch with Elizardo, then…
Not completely, but I managed to tear loose from his grasp because I already had links in Miami. The other "journalists" would tell me: "Listen, don't be stupid, you'll get to eat anything you want there, and drink whiskey."

Where were those things coming from?
From the Spanish embassy, they send him a hundred dollars' worth of food every month, and I know this, because on one occasion, when I was there, the car from the embassy came with the month's quota. The bag came with a number of bottles of cognac and very fine Spanish wine. Month after month. He's never lacked for anything since he became a "dissident". He also receives money from other places.

For example…
From the Swedish Liberal Party, who were also over at my place. I don't recall the names at the moment, but I have all of their cards.

Speaking of which, I have a very interesting anecdote about the Liberal Party. One day, Osvaldo Alfonso, who is now in jail, came over to my place to ask me to join the Liberal Party. I asked him: "Tell me something, are you from the Cuban Liberal Party? With all its tradition?" "Yes, of course…" he told me. "Damn, the party of Machado and all his murderers?" "No, no, hold on," he answered. "We have to get something clear: Machado was a Party mistake." I broke out laughing: "Give me a break, man, I don't buy it. Look, if you're from the Liberal Party, then I'm from the Conservative Party. So take a hike…"

When did you establish the Cuban Association of Independent Journalists (APIC)?
With Elizardo. I got congratulations from Miami, tokens of love and affection. They thought I was the bravest of patriots. Reporters Without Borders praised me everywhere and sent me money. That was incredible. As soon as news got out that I was in charge of the Agency and was handing out money, the "journalists" started

descending on my house like ants. Do you know I had no idea that Cuba had so many "journalists" hidden in the most unlikely jobs and professions? I had a correspondent who was a railway worker in Cienfuegos, who had spent his life hammering away at the railway lines. He's in jail now.

But they know how to write, no doubt, because there are so many newspapers and websites that publish their articles?
If they made "spelling" errors while talking, can you imagine how well they wrote? It was very painful for me to have to fix up some of that rubbish.

Why did they approach an agency that was allegedly made up of serious journalists?
There were two main things that attracted them.

Firstly, the visa they would automatically obtain. It sufficed to have been writing in the agency for a month to be put on the first plane to the United States. They were spared the line-ups, the unpleasant moments and the humiliation one endures in the U.S. Interests Section.

Secondly, the pay. Something from 20 to 40 dollars a month, just for twiddling their thumbs. There was a time when so many people showed up that I could hardly manage it. During that time, Raúl Rivero decided to leave the APIC and found his own agency.

How was your relationship with Rivero?
It was very good. I felt for Raúl Rivero. He was the one true journalist that I knew in that world, a man who had had prestige at one point or other, because of his poetry, because he had fought at the Bay of Pigs. A man who owed his life to the Revolution.

In what sense?
I was the closest friend that he had and we knew each other well. He was an alcoholic and suffered greatly. Everyone turned their backs on him, he had no money, his house fell down. He became seriously ill, and he was placed in a hospital under the Revolution. He got to be so well that he quit drinking.

And what happened to him?
He was bought. Raúl Rivero has thousands of dollars deposited in the United States thanks to the awards that he's received. All of the leaders of subversive groups also have money outside of Cuba, because they obviously wanted to keep it safe, at a distance from the greed of others and from the interventions of the government, for reasons I needn't explain. Even a child can realize that the life of a "dissident" in Cuba is great business.

How would you receive the money?
Through Transcard; I refused to receive anything from those messenger-people that are continuously coming over from Miami or other places. That's why I was the one who received the least money and gifts.

Why?
My dissident articles were different from others. My articles were respectful. For example, I would refer to the Commander in Chief by saying, "the President of Cuba, Fidel Castro," while others would refer to him as "the dictator" or this and that.

Even the Americans were surprised. "Mr. Baguer, you don't hate Fidel Castro," they would tell me, and I would answer them, "I have no reason to hate him."

Who among the Americans told you that?
The one who was in charge of the press and cultural affairs at the time, the fat guy, Gene Bigler. He became a very good friend of mine. When he left, Bigler wrote me from Rome, telling me that should I need anything I should write him immediately.

What did you answer Bigler, when he made these kinds of comments on your articles?
That I was a member of the Royal Academy of the Spanish Language, and I couldn't bring myself to write insults. I wasn't prepared to have them expel me from there.

An "independent" journalist pointed out that I never used the word *gendarme* to refer to policemen. What a blockhead! "Look, buddy, they have *gendarmes* in France; here we have policemen," and I would write it like that.

What sorts of news would the correspondents send to the APIC?
If I hadn't taken it to heart so much, I think I would have had a lot more fun. I remember a day, for instance, when one of them called me on the phone to dictate an alleged news story, it was very urgent. The man wrote something along these lines: "In Manzanillo, there

are 10,000 people on a street corner protesting because a family is being evicted from their home." I remember yelling at him, "Look, hold on a second. What street corner in Manzanillo, or anywhere else for that matter, can fit a group of 10,000 people? And also, why are they doing it?" And he answers: "See, this family wanted to live in Manzanillo and this other one in Bayamo, and they started moving furniture from one place to the other, without papers or anything." "Please, my good man, tell me of a place in the world where you can exchange homes without legal papers. Look, I'm sorry, but bring me another story." It was like that every single day.

Can you think of another example?
A person showed up telling me that his father had told him that a cousin of his had been beaten up in jail. I asked him if his father had seen this, and he told me no, he had heard it from someone. I told him, "The first thing a journalist has to do is verify the source," and I sent him on his way.

You never caught anyone's attention with those opinions of yours?
They saw no connection between the government and myself, and I did made criticisms, but very elegantly and correctly. That's why journalists kept leaving for other agencies, which spread like fungi, where they made different kinds of attacks and were, because of this, better paid.

Around that time, we got the news that the U.S. government was going to hand out much greater sums of money through the National Endowment for Democracy (NED). I continued to work earning a modest 50 dollars a month, as head of the APIC, but part of that money started coming in and people became interested in it, especially those in Miami. I can tell you that 80 percent of those millions of dollars stayed in Florida.

You know this?
Of course I do. The stream of money would shrink from Miami to

Havana, and from here to the provinces also. Our representatives would keep the biggest piece of the pie, then came the heads of subversive groups, then the others.

In order to get a hold of the hundred and so dollars that *Cubanet* owed me, I had to go to the U.S. Interests Section to denounce the head of the agency, who had pocketed the journalists' money.

Did it work?

Did it work? The Public Diplomacy officer at the Interests Section called them on the phone and gave them a deadline to pay up the debt. They tried making excuses on the other end, saying they had no money at the time… The man from the Interests Section gave them an order: "You have to pay Baguer immediately and cancel the debt. I'm going to call him at the end of the month to see that he's gotten the money." That did it.

Cubanet

From the time of its creation in 1996, *Cubanet* has been a website devoted to publishing the "journalistic works" created by counterrevolutionaries, addressing the purported violation of human rights in Cuba. From the start, it has received federal funding from the U.S. government through the National Endowment for Democracy (NED). In 1999, it received 99,000 dollars for that fiscal year.

In the year 2000, it began to experience financial difficulties, and at the end that year, 15 "journalists" were expelled from the website, resulting in conflicts between the agency's organizers and the counterrevolutionaries, combined with a number of scandals over the lack of "professionalism" of the articles published.

In August of 2002, *Cubanet* was struck by a financial crisis and could not keep up its former publishing capacity, having to suspend the payment of the "salaries" of 25 "independent journalists" in the City of Havana who had already published their articles.

This situation led to quarrels among its collaborators, who registered their complaints with the U.S. Interests Section.

How did you become involved with Cubanet*?*
It's a culinary story. Rosa Berre, who invented *Cubanet*, would record the articles that I dictated to her. She had the phone in the
kitchen of her tiny apartment. She would receive the stories while
she cooked and would pass them on later. She led a very modest
life, and at first received a very small commission. One day she
tells me she is moving to the heart of Miami, because she had
bought two apartments there. One was to be her place of residence
and the other would house the *Cubanet* offices. She was also able
to buy a car that cost thousands of dollars, all of this with her modest
"savings", poor girl, she was very thrifty, you know.

Did her work conditions change after this?
Yes, because by the looks of it she received more money as more
and more people joined the cause of "independence." It was so
easy to earn a few dollars that you would hear of a new press
agency and people quarreling over money almost every day. The
people that stole the most money were the ones from the *New
Cuban Press* (Nueva Prensa Cubana), *Free Press* (Prensa Libre), and Rosa Berre. All of them were Cuban and they were stealing
money from the journalists.

I remember a young man who had worked at a printing press
and pretended to be a journalist. He got to be head of an agency,
then grabbed six month's pay and disappeared. There was a
change in the payments around that time, also. From the 50 dollars that they were paying, it went down to 15 or 20, even when
more or less the same sums of money were coming in for the
"bosses" to distribute. They would get 50 dollars to give out and
would hand over only 20. It was shameless theft. And everyone
knew about the quarrels that went on because of this.

Anyone could open a press agency?
More than 30 of them were opened. The more capable you were
with your insults, the higher you were on the scale of values in Miami
and the Interests Section. The more groups of alleged journalists,
the better. The more they yelled, the better.

You would review the articles and then send them to Cubanet*?*
That's why I gradually lost all of my clients. Anyone with a minimum of education and professional experience who was forced to spend a half hour with those people would end up sick, my man.

What was the reaction of the Interests Section?
If no one like myself went over there and put up a fight, they would turn a blind eye. They were more concerned with other things.

With what, for instance?
With the conspiracy to promote the "persecuted independent journalists" before international public opinion, and with supplying them with awards and the best of possible conditions to work in. And with ensuring that they weren't short of visitors and diplomats they could cry to.

Tell us about some of those visits…
The year 1995 was very intense, for instance. I have more than 60 activities I participated in jotted down in my notebook, all of them promoted by the U.S. Interests Section, which acted as a public relations center, to facilitate encounters with American visitors of every ilk, and with the representatives of the international media and journalists' organizations.

For example…
January 15: A meeting in the house of the head of the U.S. Interests Section, Joseph Sullivan. An interview with American editors.
July 20: A meeting with the American delegation that attended the immigration talks. I won't tell you what we discussed, because it's obvious.

August 12: A meeting in diplomat Gene Bigler's house, where a group of officials from the U.S. Interests Section are given details on the creation of the College of "Independent Journalists", which had been founded in my home some days earlier.

August 30: a meeting with the State Department Committee on Immigration Issues. It was announced that 20,000 visas would be handed out in 1996, distributed in the following manner: 12,000 would be given to regular citizens who requested a visa; 7,000 to political refugees; and 1,000 to be handled by the U.S. Interests Section.

September 20: Presentation of a donation from Reporters Without Borders, an organization based in France. Robert Ménard, the secretary-general, and Andrés Buchet presented me with paper, typewriter ribbons, a dozen pens and 1000 dollars to fund my so-called press agency.

September 20: I was summoned by the official Robin Diane Meyer to be reproached, along with Yndamiro Restano, Olance Nogueras, Julio Martínez and others. She was very upset over a document that had been sent to the U.S. Congress without prior consultation with her, which had the signatures of 127 Cuban citizens.

September 27: Cuban-American journalist Roberto Fabricio, who was then the executive secretary of the Freedom of Press Committee of the Inter-American Society of Journalism (SIP), met with a group of people that included myself. This man had been director of *El Nuevo Herald*. We met in the home of Yndamiro Restano's parents, and he asked us to draft a fierce denunciation he could formally present to the SIP.

November 7: Robert Witajewski and Robin D. Meyer call us to meet in the home of the former to explain why some of us hadn't signed the Cuban Council project, to which we answered, with the best face we could muster, that we were "independent journalists" and we couldn't get mixed up in politics. She thought this was reasonable.

I won't go on with this because this interview will become very boring. I had to visit the U.S. Interests Section so many times that you wouldn't be able to fit all of the meetings in one book. I have to confess one thing: every time I set foot in there, I would ask myself: "What sort of independent journalists are we? Independent from what?"

Ernesto F. Betancourt

He traveled to the United States in 1948 and studied advertising and marketing at the American University of Washington (1953-56). From 1957 to 1958, he was a representative of the 26th of July Movement in Washington, and registered himself with the State Department as a "foreign agent".

During the first months of the Revolution, he returned to Cuba. He was named Director of Foreign Exchange Control for the National Bank. He decided to return to the United States in 1960.

He worked in the Organization of American States (OAS) for a period of 16 years, where he was given the position of budget administrator. There he met the counterrevolutionary Frank Calzón, with whom he maintains close ties to the present day.

From the time of the creation of the Cuban-American National Foundation (Fundación Nacional Cubanoamericana, FNCA), Betancourt served as an adviser for the organization. In July of 1983, he participated in the Cuba Project conference sponsored by the Center for Strategic and International Studies (CSIS) of the University of Georgetown, in the United States.

In June of 1985, he was named provisional director of *Radio "Martí"*, and was replaced early in the year 2000.

He has devoted himself to drafting memorandums and other defamatory documents aimed against the Revolution and its leaders, and has promoted different campaigns to exacerbate existing tensions between Cuba and the United States, on such sensitive issues as bioterrorism and the alleged threat that Cuba represents for that country.

On a number of occasions he has been quoted as an intelligence analyst.

Talk to us about the last time you set foot in the U.S. Interests Section or its official premises…
The Day of the Cuban Press, on May 14. A workshop was held at James Cason's home, with all of the "independent journalists". They paid homage to my career in the "independent press" and gave me a diploma. They had the bad idea of asking me to direct the

discussion on the issue of Ethics. There were representatives of the U.S. government there. I told them that a single conference would not suffice to cover the issue, and that we needed a whole course on ethics, because the vast majority of those gathered there claimed to be journalists and hadn't the slightest bit of education.

Their texts were not even up to a sixth-grade standard. I apologize to all children in the sixth grade.

You also set up a section in Cubanet *devoted to language issues, no?*
I would go out and harvest examples. There were so many atrocities that I had more than enough for my section. They would be presented as though they had been taken from the Cuban press, but in truth they were written by the "independent journalists."

For example, do you know that once I saw a headline that claimed that an earthquake in Turkey had caused enormous destruction in the island of Samoa? The writer had no concept of geography. The island that was destroyed was the Greek island of Samos, the land of Pythagoras. My God, what ignorance!

It's difficult to imagine a member of the Royal Academy stuck with such duties...
Sometimes I would tell my official that nothing could pay for the suffering I had endured listening to those idiots talking and reading their stories and all of the things they did. Listen, not even a fourth-grader could write that badly.

The renowned "independent journalist" Tania Quintero has no idea what it is to write, but if you look her up in American newspapers, she is identified as one of the great, founding members of the "independent press" in Cuba.

There was a person there who was illiterate even in speaking. He was a *santero* (a practitioner of the Afro-Cuban religion *santería*), he lived in San Miguel del Padrón (a neighborhood in Havana) and you should have seen the things he wrote. The saints were definitely not with him. You couldn't even make out what he was saying.

Would the U.S. Interests Section tell you what to write?
They didn't dare do that, because they knew me well.

You would propose the topics, or were they the ones who chose them?

Not me. The U.S. Interests Section chose the topics for the mentally retarded, pseudo-journalists… And not only that, but also, after they were done writing them, before putting them out, they would go to the Interests Section so they could go over them in case there was something in there that was politically inconvenient for them. They would submit them after they had been approved. They complained about censorship in Cuba and I watched them bow down to the censorship of the United States.

Open Eyes (Ojos Abiertos)

On January 16, 2003, the launching of the book *Ojos Abiertos* was held in the home of Héctor Palacios Ruiz, a member of the Center for Social Studies. The event was attended by a group of counterrevolutionaries and several members of the diplomatic corps accredited in Havana. James Cason, head of the U.S. Interests Section, was the highest ranking diplomat in attendance.

Printed in Mexico in November of 2002 and presented at the Book Fairs in Guadalajara, Mexico and Madrid, Spain, the book is the fruit of a contest sponsored by counterrevolutionary organizations in Miami. It is 248 pages long and gathers the writings of 20 counterrevolutionaries and the works of various Cuban artists residing abroad.

This contest was preceded by another held in the year 2000, marked by scandalous manipulation of the selection and award process, which was overseen by Raúl Rivero, as president of the jury, Elizardo Sánchez Santacruz, and Héctor Palacios from the Center for Social Studies. The latter received the top prize.

Between this and the moronic things they were saying, it was all becoming unbearable. The Americans put some effort into raising the standard of the "independent" journalists, who were the butt of jokes and a cause for quarrels within the ranks of the "dissidents". They proposed to both Raúl Rivero and myself that we establish a school within the U.S. Interests Section. Neither of us accepted. Later on, Ricardo González Alfonso asked me for the same thing: to give the journalists lessons.

When was this?
This happened not so long ago. Ricardo was already the head of Manuel Márquez Sterling Journalists Society.

A school open to everyone?

No. Only for his people. It was going to be over in Miramar (a neighborhood of Havana), where he lives. I accepted and asked him how much he was going to pay me for giving the lessons. He asked whether I expected to earn more than Raúl Rivero and himself. I told him, "Why not? Rivero is a journalist, but you don't even know how to write your own name." He promised to tell me how much he would pay me, but then the Comandante showed up and the party was over *(Translator's note: This is a line from a Cuban song).*

What was Raúl Rivero's opinion of those people?
He thought they were all idiots. He was in complete agreement with me. When the U.S. Interests Section wanted us to give lessons, he said, "No, no, how can we get involved in that? They're all idiots, ignorant people. They don't know anything about grammar or composition, they don't know anything, period. We're going to bust our heads with those imbeciles, for nothing. Let's turn them down." That's what we did.

Did you ever interview a U.S. high official on the request of the U.S. Interests Section?
The last was my friend James Carter. I call him "friend" because, when he was president, he invited me to the United States to give Spanish classes at the university where he had studied. When he came to Havana, he sent for me to have lunch with him.

In private?
No, there were other people there. He had me sit close to him, with a single person between us, to talk with me. He asked me about the "Varela" Project, and I spoke to him in all honesty.

What did you tell him?
That it's a failure. That Oswaldo Payá is nothing more that a frustrated altar boy. No one in Cuba pays attention to him. Payá would constantly show up at my place: "Hey, Baguer, do an

interview with me." He would show up a month later with the same story, and I would send him on his way.

Roberto Rodríguez Tejera

In 1985, he worked as a commentator on Miami TV's *Channel 51* and later as editorial and news director.

In 1988, he worked as a journalist for the *Cadena Azul* network.

In 1990, he acted as director of *Television "Martí"* in Miami.

He has ties with the counterrevolutionaries Hubert Matos Benítez and Ramón Saúl Sánchez Rizo.

He is closely linked to the Miami extreme right wing. He is one of the sources of funding for the "independent journalists", notably Raúl Rivero Castañeda.

I knew him from the Cerro neighborhood, where we both lived. I used to see him walking around in ripped pants, and now he goes around like a president, in a minivan. He claims the Church gave it to him, but we all know he bought it himself. One day I told him straight what most of the "dissidents" were saying: that he paid for the signatures (on the "Varela" Project).

And what did he answer?
That it wasn't true, that it was something made up by the communists. It was the counterrevolutionaries themselves who had told me this, that this is what he had done in eastern Cuba. Furthermore, I know of "dissidents" whose signatures have appeared on the project when they have not actually signed it, because they can't stand Payá. That's the case with María Valdés Rosado.

Those people just go on cheating one another and fighting among themselves to become the leader who finally gets a hold of the cake, to start handing out scholarships, money, positions, exactly what takes place everyday in almost every country of the world.

With Payá, that's two "future presidents" of Cuba that you know. Were they the only ones who presented themselves as such?
No way! You have to include that other gangster, Ricardo Bofill, on the list of candidates for president of the New Republic of Dependent Cuba. There are many aspiring candidates, really, many press agen-

cies and many political parties. The only thing missing is people to follow them. Just like that new press agency I ran across in Santiago, made up of a mother and son, neither of them journalists.

What can I say about the political parties? I know of four members that make up the Christian Democratic Party, for instance. Oh, and I was forgetting about another "president": Vladimiro Roca.

Why do you say that?
Because he had delusions of grandeur. Vladimiro's wife — his former wife, not his present wife — was a friend of mine. I would pay her visits and she invited me to lunch on more than one occasion. If I visited that house, it was because of her, she was a good person.

I'm going to say something blasphemous: may Blas Roca forgive me, but how annoying and idiotic his son is! He's unbearable. One day, I told him something I just couldn't keep inside: "If your father could hear you, he would rise up from the grave and spit on you." Blas was a man who was loyal to the Revolution and a good person all in all.

Do you know what his son told me about him? That his father had been an idiot, because when the Revolution triumphed he had handed his party over to Fidel, who gave him a worthless little position in turn. Just think! I had known the old man. Just look at the mind of this little scoundrel!

When you met up with the other agents, now their true selves, who surprised you the most?
Tania was my biggest surprise.

Why?
I would have never thought it. She was my friend, but she was one of the oldest and fiercest "dissidents". A real tigress.

Who else?
Orrio, or Agent Miguel. We would have quarrels of Olympic proportions, and when we saw each other then, at the moment of truth, we hugged each other and I couldn't help telling him: "Look at you here, and you were such a bastard! And we're even having a drink together, damn it!"

I TOOK MY ORDERS FROM THE U.S. INTERESTS SECTION ALONE

ODILIA COLLAZO VALDÉS

Minutes before the trial, Odilia absently took out a CD of songs by Fito Páez. She was tense. In a few minutes, she would be giving evidence in front of several of alleged "dissidents", after having been one of them until just a few hours earlier.

Not that she was afraid; she was just unsure whether she'd be able to throw off completely the guise and vernacular of the hard-line counter-revolutionary, which the real Odilia Collazo Valdés, Lily — otherwise known as Agent Tania of the State Security Service — had been hiding behind.

She opened the CD case and, to while away the minutes before they called for her, she started to read the insert. There was one song, set to music by Fito, with words by an anonymous poet. She read: "I offer you my yesterday / my before / my after / my always / my perhaps / and my already." "It can't be," she said to herself, and from that moment her doubts evaporated.

Those lines didn't come to her by chance. Her last words at the trial, after one of the most devastating depositions ever heard in the Supreme Court, were those very words: "I offer you my yesterday / my before / my after...." *Her voice was strong and clear.* "Here," *she said, looking at the accused,* "is what Odilia Collazo thinks. And I want to dedicate this poem to Fidel."

AGENT TANIA

What sort of schooling did you have?
I learned crafts from a very early age. When my children were eight and nine, I started working at an army base, in the artillery. The officers there told me I should study, that it was a shame that I didn't. Then there was a recruitment drive by the local authority, and I went along.

Really, I would have liked to be a doctor or a nurse. Or a journalist. In the end, the Revolution rewarded me.

In what way?
In 1988, State Security in the San Miguel de Padrón district approached me and said they needed me to get in with some people in the human rights groups operating in the area. San Miguel is a district that's had its problems. Ricardo Bofill was living in the neighbouring Mañana district. After a spell in jail, he worked in the canning factory and started recruiting people there.

What did you say to them when they asked you to do this?
That I couldn't. But they talked me into it. That year, I was managing a grocery store very near where they were holding their meetings.

Who did you make contact with?
I was living next door to the mother-in-law of Roberto Bahamonde Masó, the counterrevolutionary who's now in the United States. I'd known the family from when I was a girl.

Was that the birth of Tania?
No, that was the birth of Betty. Betty was my first codename. Tania

came later, in honor of Tamara Bunke, Che's comrade-in-arms in the guerrilla war in Bolivia.

On May 20, 1988 I joined the Cuban Pro Human Rights Party (Partido Pro Derechos Humanos de Cuba). In 1993, I was elected its president.

How did this promotion come about?
It all started because of a telephone. I was the only activist in the Party who had a phone. So in 1991, I became the spokesperson on the National Executive. Where I lived had other advantages: it's in the basement and its got a patio at the front... All these things made the work easier.

Juan Betancourt Morejón, who at that time was party secretary, started visiting me with Carlos Orozco and Nelson Torres Pulido. My home became the scene of anti-government plotting, and there were a lot of fric-

Roberto Martínez

tions, because I'd taught my children from an early age to love the Revolution, and they didn't understand this sudden change. My family slammed the door on the counterrevolutionaries, set the dogs on them, did all kinds of unpleasant things to them.

How did you resolve the dilemma?
Sometimes I had to go out on urgent assignments for headquarters; at home they thought I was in love with a State Security agent, who they had seen me talking to occasionally.

He was much younger than me and they asked me if I realized I was cradle-snatching. I was single at that time and this situation was a real problem. They disconnected the phone cable so the phone wouldn't work. Things improved later, after I met my present husband, Roberto Martínez Hinojosa.

How come?
He's more my age and his support and affection have been fundamental. He's also a State Security agent.

What operations were you involved in?
In 1991, I helped get Bahamonde out of the country. That was one of the most difficult jobs, because the man's paranoid and imagined all kinds of things. When he finally got on the plane on September 28 that year, I could hardly believe it. I've since found out that he's in Miami and is suffering from Alzheimer's disease.

Was there anyone representing the Pro Human Rights Party in Miami?
Yes: Samuel Martínez Lara and Evelio Ancheta, who were both members of the Cuban Democratic Consensus (Concertación Democrática Cubana) which included several groups: the Independent Medical Association (Colegio Médico Independiente), November 30 Party (Partido 30 de Noviembre), Harmony Group (Grupo Armonía), Cuban Democratic Directorate (Directorio Democrático Cubano) and others. They sent me my instructions, until one fine day I started getting them directly from the U.S. Interests Section.

Through whom?
Victor Vockerodt and Timothy Brown.

What did they want you to do?
They told me they needed surveys. We did one of people's attitudes to the embargo, whether they were for it, against it, or abstained from answering. We set up a team: Horacio Casanova, other people and me. We sat around a table with a map of Havana and started the survey in San Miguel del Padrón, then in the Cotorro district, in Havana Vieja and Centro Habana... without leaving my place. We invented all the information, from one end of the city to the other. Casanova told me to avoid even numbers, that odd numbers were more convincing. So we decided that 71% were in favor of lifting the embargo, 17% were against, another group abstained from voting and the remaining fraction refused to speak at all. All the numbers we quoted were odd.

What were relations like with the U.S. Interests Section officials?
One day in 1991, Jeffrey De Laurentis — the vice consul at the time — was talking with counterrevolutionary Nelson Torres. I walked into the office with Horacio Casanova and Nelson Pérez Pulido to deliver one of those famous surveys. De Laurentis started abusing Nelson Torres and Horacio. He was a cold man, a real tyrant, who always looked down his nose at us. I faced him and said, "Look, I'm out there in the streets with State Security on my trail day in, day out. You should respect us; this is our country," and a few more things. He took off his glasses and asked me what I wanted. "I don't want anything," I said, "You're the ones who wanted the survey and now you've got it."

After that, whenever I went to the Interests Section, they called me in first, ahead of all the other counterrevolutionaries sitting there waiting to talk to him. That's how I got in with them.

Did they ever suggest that you emigrate?
Yes. Before I started bringing them information and surveys. In 1992, they gave me an immigration form to fill in. I was in a terrible state, because I didn't want to go. They told me I had to fill it in and send it off. I filled in the form, because I was sure they wouldn't give me a visa. I knew several people in my neighborhood who wanted to emigrate for family or economic reasons and had lined up outside the Interests Section offices; none of them got a visa, even by mistake. I got the reply straight away. I'll never forget it; the appointment for my interview was for December 12, with Mr. De Laurentis again. He approved my application on the spot. But I didn't want to go.

Did you also provide endorsements for people who wanted to get visas?
Loads of them.

Were you paid for them?
Of course not.

Council for Cuba's Freedom (Consejo por la Libertad de Cuba, CLC)

Established on October 9, 2001 and registered on August 22 of that same year as a non-profit organization. It is directed by a board of eight members, made up of Luis Zúñiga Rey, Alberto Hernández, Diego Suárez, Elpidio Núñez, Horacio Salvador García Cordero, Ninoska Pérez Castellón, Feliciano Foyo and Ignacio Sánchez.

Its political stance consists of an unshakable refusal of all dialogue, working principally with the counterrevolutionary movement in Cuba. It has actively lobbied against our country in the U.S. Congress.

It is against all negotiations with Cuba and it declares the elimination of the present government of President Fidel Castro and his followers, be it through peaceful or violent means, to be its first priority.

The chief leaders of the organization have been linked to the terrorist activities carried out by the FNCA during the 1990s, particularly to Luis Zúñiga, Alberto Hérnandez and Horacio García, who directed the organization's paramilitary arm and supplied the means and the funding for the violent actions they secretly carried out through other organizations.

The ties between Alberto Hérnandez and the terrorists detained in Panama — Luis Posada Carriles and Gaspar Jiménez Escobedo — are well known; with the support and guidance of the CLC's principal directors, these terrorists have planned several assassination attempts against the Cuban president during his trips abroad, including the one intended for the 10th Ibero-American Summit held in Panama.

They have increased their ties to leaders and members of counterrevolutionary groups in Cuba, systematically supplying them with significant financial resources, promoting the creation of clandestine organizations and encouraging them to assume ever more aggressive positions in their actions against the Revolution.

At the time there were rumors that political endorsements for visa applications were being sold, weren't there?
That's right. In fact, I told De Laurentis something that was very true: that people were saying the Interests Section was involved in this business, and I said I knew which people were selling their signatures at that time. One of them was Carlos Orozco. Then he asked me why I'd filled in the form to see him, and I told him that was the only way I could get to talk to him.

At the second interview, they started playing with me, saying they didn't know what "vocera" (spokesperson) of the Pro Human Rights Party meant. They looked the word up in a dictionary and asked me why I had applied to join the Political Refugee program if I didn't want to emigrate. I explained that what I wanted was to talk to Mr. De Laurentis, to tell him about all the scams that were going on. They told me my application was approved and then started laughing, "No, no it isn't approved," because they needed me at the Interests Section to continue passing them information.

Didn't they find it strange that a "dissident" was coming to them with tales against her cohorts?
They saw it as a positive sign for their work. They knew I was quite well placed in the Party and decided it would be a good idea to keep me close. In the end, they sent me a letter turning down my visa application, and they were left convinced that I was a genuine defender of human rights, that I hadn't been going to the Interests Section to hustle a visa.

Those were the toughest years of the Special Period ...
In 1993, the situation was pretty tense, what with the power cuts and the shortages; there were problems, social, political, as well as economic. On instructions from State Security, I went on feeding the Americans the message they wanted to hear, or that my government wanted them to hear.

Horacio Salvador García Cordero

One of the top leaders of the counterrevolutionary organization known as the Council for Cuba's Freedom (Consejo por la Libertad de Cuba).

He left the country in 1960. He had ties to the terrorist group known as the Student Revolutionary Directorate (Directorio Revolucionario Estudiantil), with which he promoted different terrorist acts against Cuba. He was one of the leaders of the Cuban-American National Foundation (Fundación Nacional Cubanoamericana, FNCA) until August of 2001.

During his membership in the FNCA, he was tied to its most recalcitrant terrorist group, substituting Luis Zúñiga Rey in 1995 as head of the paramilitary arm of this organization.

He continued facilitating funding for similar actions on behalf of the Foundation.

He has been involved in the illegal smuggling of artworks into the United States and the introduction of counterfeit dollars into Cuba.

He is the millionaire co-proprietor of García Menéndez Enterprises Inc. and a McDonald's chain in Miami.

He has participated in the recruitment of counterrevolutionaries within Cuba, who have received instructions from him to organize clandestine cells and to carry out acts of sabotage and terrorism.

In the year 2001, he gave orders to carry out such activities to members of counterrevolutionary groups, who established a conspiratorial structure and received systematic funding for their purposes.

He supports the activities of counterrevolutionary leader Félix Navarro Rodríguez, who lives in the province of Matanzas, sending him financial aid on a regular basis.

In June or July of 1994, I was talking to Robin Diane Meyer, the second secretary at the Interests Section, and I told her I was going to make a prophesy: "If you keep on refusing visas and boats keep getting stolen, there's going to be a revolt." I just wanted to know how she'd react. "This country's a pressure cooker and the only escape valve is emigration," I said. She told me her government wouldn't allow it. I told her firmly that whether Washington liked it or not, there was going to be a mass exodus. She answered, shouting: "Clinton won't let it happen!" After that came the rafters crisis and the U.S. government had to rethink things.

Did the Interests Section ask for your cooperation at that time?
Yes. They wanted me to hand out leaflets saying that the people who were leaving on rafts were going to the Guantánamo naval base, and that they weren't going on to the United States from there.

Did they explain why they wanted you to distribute the leaflets?
Look, they didn't want to believe there would be a mass exodus due to the policies Washington had applied up to that time. They were obsessed with the publicity the crisis was getting and were sure it would wear down the Cuban government. We wanted them to do something to discourage the people planning to risk their lives at sea and hoped they would agree to migration treaties.

I invited her to my place. The neighbors were doing some carpentry and repairs, and it was really noisy all the time. She asked me about the hammering and I told her, "They're making rafts," and gave her a story about all the people in the neighborhood getting ready to leave. She was horrified. So a couple of days later, there was Odilia Collazo, the faithful servant, handing out leaflets in Cojímar.

The Americans were presumably grateful to you ...
They put their seal of approval on my appointment as president of the Pro Human Rights Party when Nelson Torres Pulido left, on September 2, 1994. And I've been president ever since, up until a few days ago.

How did you make contact with the counterrevolution in Miami?
By radio, over the Internet, by phone ... I was a regular on the roundtable discussions broadcast on *Radio "Martí"* Tuesday and Thursday nights, with Luís Aguilar León, a writer whose stuff appears quite often in the *Nuevo Herald* and is heard on the radio

in Miami. In spite of being totally hostile to the Revolution, he is always saying that it's a mistake to underestimate Castro. I was also on this program with Omar López Montenegro. They were always phoning me.

What other radio stations called you?
La Cubanísma, Radio Mambí, La Poderosa ... I've lost count. Through Nancy Pérez Crespo, I started working with Agustín Tamargo, on a program broadcast every Monday, called "Round Table". I worked with him for years.

Joe García

A member of the Cuban-American National Foundation (Fundación Nacional Cubanoamericana, FNCA).

In 1988, he was the coordinator for the FNCA Exodus Program, which re-located to the United States nearly 10,000 Cuban émigrés who had been living in Spain, Panama, Peru, Venezuela, Costa Rica and the Dominican Republic, among other countries. He traveled to more than 20 nations to carry out this mission.

In late 1992 and early 1993, he traveled to Moscow, accompanied by Roberto Martín Pérez, to organize a similar re-location of Cuban émigrés residing in Russia. Both met with officials of the Ministry of Foreign Relations, Immigration, and the Russian Vice-Minister of the Interior.

On May 19, 2000 he was named executive director of the FNCA, with a salary of 120,000 dollars a year. He replaced the terrorist Francisco José "Pepe" Hernández Calvo.

His designation was considered one of the steps taken by the organization to salvage the tarnished image of the Foundation, brought about by its participation in the kidnapping of Elián González.

On the radio in Miami, Agustín Tamargo called you "the Mariana Grajales of the dissidents." Why?
He himself used to tell me I was his Mariana Grajales. He fell in love with my image as a tough fighter against the "Castro regime". Whenever something happened in Cuba, or at election time, or in

the run-up to Geneva, Agustín would always put on a special program with me. He loved to hear me talk tough, shoot my mouth off. All I did was tell him and his Miami audience what they wanted to hear. He would tell me beforehand what the topic was going to be, of course. They would play the first notes, and I would sing the rest of the song for them, you could say.

When was the last time you talked to Tamargo?
A few hours before my cover was blown, in March. They had just arrested Raúl Rivero, Omar Rodríguez and the rest of them. I still didn't know that my real identity was going to be revealed. On the programme, I said, "The people who've been arrested in Cuba are not terrorists. They are fighters whose weapons were pen and paper; their bullets were medicines." Between the lines I was rubbing in the fact that everyone knows, whether they are "opposition" members or not: that smuggled medicines are being supplied to the "dissidents" to demoralize the Cuban public, thanks to Frank Hernández Trujillio, Democratic Action (Acción Democrática), the Democracy Movement (Movimiento Democracía), New Generation Cuba (Nueva Generación Cuba), Cuban National Resistance (Resistencia Nacional Cubana), Lincoln Díaz-Balart and the rest of the "exiles".

Did you write as well?
Yes. I wrote denunciations. Those reports on human rights violations in Cuba, the ones the Interests Section sent to the State Department, were written by me. At the beginning, I wrote them by hand; they must have a lot of reports in my handwriting and with my signature stored away. Later, I started using a typewriter and finally a computer. They arranged the copying. Things developed to the point where I was practically the secretary of Ricardo Zuniga, the political/economic chief at the Interests Section.

How did that come about?
He came to trust me so much that I would write the reports they asked for on the computer, send them in by e-mail, and he would pass them along to the State Department without changing so much as a comma.

Where did you learn to use a computer and the Internet?
There in the U.S. Interests Section. A Cuban woman there taught me. It was part of her job to help us "independent journalists" with our work, although she actually hindered it a lot of the time.

Luis Zúñiga Rey

He left the country illegally through the Guantánamo Naval Base in 1970. He was arrested and sentenced in 1974 when he attempted an armed infiltration of the Island. Out of the country once again, he became the vice-president of the counterrevolutionary organization known as the Association for Continental Peace (Asociación por la Paz Continental, ASOPAZCO), based in Spain and funded by the Cuban-American National Foundation (FNCA).

During the 1990s, he began to play a more active role within the FNCA as a member of its paramilitary arm.

He sought out, recruited and supplied Cuban citizens temporarily visiting the United States, whom he instructed to sabotage economic targets in Cuba.

He has also maintained ongoing ties with the heads and members of counterrevolutionary organizations, whom he has attempted to involve in violent acts against Cuba. In April of 1994, he was removed from the leadership, although he continued his involvement in violent activities aimed at Cuba.

He subsequently directed the FNCA project known as the Human Rights Foundation (Fundación para los Derechos Humanos), and was accredited for numerous consecutive years as a member of the Nicaraguan delegation, in order to intervene against our country at the Commission on Human Rights in Geneva.

He left the FNCA in August of 2001 and joined the terrorist organization known as the Council for Cuban Freedom (Consejo por la Libertad de Cuba), maintaining an intransigent and violent stance.

What sort of information about human rights did the Section ask for?
About social, political and economic problems; what was happening to the prisoners; what the general gossip was about.

After my success as a "forecaster" of the rafters crisis, in December they wanted my predictions about what would happen the following year. You can imagine what sort of workload that created for my comrades in Security.

This monitoring was confined to Havana?
No, no. It was coast to coast. On my visits to the Interests Section, they would sometimes ask me to show them on a wall map which region had the most problematic political scenario. They usually ended up deciding to visit the place I picked, and took me along so I could tell them who to get in touch with.

Officially, the visits were to check if the migration treaties were being observed. That was the pretext, but they really went to see for themselves what was happening in those provinces. They wanted to confirm what they were being told.

Did they pay you at the Interests Section offices?
No. I never got money there. Meals and bags full of all sorts of things, but money, never. My pay arrived via Frank Hernández Trujillo and Democratic Action. At the trial, I was able to show the court all the equipment they had given to me as "gifts", the documentation for medicines, clothes and money that arrived from Miami. The month when I got the least money was when they sent me 100 dollars.

How did the money arrive?
By Western Union, using a Transcard card. They also sent it with "mules", people who came from Miami and got a commission for bringing us our money.

Did you have meetings with officials at any other embassies?
Plenty. In fact, my last "job" as a dissident was on March 12 of this year, at the Spanish embassy. I met with José María Fernández López de Turiso, who had just arrived in Cuba to begin work at the embassy. The Interests Section instructs you to visit other diplomatic missions, and not just the EU, Poland, Canada. They send you to the Caribbean, Latin American and African embassies as well.

Why?
To inform these embassies about the reports of human rights violations, so that this wasn't seen as something done solely by the Americans, or the people at the Interests Section, in particular; our job was to give them a "local" veneer. The idea was to put on a show to convince them that the denunciations were coming from us, the Cubans. There were some cases of genuine interference...

For example?
On January 6, 1995, Ryan Stevenson Jr., an official from the Canadian department of foreign affairs, asked for a meeting with some of us at the Canadian embassy. The people who participated were Héctor Palacios Ruiz, Aida Valdés Santana and me. He didn't just want to know about everything we were doing, but also the numbers of counterrevolutionaries, what the Americans thought, if they supported us; it was a real interrogation. At the end, he asked us what Canada could do to help the "opposition" and assured us they would keep up this kind of contact until we had achieved "real democracy" here. Meetings of this kind with visitors and accredited diplomats were pretty frequent.
    More examples?

Go ahead.
A lot of these documents travelled in the Spanish Embassy's diplomatic pouch. Support from Spanish diplomats has been consistent, at least up to when I stopped being president of the Pro Human Rights Party. The present ambassador is particularly obliging. He told us we could count on him for anything we needed. His people were also very nice to us: they copied documents for us, gave us pens, paper, typewriter ribbons ... In reality, they were a significant factor in supplying what we needed for our work.

Were your instructions from the Interests Section to visit embassies just to report on human rights violations?
No. Sometimes they would ask us to go there to promote particular individuals, who were up for awards. I saw this myself from inside the Interests Section, so no one can tell me any different: the awards,

all the awards, originally come from there. I saw how they set things up for the ones presented to Payá, to Oscar Elías Biscet, to Elizardo, to Vladimiro Roca ... These people were nobodies, who were transformed overnight into "generals without armies". The Americans are experts at manufacturing "celebrities," especially out of people short on charisma or whose egos need a boost. The same thing happened with certain "journalists" and a few magazines.

Such as?
Such as *Vitral* magazine. I learned of its existence at the German embassy. At a reception, Wilfried Krug, an advisor there who looked after us "opposition" members, told us the embassy would be donating computers, printers and other supplies to the church in Pinar del Río, so it could start a magazine. Naturally, it would challenge the Havana regime. I remember asking him, "And you think the government is going to allow that?" "Yes of course," he replied, "They won't try to stop it now, just before the Pope's visit. We have to take advantage of the present circumstances." And that's how it worked out.

I heard similar arguments when the Cuban Council (Concilio Cubano) and the "Varela" Project emerged, but that was in a different diplomatic setting.

Where?
The U.S. Interests Section.

How did you become connected with the Cuban Council?
Robin Diane Meyer and her assistant, Hilda Esquivel, introduced me there to Leonel Morejón Almagro, who'd been appointed national delegate ... The two officials themselves gave me the first draft of what became the charter of the Cuban Council, and asked me to read it. There were no signatures of course, and I was probably one of the first Cubans to see it.

Did you agree to join?
Not then and there. I told them I needed to discuss it with my Party executive; you know who I actually had to consult. But they insisted,

"Please, tell us what you think. Now's the time to put pressure on the Cuban government to sit down with us and the opposition." I was a witness to the birth of the Cuban Council there in the U.S. Interests Section. I signed its charter a short while later, at the home of Héctor Palacios, who was appointed president. I was a member of Commission 6 of the organization.

What was the Cuban Patriotic United Front (Frente Unido Patriótico Cubano)?
It was created by my party. There was nothing unusual about it. Every time a group was formed and the top positions were divvied up, the people left out formed another group. Aida Valdés Santana created her own bloc; I formed mine. The Cuban Council started going downhill, without needing much help.

What about the Front?
Within two days I had 50 signatures of presidents of different groups. The Americans raved about my charisma and leadership ability, and said that it was amazing how quickly I'd got the signatures. I was laughing up my sleeve, because I knew just how much "help" I'd been getting.

Then one day the Security Service told me to put the brakes on the Front, which was on a collision course with the Cuban Council. Actually, Leonel Morejón called me begging for mercy: "Please, stop the Front. A lot of people are going over to your side and it's weakening the cause." The Interests Section gave me a warning too. I was ready to stop anyway, because by that time the Cuban Council was dead in the water. However, I managed to persuade the Americans that the Front also had a role to play in the "democratic transition".

What was the argument?
Theirs: that several parties should be groomed, to strengthen civil society. I told Robin Meyer, "We've already got three camps for a democratic regime: the Communist Party on one side, the Cuban Council — the liberals — on the other, plus the Front, which represents the hard line." I told her we even had a slogan: "We're

fighting in the front line." Robin Meyer got all excited, saying yes, that would be real democracy. And I said to myself: "That's what *you* think!"

What went wrong with the Cuban Council?
They started stealing the money; there were conflicts of interest. That was why the so-called Group of Seven appeared, which met secretly on February 10, 1996 in Diez de Octubre. Those of us who were left out started to protest. Who had elected Oswaldo Payá, Martha Beatriz Roque, Gustavo Arcos Bergnes, Félix Bonne Carcassés, Elizardo Sánchez, René Gómez Manzano and Jesús Yáñez Pelletier? In reality, they were the ones with the most clout, the ones with the strongest links with Miami and the Interests Section at that time. The "sacred cows". That created problems among the committees, because no one would accept them, without having been elected, as the representatives of the Cuban Council.

The seven started monopolizing the money and ousted Leonel Morejón Almagro, who was supposed to be the Council's guiding hand and apparently had the backing of the Interests Section. The way they creamed off the money that came in from the "NGO's" in exile was outrageous and amounted to thousands of dollars, to judge by the standard of living of those people.

Do you have evidence of how the money was getting through?
The money sent to the Council for the February 24 celebrations was collected by Arcos Bergnes from the Czech Republic embassy. It had already been earmarked: for the festivities (dinner, snacks, drinks) and a sum to be delivered to each member. They said Ricardo Bofill had sent it, but that wasn't true; he never would have sent it, because he would have kept it for himself.

I went all over the country sharing out the money among the members of the "opposition", on behalf of the Cuban Council. That gave me the chance to meet people in the provinces who were hurting Cuba and playing along with the Yankees.

Gustavo Arcos Bergnes told me that 30 dollars was to be shared among the prisoners, the ones that Elizardo — who was notoriously cautious — would never help because he saw them as terrorists. That was true: they were serving time for acts of terrorism, for violence against Cubans and Cuban institutions.

Do you remember any of the operations those prisoners had taken part in?

I will never forget one of them, who came from Holguín. Batista was his surname. He's in Miami now. He'd lost some fingers. He was jailed for planting bombs in workplaces and had injured people and seriously damaged businesses that way. This man was vicious to the point where he used to burn his own arms with cigarettes. I've never seen anything like it. When I asked him why he did it, he told me he had to prepare himself psychologically for when they started torturing him. That was crazy, because he'd all but finished his sentence and nobody had laid a finger on him.

Who gave you the list of people to be given money?

Arcos Bergnes, who also asked Elizardo for names. Elizardo avoided getting getting his hands dirty, but he had his own private list of terrorists. Money also went to Lázaro González Valdés, Héctor Palacios and Leonel Morejón Almagro. Very little of the money they gave me to distribute was allocated to the passive "dissidents". Most of it was for prisoners who'd been involved in terrorism.

What were your relations with Elizardo like?

Very strained, for one simple reason: when they appointed me Party president, he wanted to get rid of me and used Lázaro González Valdés to split my organization. Lázaro set up another Human Rights Party, affiliated with the Andrei Sakharov Foundation. The president was René Montes de Oca, who's currently in jail. This new group got started at Elizardo's home.

Why was that?

Odilia Collazo didn't let herself get pushed around by Elizardo Sánchez. I've always been assertive. They couldn't get me to do what they wanted. I made a scene that has become legendary. I turned up at his house with 12 other people, on bicycles, and we knocked him about a bit. I was going to make him respect me, one way or another. He ran out of the house. We went there to give it to him, eight women and four men from the Front.

He was scared of me after that, and started inviting me to all his receptions and distancing himself from Lázaro.

Why did he want to take over the Pro Human Rights Party?
Because it had been around the longest. It was an offshoot of the Cuban Committee for Human Rights (Comité Cubano por los Derechos Humanos). It's the only one with a certain amount of history. The Committee dated back to 1976. That was why he wanted to get rid of me, there was no other reason. Elizardo tried to give me instructions, but in a world where you could smell crooks a mile away, I only accepted instructions from the Interests Section.

How did you get along with Payá?
Really well, but we were never very close, because he's sexist and racist.

Why do you say that?
Do you know of any close collaborator of his who is a woman or black? Moreover, he accuses the government of being totalitarian, anti-democratic and exclusionary, and says he wants national reconciliation, when in reality, everything he does is completely centralized, he adopts decisions unilaterally, he makes declarations on behalf of a committee that did not elect him as its leader, and which neither knows of nor approves his stances and statements beforehand. As far as I know, there have never been elections in his group.

How are relations between Payá and the other mercenaries?
Abysmal. He is constantly attacking those who don't agree with his project. His favorite insult is accusing them of being State Security agents, and he refuses to discuss any points in common with them to reach a consensus. A classic example is his feud with Martha Beatriz, who hates him. Payá does not accept the Assembly to Promote Civil Society in Cuba. He also vehemently

prohibits those who support the "Varela" Project from joining in other initiatives they consider to be viable. He is opposed to those who defend pluralism.

Payá's image abroad is one of a very austere man...

They present him as an "average Cuban". They show pictures of him riding a bicycle, like anyone else on the streets. What the journalists don't say is that he has a Volkswagen minivan, with nine seats, white, license plate number HS 00712. He drives his family around in it, and takes them to Varadero in it now and them.

Listen, this will give you a good idea of what he's like: in his living room, where he receives the diplomats, foreign correspondents and other visitors from abroad, he has old furniture and a Russian television. He puts on a real show. But in the rest of the house, he has every modern convenience you can imagine in a very comfortable home: color television, VCR, video games, a top-of-the-line stereo system, computer...

Did you sign the "Varela" Project?
Yes, Vicky asked me to.

Who supports Payá?
The U.S. Interests Section, especially. And also the Spanish government.

But he claims he has never received help from abroad...
He might be able to get other people to buy that story, but not me. He has received economic support from organizations, parties and governments. It's impossible to carry out a national campaign of the scope of the "Varela" Project relying solely on the salary of an electro-medicine engineer working for the Ministry of Public Health, who also happens to be the only member of the household who works.

Everyone knows he has stable and public ties with the leaders of the Cuban-American National Foundation — namely Joe García, Pepe Hernández, Fernando Canto, Domingo Moreira, Josefina Vento and Ramón Humberto Colás Castillo — and with the Cuban Democratic Directorate. And also with Francisco Zúñiga, Carlos Alberto Montaner and Father Francisco Santana.

The priest from the kidnapping of Elián?
The very same, one of his main public relations agents outside Cuba. This is a man who belongs to the Cuban-American National Foundation.

Do you recall any personal anecdotes involving Payá?

I was a witness, sitting at the same table, with him and Vicky, when she personally instructed him to seek support for the "Varela" Project in the European Union, primarily in the embassies of Belgium and Germany, and especially in Spain, when Aznar was president of the European Union.

I remember Payá telling the head of the Interests Section that "if they touched one of his activists again, the political scene in Cuba would turn very dark." This is typical of Payá: threatening the Revolution from the shelter of the support he's getting from the U.S. government. Those poor fools just can't get it through their heads that we Cubans aren't afraid of anything.

Incidentally, how often did you go to the Interests Section offices?
Not every day, but quite often. I mean, I didn't have set days, but I'd go whenever I needed to work on the computer or check my e-mail, or when they called me, or when there was a reception or a party... I couldn't tell you how many times I went, because I lost count. Like other "dissidents", I have an open pass; they haven't taken it back yet.

Did they ever invite you to the United States?
Sure, I got invitations. But I never wanted to go.

What sort of relations did you have with Vicky Huddleston?
Very good.

Samuel Martínez Lara

One-time general secretary of the Pro Human Rights Party.

Former counterrevolutionary prisoner, organizer of demonstrations and conspiratorial meetings; publisher, together with Tania Díaz Castro, of subversive documents. Had links with Gustavo Arcos Bergnes and Elizardo Sánchez Santacruz.

And with James Cason?
Excellent. I got on well with his wife and got the chance to be one
of the first members of "the opposition" to meet with him. He offered
me the use of his residence for meetings with all the provincial
delegates of the Human Rights Violations Reporting Office, or for

any other event.

His wife, Carmen, is from El Salvador; she told me how much
she liked the old quarter of Havana. She said the Cubans didn't
appreciate their cultural heritage, that she'd been all over the world
and that she loved Havana. I realized from the way she talked that
she was trying to gain my trust. She's someone it would be a mistake to underestimate, a very cultured person, perhaps more so
than her husband. She was the one who handled protocol, and
was constantly trying to win us over.

Did all the officials behave the same way?
No. I must be fair: not all the American diplomats used us and
underestimated us. Among all the send-offs of Interests-Section
officials I attended, the one for Section Chief Michael Kozack
was the only one that made me feel a pang of regret. He had
been involved in plots too, and called me to meetings and gave
me instructions. He did the same as the rest, but with a lighter
touch.

He and his wife hugged me and told me they didn't want to
leave Cuba with hard feelings, that they loved my country, my island. His wife said they had met a people here with values that
weren't common in other countries. She cried. She's Mexican and
she told me she was fonder of Cuba than her own country, because her children were safe and she could let them play with the
other kids in the neighborhood without worrying what might happen to them. That goodbye made a real impression on me, because I realized they hadn't come here just to do a job, and were
leaving their hearts in Cuba.

There were subtle differences between the American diplomats?
I also remember Steve Rice, Kozak's vice-consul, a militant
conspirator with close ties to the counterrevolution. He came to

my place several times and once, in April of 1997 if I remember correctly, he told us at a dinner given by Martha Beatriz Roque that the "dissidents" in Cuba were not really all that persecuted, and every time he had to attend meetings with them, he came away dizzy. He preferred talking to us, "the chosen ones".

Did you meet any CIA officials or agents?
Yes, Timothy Brown. He told me himself, personally. One time he had lunch at my place with my husband and me. We talked about all kinds of things, not just work. He tried to protect me. He would squeeze my arm discreetly to stop me from saying too much and getting myself into trouble, when he thought State Security might be listening in.

Did they think there were Cuban State Security agents inside the Interests Section?
They distrusted the Cubans who worked there. They didn't trust them and set traps for the domestic staff, who were Cuban, so they could tell whether they'd touched their documents.

Often, when they wanted to tell me something that no one else was supposed to know about, they'd write it on a slip of paper; after I answered, they'd keep the slip of paper.

If they were so fearful, why did they keep open house for the "opposition"?
I sometimes got the impression it didn't matter to them that much. The important thing was to have faces and names to put forward for the benefit of public opinion as "opponents of the Castro regime". They opened their doors to all of us also to show us the benefits of capitalism, like how you could have a big house and lots of possessions, how generous you could afford to be as a master.

Tell us what happened when it came to handing out the gifts at the Interests Section offices or at the American diplomats' residences.
It was a free-for-all, like breaking a piñata. I didn't take part in those scrums. I sent my husband to collect the gifts. People descended

like vultures on the gift bags and the trays of prawns and lobster, to the point where the actual diplomatic corps got nothing to eat. When the gift bags and food appeared, protocol went out of the window. It was like a feeding frenzy among sharks. In the end, James Cason reorganized the receptions: there was one bag per person and that was that.

What was in the bags?
Radios, flashlights, literature, battery chargers, the Universal Declaration of Human Rights in huge batches, speeches by U.S. politicians, pronouncements by Bush, counterrevolutionary magazines…

Was it your idea to set up the National Human Rights Violations Reporting Office?
Yes. The Interests Section wanted representation from all sectors of civil society. Since there was already a Group of Four (Vladimiro, Martha Beatriz, Bonne and Manzano) and a Group of Seven, we set up that office, which was joined by a youth movement, the Independent Medical Association and the Pro Human Rights Party. Our mission was to record and expose all violations.

All this was done in the wake of the arrival of Bill Barker, a Presbyterian, who wanted to see an office represented by young people "who are the ones who've changed things throughout history," as he used to say. They chose my party because it had the biggest membership and branches all over Cuba, including the Isle of Youth.

Bill Barker admitted to us in confidence that he had been sent by Lincoln Díaz-Balart. He told us they could give us what we needed, that we could even choose what sort of weapons we wanted.

At that time, my representative in exile was Democratic Action (Acción Democrática), which supplied me with clothing and equipment.

Some of us also met with Spanish economists. They wanted to work with the economists to lay the foundations for a change in the future. They asked Martha Beatriz and me to make a call to businessmen and ask them not to invest in Cuba.

They respected me for many reasons.

Nancy Pérez Crespo

Born in Cueto, Holguín. She is the representative in Miami of the counterrevolutionary group known as Cuba Press, run by Raúl Rivero. She is a CIA agent, executive director of the Florida Israeli Cultural Institute, and and an announcer for the radio station *Voice of the National Democratic Affinity Party* (*Voz del Partido Afinidad Nacional Democrático*).

She sends money on a regular basis to the head of the Havana Press group, Jorge Olivera, and his family, as well as to Raúl Rivero, through his wife, Blanca Reyes. She has also sent money to Elizardo Sánchez Santacruz.

She is the editor of a magazine called *Nueva Prensa Cubana* (New Cuban Press), which publishes articles written by so-called "independent journalists". This publication has circulation in Spain, Panama and Miami. She has also traveled to Europe to coordinate new actions.

She has used foreign and Cuban-American emissaries to send instructions, as well as money and materials, to members of the counterrevolutionary press.

She works for the subversive radio station known as *Radio "Martí"* and runs her own gallery, which features works by so-called "dissident" Cuban artists.

She is a member of the International Society of Journalism (Sociedad Internacional de Periodismo, SIP).

She has friendly ties with the terrorist Orlando Bosch.

She has organized, along with leaders of the Cuban American National Foundation, the Cuban Democratic Directorate and other counterrevolutionary organizations, hostile actions against Cuba at the U.N. Commission on Human Rights.

Such as?
They all knew my father had been locked up in the Cabaña with the "political" prisoners for six years. As far as the counterrevolutionaries in Miami and the ones who knew him in Cuba were concerned, he was a hardliner's hardliner. For me, that was a major

endorsement. They respected me not just because of my position in the Party, but because of my father too.

Who was your father?
He was in the Cuban Navy for 31 years and fought with the U.S. Army in the Second World War. He fought in the Bay of Pigs, and during the October Crisis they discharged him for conspiring with some of his fellow Navy members. He was stripped of his rank and treated as a traitor to the nation. He was jailed on July 12, 1963.

What was his rank?
He was a sergeant and used to give classes on navigation. He had been a sponge diver, of very humble, rural origins. He had a very difficult life before the Revolution.

What do you remember about that time?
He left the house one day and never came back. They put him in jail. I was very young, 12 years old, but I've always been pretty sharp. It stuck in my mind that before he went, he picked out three songs from the records we used to play and told me to listen to them and think of him. That really intrigued me, also the fact that he left me his diary; it was as if he was leaving to fulfil some sacred duty.

What were the three songs?
One was "Reloj" (Clock); it goes, *"Clock, don't mark the hours…"* It was as if he wanted time to stand still. The second was "La Barca" (The Boat): *"My beach is a sorrowful place today, because your boat must sail…"* And the third, a ballad sung by Barbarito Diez: *"Birds fly home to the nest, but when those you have loved depart, they never return…"* I felt he was trying to tell me not to stop loving him, not to forget him. And I didn't, of course.

Did you visit him in prison?
Yes. He'd left me the key to where he kept money and his tools. Bit by bit he told me where all his things were.

I should explain, there were four of us children, but I was the oldest and the closest to him.

I went to visit him in the Cabaña. We would talk through the bars; I went every three months. He always asked me how I was doing at school, what I did with myself. He kept a bit of wire in his belt, which he used to pass me notes, because talking was so difficult. I would write back and he would hide the bit of paper under his dental plate.

What did he say?
In his notes he always told me never to stop loving the Revolution, to be a good girl at school and to listen to the songs, because one day I'd understand why he'd left them for me.

A "political prisoner" telling you to love the Revolution …?
That used to confuse me a lot.

What did you do?
I often asked my comrades in State Security. I told them I didn't understand about my father.

And what did they tell you?
Nothing. My mother and brothers and sisters had no answers for me either. As far as they were concerned he was a traitor to his country. Full stop. To give you an idea: my mother is from the countryside and is a real revolutionary. Luckily she lives in Batabanó, well away from my work among the "dissidents". If she and my grandmother had found out what Odilia was mixed up in, I don't think I'd be here telling you all this.

Whenever I mentioned my father, my officials always gave me the same answer: that there were things that couldn't be discussed, that the files were classified and they had no access to them. But something inside me made me keep trying to find out more.

Ruth Montaner (Chuni)

Her maiden surname is Morán. She was married to Ernesto Montaner, brother of Carlos Alberto Montaner. She prefers to use her ex-husband's surname. She is known as Chuni. She is currently the director of radio station WQBA and has close ties with extreme right-wing groups based in Miami. She is in favor of the blockade. In 1997 she was the top representative in the United States of the organization known as the Internal Dissidence Work Group (Grupo de Trabajo de la Disidencia Interna, GTDI).

She lobbied intensively to prevent President Fidel Castro from being invited to the 7th Ibero-American Summit held in Margarita Island on Novemer 8 and 9, 1997. In all of her efforts, she has had the support of anti-Cuban congresspeople Lincoln Díaz-Balart and Ileana Ros-Lehtinen.

She waged an aggressive propaganda campaign targeting diplomatic missions accredited in Cuba, demanding that they distribute the counterrevolutionary document entitled "La Patria es de Todos" (The Nation Belongs to Everyone), released on June 27, 1997.

She has close ties to Félix Antonio Bonne Carcassés, René Gómez Manzano, Vlamidiro Roca and Martha Beatriz Roque.

In June of 1999 she took part in an anti-Cuban campaign during the summit meeting between the European Union and Latin American countries, held in Río de Janeiro, with the aim of denouncing alleged human rights violations in Cuba.

She has received significant sums of money from U.S. government federal funds. She has been accused of embezzlement on more than one occasion, which has led to her removal from the Dissidence Support Group (Grupo de Apoyo a la Disidencia, GAD). She shares the political stances of her former brother-in-law Carlos Alberto Montaner.

Félix Rodríguez Mendigutía

Colonel of the CIA. Known as "El Gato" (The Cat), he also called himself Félix Ramos. Of Cuban origins, he pretended to be a captain in the Bolivian army in order to capture guerrilla fighters. He claims to be the assassin of Che Guevara.

He is now an insurance agent and consultant; he is a trusted employee of Trident Investigative Services Inc. The agency is represented in Argentina by John Battaglia Ponte, a naturalized U.S. citizen of Uruguayan birth who is a former CIA agent and participant in the so-called "Condor Plan" in the 1970s. He later worked in Central America, where he helped Anastasio Somoza flee from Nicaragua.

He took advantage of his contacts in El Salvador to use the runway at the Ilopango air force base as an operations center for a number of aging planes that would deliver weapons to the Contra forces; the planes belonged to the Corporate Air Services company. The owner of the company was a former major-general of the U.S. Air Force, Richard Secord, a friend of Oliver North.

During the Iran-Contra operation, he worked alongside José Basulto in Ilopango to deliver "humanitarian aid". Together, they took part in the execution of all the actions under the command of Oliver North. A DEA agent once said in an interview with *The New York Times* that he had compiled convincing evidence in Guatemala that the Contra supply operations carried out at the Ilopango air force base in El Salvador — where Félix Rodríguez Mendigutía and José Basulto were working — were also a front for the smuggling of cocaine and marijuana.

In this home in Miami, Félix Rodríguez Mendigutía keeps two trophies from his assassination: a GMT Master Rolex and pipe that belonged to Che.

He is a friend (and was his subordinate in the CIA) of Donald Gregg, a security adviser to former president George Bush.

A few months ago, when things got really tense in my secret work, I told my official that if I died, he would have it on his conscience that he'd held back the truth from me. And that I would go on loving my father no matter what. I was sure he loved me too, and had let me know it in many ways. I kept asking over and over.

A few days later we talked about it again. It's like I can see his face right now. He had spoken to his superiors, and he told me, "Odilia, you're going to have to keep this secret close, because it could cost you your life. Your father was one of us." We both wept. My heart hadn't deceived me.

How did your mother react?
You can imagine! She found out from me, and so did my brothers and sisters, when they heard me speak on television during the trial.

And your father really never told you anything?
Never. This work is just too risky. He came out of prison in 1969 and died in 1988. He took his secret with him to the grave.

Odilia Collazo Valdés.

Néstor Baguer Sánchez Galarraga.

Roberto Martínez Hinojosa.

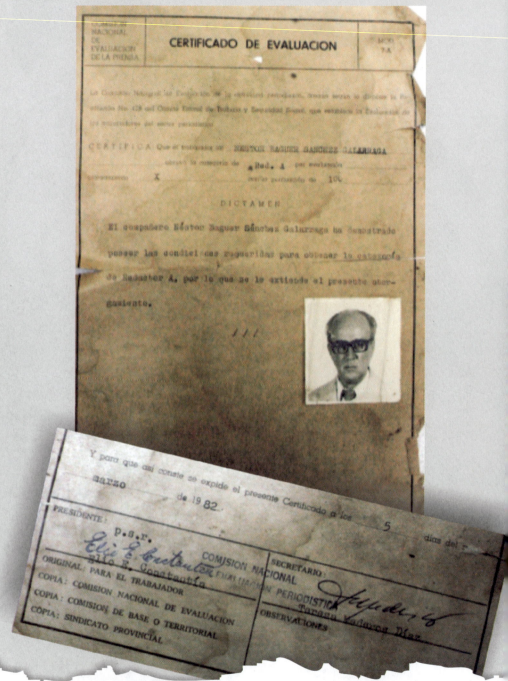

Certificates accrediting Néstor Baguer with the degree of Bachelor in Journalism. It was approved by a National Commission headed by a master journalist, the late Elio Constantín.

Diploma given to Néstor Baguer as a member of the Spanish Royal Academy.

┌ D I S I D E N T E   U N I V E R S A L   D E   P U E R T O   R I C O ┐

disidente

AÑO 16   NUM. 164   **E D I C I O N   I N T E R N A C I O N A L**   FEBRERO 2001

LLAMAMIENTO
Desde La Habana

ELIZARDO SÁNCHEZ

OSWALDO PAYÁ

Los representantes de las organizaciones cívicas, sociales, culturales y políticas independientes que dentro de Cuba promovemos y defendemos pacíficamente los derechos civiles, el pluralismo y la reconciliación nacional hacemos, **TODOS UNIDOS**, un llamado a la comunidad internacional para que contribuya a detener la ola represiva desatada por el Gobierno de Cuba, desde noviembre de 1999, víspera de la IX Cumbre Iberoamericana que se celebró en La Habana.

En nuestro mensaje desde Cuba a la X Cumbre Iberoamericana del pasado 29 de octubre, declaramos que no pedíamos el aislamiento del gobierno cubano. Las posturas asumidas por las autoridades de nuestro país en los últimos tiempos, pudieran reflejar el irracional propósito de autoaislarse de una comunidad internacional que cada día asume con más fuerza los principios democráticos y el respeto a los Derechos Humanos.

Durante el año 2000 se registraron más de mil actos de represión política contra pacíficos disidentes y por lo menos 18 de ellos permanecen en prisión provisional como parte de los centenares de prisioneros por motivos políticos que languidecen en las cárceles desde hace años.

En el pasado mes de diciembre la desproporcionada maquinaria represiva del Gobierno de Cuba rompió todo los récords al registrarse más de 300 acciones de represión política, de las cuales por los menos 270 fueron detenciones arbitrarias de opositores no violentos.

Reclamamos la liberación de los presos por motivos políticos y que se ponga fin a las prácticas de hostigamiento, juicios parcializados, condenas injustas y desproporcionadas, detenciones e incomunicaciones arbitrarias, prohibición de libre acceso a los juicios públicos, así como a todos los actos que transgreden los derechos esenciales de la persona humana.

TODOS UNIDOS, hacemos un llamado para que se solidaricen con este reclamo los gobiernos democráticos, parlamentos, organizaciones humanitarias, internacionales políticas, organizaciones de la prensa, sindicales, académicas y religiosas de todo el mundo.

Los cubanos aspiramos a la solidaridad de la Comunidad Internacional en la lucha por la conquista: DE NUESTRO DERECHO A LOS DERECHOS.

La Habana, 16 de enero de 2001

Lista de firmantes en la página 3

EN ESTE NUMERO

Disidente magazine is published in Puerto Rico. It is one of Elizardo Sánchez's business enterprises.

disidente

A CALL FROM HAVANA

ELIZARDO SÁNCHEZ

OSWALDO PAYÁ

The representatives of the independent civic, social, cultural and political organizations that peacefully promote and defend civil rights within Cuba, working for pluralism and national reconciliation, ALL OF US UNITED call on the international community to help put an end to the wave of repression unleashed by the Cuban government since November of 1999, on the eve of the 9th Ibero-American Summit held in Havana.

In our message from Cuba to the 10th Ibero-American Summit last October 29, we stated that we were not asking for the international isolation of the Cuban government. The stances recently assumed by our country's authorities, however, could well reflect the irrational objective of self-isolation from an international community that is ever more concerned about respecting democratic principles and human rights.

During the year 2000, more than a thousand acts of political repression against peaceful activists were registered; at least 18 of these activists remain in pre-trial detention, among the hundreds of political prisoners who have been languishing in jail for years.

Last December, the repressive apparatus of the Cuban government broke all records in registering more than 300 acts of political repression, of which at least 270 were the arbitrary arrests of non-violent dissidents.

We ask for the freedom of all political prisoners and for an end to the practices of harassment, biased trials, unjust and exorbitant sentences, arbitrary arrests and isolation, the prohibition of free access to public trials, as well as to every action that violates the fundamental rights of human beings.

ALL OF US UNITED call for support for this just demand from democratic governments, parliaments, humanitarian organizations, international political organizations, and press, trade union, academic and religious organizations throughout the world.

We Cubans hope for the solidarity of the international community in the struggle to attain OUR RIGHT TO HUMAN RIGHTS.

Havana, January 16, 2001

Vicky Huddleston llama a apoyar los cambios

La jefa de la Sección de Intereses de EU en Cuba, Vicky Huddleston, elogió ayer la labor desarrollada en los últimos años por la disidencia interna en Cuba y exhortó a la comunidad internacional a trabajar por una transición pacífica hacia la democracia en la isla comunista.

"En mis tres años de gestión aquí he notado un crecimiento notable en la oposición interna, que realiza un gran trabajo en materia de vigilancia de los Derechos Humanos y en fomentar el desarrollo de la sociedad civil", dijo Huddleston.

"Creo que pude haber contribuido en una pequeña forma a centrar la atención en la situación de los derechos humanos", agregó la diplomática, quien arribó a la isla en septiembre de 1999.

La diplomática, jefa de la Sección de Intereses de Estados Unidos en Cuba, oficina que cumple funciones de enlace entre ambas naciones, sin relaciones desde hace más de 40 años, culmina este mes su labor en la isla tras ser designada como embajadora en la República de Malí, en África.

De 59 años de edad, Huddleston fue una crítica permanente del gobierno de Fidel Castro, al que le ha reclamado públicamente que promueva una apertura política y permita el libre accionar de sus opositores.

"Las Organizaciones No. 13 Gubernamentales y los gobiernos deberían tratar de apoyar más a los disidentes cubanos, siempre en una forma legítima, así como se hizo con los países de Europa del Este", dijo la diplomática al demandar un mayor protagonismo de la comunidad internacional respecto a la situación en Cuba.

Consideró que en la isla ya se vive un momento de transición, a pesar del inmovilismo que quiere imponer el gobierno a la sociedad, y advirtió que "no puede haber castrismo sin Fidel Castro", al ser consultada sobre las perspectivas políticas en el futuro de Cuba.

Huddleston afirmó que el Proyecto Varela, una iniciativa disidente que promovió la convocatoria a un referéndum para modificar leyes electorales y exigir la libertad de presos políticos, "marcó uno de los momentos más importantes de la historia cubana reciente".

"La respuesta del gobierno de Castro fue drástica, pero le hizo perder credibilidad ante la comunidad internacional", precisó la diplomática y reiteró su pedido de apoyar a los opositores que operan en Cuba.

"Hay una generación de cubanos que está pidiendo cambios y hay que apoyarlos. Hay que fomentar una transición pacífica" que

VICKY HUDDLESTON

permita una salida ordenada al sistema socialista, vigente en la isla desde hace 43 años, agregó.

Huddleston negó las acusaciones oficiales sobre el presunto financiamiento de la disidencia por parte de los diplomáticos estadounidenses acreditados en la isla y afirmó que esa "es una mentira del Estado" cubano.

"Los disidentes trabajan por sus ideas y sus creencias, no por un sueldo que le podamos pagar nosotros. Nunca les hice siquiera una sugerencia", enfatizó la diplomática.

Luego de señalar que se retiraba conforme con el trabajo realizado en los últimos tres años, donde tuvo que enfrentar desde la crisis generada en 1999 por la zaga judicial del niño Elián González y la visita del ex presidente Jimmy Carter, en mayo pasado, Huddleston dijo que no se lleva "malos recuerdos de La Habana".

Algunos de sus líderes, como Oswaldo Payá, promotor de "Proyecto Varela", que reclama un referéndum para introducir reformas en la Constitución, y el recientemente liberado Vladimiro Roca, asistieron anoche a la recepción de despedida de la embajadora.

Huddleston reconoció que "hemos recibido una cooperación bastante buena de Cuba en la base Guantánamo", quien no específico en qué consistió ésta. En la base norteamericana de Guantánamo, enclavada en el extremo oriental de la isla caribeña, hay actualmente 564 prisioneros sospechosos de pertenecer a la red terrorista Al Qaeda o a las fuerzas talibanes durante la guerra de Afganistán.

"En un futuro, con democracia, Cuba será el motor económico del Caribe", indicó la diplomática.

El Nuevo Herald, Miami, FL
Sábado 7 de septiembre del 2002

Grupo disidente cubano pide solidaridad con presos en huelga de hambre

LA HABANA - El opositor Movimiento Cristiano de Liberación llamó en La Habana a gobiernos, instituciones e iglesias, para que "defiendan la vida" de varios presos políticos cubanos que mantienen una huelga de hambre, y están "en peligro de muerte".

"Llamamos a todos los gobiernos, instituciones, iglesias y personas de buena voluntad para que, con urgencia, defiendan la vida y libertad de estas personas en peligro de muerte, debido a la arbitrariedad y la injusticia del gobierno de Cuba", dijo el llamamiento *No les dejen morir* que firma el presidente del Movimiento, Oswaldo Payá Sardiñas.

Los presos, cuyo número no precisa el texto, se encuentran en las prisiones de Valle Grande, en Ciudad de la Habana, y Quivicán,

en la provincia La Habana, y recurrieron a la huelga "como último y dramático recurso para reclamar su liberación".

Cita el caso de Emilio Leyva Pérez, presidente del ilegal pero tolerado Partido Pro Derechos Humanos, que la víspera cumplió 20 días sin ingerir alimentos y "ya no tiene fuerzas para levantarse".

Otro opositor preso, Leonardo Brazón, también está en huelga de hambre.

El ilegal Movimiento Cristiano de Liberación señaló que "no apoyamos ni incitamos huelgas de hambre, ni otras acciones en la que pueda dañarse la salud o poner en peligro la vida de personas".

Diario Las Américas, Miami, FL
Jueves 19 de septiembre del 2002

A page from *Disidente* magazine. The U.S. Interests Section has become the main promoter of this publication, using it to send instructions to puppet governments.

Vicky Huddleston calls for support for changes

Yesterday, the head of the U.S. Interests Section in Havana, Vicky Huddleston, paid tribute to the work carried out by dissidents within Cuba in recent years, and called on the international community to help bring about a peaceful transition toward democracy on the communist island.

"In my three years of work here, I have witnessed a remarkable growth in the internal opposition, which works to monitor Human Rights and to encourage the development of civil society," said Huddleston.

"I think I may have had a small part in drawing attention to the situation of human rights here," added the diplomat, who arrived on the island in September of 1999.

The diplomat, head of the U.S. Interests Section in Cuba, an office which oversees relations between the two nations, which have had no economic relations for over 40 years, will be saying goodbye to her work on the island this month, after being re-assigned as ambassador to the Republic of Mali, Africa.

Fifty-nine years old, Huddleston has been a permanent critic of the government of Fidel Castro, and has publicly demanded that it promote a political opening and give the opposition free rein to carry out its activities.

"Non-governmental organizations and governments themselves should try to offer more support to Cuban dissidents, and always in a legitimate manner, just as was done with countries in Eastern Europe," the diplomat said, demanding greater involvement of the international community with respect to the situation in Cuba.

She maintained that a time of transition is already underway in Cuba, despite the paralysis the government hopes to impose on society, and said that "there can be no Fidelismo without Fidel Castro," on being asked about the political perspectives of Cuba's future.

Huddleston stated that the Varela Project, a dissident initiative promoting a call for a referendum to modify electoral laws and demand the freedom of political prisoners, marked one of the most important moments in Cuba's recent history."

"The response of the Castro government was drastic, but it led to a loss of credibility before the international community," the diplomat explained, reiterating her appeal for support of the dissidents working within Cuba.

"We have a generation of Cubans who are asking for changes and we have to support them. We have to encourage a political transition" that will allow for an orderly departure from socialism, in place on the island for 43 years, she added.

Huddleston denied official accusations of alleged funding given to dissidents by U.S. diplomatic officials accredited on the island, and stated that this was a "fabrication of the Cuban state."

"The dissidents are fighting for their ideas and their beliefs, not for any salary we might pay them. I never even gave them a suggestion," the diplomat emphasized.

Stating that she was leaving satisfied with the work carried out during the past three years, having experienced everything from the crisis generated by the legal saga surrounding Elián González to the visit of former president Jimmy Carter this past May, Huddleston added that she was taking with her "good memories of Havana."

Some of the opposition leaders, such as Oswaldo Payá, promoter of the Varela Project, demanding a referendum to bring about changes in the constitution, and the recently released Vladimiro Roca, were present at the farewell reception held for Huddleston last night.

Huddleston acknowledged that "we have received fairly good cooperation from the Cuban government in the Guantánamo Base," although she refrained from specifying what this cooperation consisted of. In the U.S. naval base in Guantánamo, located in the easternmost region of the Caribbean island, there are currently 584 prisoners suspected of belonging to the Al Qaeda terrorist organization or to the Taliban army during the war in Afghanistan.

"In a democratic future, Cuba will be the economic engine of the Caribbean," the diplomat stated.

El Nuevo Herald, Miami, FL
Saturday, September 7, 2002

Cuban dissident group calls for solidarity with prisoners on hunger strike

HAVANA- The opposition group Christian Liberation Movement made a call from Havana to governments, institutions and churches to "defend the lives" of a number of Cuban political prisoners who are on a hunger strike and "in danger of dying."

"We call on all governments, institutions, churches and people of good will to urgently defend the lives and freedom of these individuals in danger of dying, due to the arbitrariness and injustice of the Cuban government," stated the declaration entitled "Do Not Let Them Die", signed by the president of the Movement, Oswaldo Payá Sardiñas.

The prisoners, whose number is not specified in the document, are being held in the Valle Grande Prison in the province of Ciudad de La Habana and the Quivicán Prison in the province of La Habana. They have resorted to the strike "as a last and dramatic resort to demand their freedom."

The document cites the case of Emilio Leyva Pérez, president of the illegal but tolerated Human Rights Party, who had not eaten in 20 days as of the previous night, "and no longer has the strength to stand up."

Another jailed opposition member, Leonardo Brazón, is also on a hunger strike.

The illegal Christian Liberation Movement stressed that "we do not support or encourage hunger strikes, or any other actions that could harm the health or threaten the lives of individuals."

Diario Las Américas, Miami, FL
Thursday, September 19, 2002

Mas y Sánchez conversan en discreto encuentr

Por PABLO ALFONSO
Redactor de El Nuevo Herald.

En el marco de una serie de discretas reuniones con dirigentes políticos del exilio, el disidente cubano Elizardo Sánchez se reunió la pasada semana con el presidente de la Junta de Directores de la Fundación Nacional Cubano Americana (FNCA), Jorge Mas Canosa, informaron a El Nuevo Herald fuentes fidedignas.

La reunión, según las fuentes, tuvo lugar en la residencia de Mas Canosa el pasado 25 de diciembre, Día de Navidad, y a la misma asistieron también Francisco "Pepe" Hernández y otros directivos de la FNCA. Los temas discutidos continúan sin embargo bajo un manto de silencio.

Dirigentes de la FNCA consultados por El Nuevo Herald negaron enfáticamente la información, en tanto que Sánchez señaló que "no ha habido un encuentro formal todavía con el ejecutivo de la Fundación pero esperamos que pueda haberlo".

Preguntado sobre si por "formal" quería decir que había sostenido reuniones informales con dirigentes de la Fundación, Sánchez se limitó a contestar: "Quiere decir exactamente que no nos hemos reunido formalmente".

El encuentro entre Sánchez y Mas Canosa, cuyas respectivas organizaciones mantienen posiciones y estrategias políticas contrapuestas en torno a la situación cubana, pudiera interpretarse como un esfuerzo mutuo por acercar esas posiciones en aras de lograr sus objetivos comunes de democratización en la isla.

Sin embargo, para Sánchez que salió de Cuba con un permiso temporal, la reunión con la FNCA puede tener un alto costo a su regreso a la isla. El gobierno de Fidel Castro es particularmente agresivo con la FNCA que ha auspiciado proyectos como la reciente Ley Helms-Burton, que refuerza el embargo económico estadounidense contra Cuba.

"No hay nada nuevo en esto, porque cada vez que salgo al exterior en forma temporal me reuno con representativos de todo el arco político cubano", dijo Sánchez. "Por lo demás, ya sabemos que a los actuales gobernantes cubanos no les gusta nada que signifique convergencia de la oposición democrática".

Sánchez, presidente de la Comisión Cubana de Derechos Humanos y Reconciliación Nacional, llegó a Miami el pasado 23 de diciembre, tras recibir en París el Premio a los Derechos Humanos de la República Francesa. A su paso por España, Sánchez fue recibido por importantes figuras políticas de ese país, entre ellas el presidente del gobierno, José María Aznar, y el ex-presidente Felipe González.

Desde su arribo a Miami ha sostenido aproximadamente una docena de discretas reuniones con representantes de otras tantas organizaciones políticas y de derechos humanos.

Sánchez dijo que aunque el proyecto y la agenda de su organización es exclusivamente de derechos humanos, eso no impide que sostenga intercambios con organizaciones políticas.

"No puedo desconocer que corresponde un papel muy relevante a las organizaciones políticas de la oposición y el gobierno para lograr un mejoramiento sostenido e irreversible de la situación de derechos humanos en el país", afirmó.

El sábado Sánchez se reunió con Ricardo Bofill, presidente del Comité Cubano Pro Derechos Humanos, en un encuentro en que ambos dejaron a un lado viejas rencillas personales y desavenencias políticas de casi una década.

Sánchez y Bofill, dos de los más connotados dirigentes fundadores del movimiento de derechos humanos en Cuba, se sentaron en torno a una mesa por primera vez desde que ambos se distanciaron en La Habana en 1987 y Sánchez salió del Comité para fundar su propia organización.

"Nadie entró a hablar del pasado, sólo se habló del futuro, de las cosas que en conjunto podemos hacer", afirmó Bofill, refiriéndose a la agenda de la reunión.

Bofill dijo que en la reunión se acordó la colaboración para trabajar con organizaciones internacionales de derechos humanos; aunar esfuerzos para que el movimiento de derechos humanos de Cuba pueda alcanzar estatus de Organización No Gubernamental ante la Comisión de Derechos Humanos de Naciones Unidas y coordinar la asistencia a los cubanos repatriados por Estados Unidos a Cuba, entre otros temas.

Por su parte, Sánchez calificó el encuentro como una "minicumbre cubana de derechos humanos". A la reunión asistieron, además, Ramón Cernuda, representante en el exterior de la Coordinadora de Organizaciones de Derechos Humanos de Cuba; Roberto Bismarck, vicepresidente del CCPDH; así como Lino Sánchez y Héctor Aguilera, ambos de la CCDHRN.

"Aprovechamos la reunión para identificar importantes áreas de cooperación", afirmó Sánchez.

Entre las organizaciones con las que Sánchez se ha reunido figuran El Buró de Información del Movimiento de Derechos Humanos, la Coordinadora Social Demócrata de Cuba, el Partido Demócrata Cristiano, la Unión Liberal, el Directorio Revolucionario Democrático Cubano, el Movimiento Democracia, el Partido de Unidad Nacional Democrática (PUND) y Cuba Independiente y Democrática (CID).

"He encontrado en todos un ambiente muy cordial, de mutua comprensión, aunque reconozco diferencias en cuanto a ámbitos y métodos de trabajo", dijo Sánchez.

Hubert Matos, secretario general del CID, dijo que la reunión con Sánchez se realizó en el local de esa organización y que en la misma se trató el problema cubano a fondo, destacándose las diferencias y coincidencias de ambas organizaciones.

"Nosotros apoyamos por principio a toda la resistencia interna", dijo Matos.

Añadió que el CID le señaló a Sánchez, que su propuesta para que Castro encabece un proceso de democratización en Cuba "es totalmente irrealizable, porque Castro ha dado sobradas muestras de que no está dispuesto a ceder nada".

Matos dijo que el CID se mostró también en desacuerdo con Sánchez en su planteamiento de que una proceso negociador previo entre Estados Unidos y Cuba es una condicionante para la democratización de la isla.

"El problema es de un régimen despótico con un pueblo que no quiere vivir en despotismo, las diferencias entre Estados Unidos y Cuba son otra cosa", subrayó Matos.

Sánchez explicó que su reunión con el PUND, una organización que promueve las acciones armadas para derrocar al gobierno cubano, fue motivada por la necesidad de obtener información familiar que facilite la defensa de los comandos de esa organización arrestados en acciones de infiltración en la isla.

"La organización que yo represento se ha hecho cargo de la defensa de esos hombres y en particular de Humberto Eladio Real Suárez, condenado a muerte", dijo Sánchez. "En estos momentos estamos encabezando una campaña mundial para que le sea conmutada la pena de muerte".

Sánchez viajó el sábado en la noche a Nueva York para reunirse con el ex presidente venezolano, Carlos Andrés Pérez con quien,

---

Translation of the article on the previous page:

Mas and Sanchez hold discreet encounter

During a series of meetings held with Cuban political leaders living in exile, the Cuban dissident Elizardo Sánchez met last week with the president of the board of directors of the Cuban-American National Foundation (FNCA), Jorge Mas Canosa, reliable sources told us.

According to the same sources, the meeting was held in the home of Mas Canosa this past December 25, on Christmas Day, and saw the participation of Francisco "Pepe" Hernández and other directors of the FNCA. The topics of discussion, however, remain under a veil of secrecy.

Directors of the FNCA approached by reporters from *El Nuevo Herald* emphatically denied the rumor, and Sánchez insisted that "there has not yet been a formal encounter with the executive of the Foundation, although we are hoping to have one."

When asked if, by using the word "formal", he meant there had already been "informal" meetings with leaders of the Foundation, Sánchez limited himself to answering: "It means we have not yet had any formal meetings."

The meeting between Sánchez and Mas Canosa, whose respective organizations maintain positions and strategies that are entirely opposed with respect to the Cuban situation, could be interpreted as a mutual effort to reconcile these positions with the aim of achieving the shared objective of bringing democracy to the Island.

Nevertheless, for Sánchez , who left Cuba with a temporary permit, the meeting with the FNCA can bring serious repercussions upon returning to the Island. The government of Fidel Castro is especially aggressive toward the FNCA, known for sponsoring such projects as the recent Helms-Burton Act, which toughens the U.S. embargo on Cuba.

"This isn't new; every time I leave the country, I meet with representatives from the entire Cuban political spectrum," said Sánchez. "Beyond that, we all know that the Cuban leaders dislike anything that can mean a convergence of the democratic opposition."

Sánchez, president of the Cuban Commission for Human Rights and National Reconciliation, arrived in Miami this past December 23, after receiving in Paris the Human Rights Award of the Republic of France. During a stopover in Spain, Sánchez was received by important political figures of the country, including President José María Aznar and former president Felipe González.

Since his arrival in Miami, he has held about a dozen discreet meetings with representatives of political and human rights organizations.

Sánchez said that the fact his organization has an exclusively humanitarian agenda does not prevent him from holding meetings with political organizations.

"I can't deny the fact that both political organizations of the opposition and the government itself play an important role in bringing about a sustained and irreversible improvement to the human rights situation in the country," he stated.

On Saturday, Sánchez met with Ricardo Bofill, president of the Cuban Committee for Human Rights, in a meeting that forced both leaders to put aside old personal quarrels and political disagreements.

Sánchez and Bofill, two of the most renowned, founding leaders of the human rights movement in Cuba, sat at a table facing one another for the first time since parting ways in Havana in 1987, when Sánchez left the Committee to found his own organization.

"No one has come to talk about the past, we'll speak only about the future, about the things we can do together," Bofill stated, referring to the meeting's agenda.

Bofill mentioned that both had agreed to work with international human rights organizations, to join efforts so that the human rights movement in Cuba could obtain the status of a non-government organization before the United Nations Commission on Human Rights, and to coordinate assistance for Cuban citizens repatriated to Cuba by the United States, among other things.

Sánchez qualified the meeting as a "mini-Cuban summit on human rights." The meeting was also attended by Ramón Cernuda, the representative abroad of the Coordinator of Human Rights Organizations of Cuba, as well as Roberto Bismarck, vice-president of the CCPDH, and Lino Sánchez and Héctor Aguilera, both from the CCDHRN.

"We took advantage of the gathering to identify important areas where we can collaborate," stated Sánchez.

The Bureau of Information for the Human Rights Movement, the Social Democratic Coordinator of Cuba, the Christian Democratic Party, the Liberal Union, the Cuban Revolutionary Democratic Directorate, the Democracy Movement, the National Democratic Unity Party, and Independent and Democratic Cuba are among the organizations Sánchez has met with.

"I've encountered with all of them a very friendly atmosphere, of mutual understanding, although everyone recognizes their differences with respect to methodology," said Sánchez.

Hubert Matos, general secretary of the CID, said that the meeting with Sánchez took place in the headquarters of the organization, and that the Cuban question was seriously taken up, bringing to light the differences and similarities of both organizations.

"In principle, we give our support to all of the internal opposition," said Matos.

He added that the CID had told Sánchez that his proposal for Castro to head up a process of democratization in Cuba was "totally unworkable, because Castro has given abundant evidence that he is unwilling to concede anything whatsoever."

Matos said that the CID also expressed disagreement with Sánchez with respect to his premise that in order to bring democracy to the island, prior negotiations between the United States and Cuba were necessary.

"The problem lies with a despotic regime and people who don't want to live under despotism; the conflicts between the United States and Cuba are another issue," Matos emphasized.

Sánchez explained that his meeting with the National Democratic Union Party, an organization that promotes the use of armed force to overthrow the Cuban government, was motivated by the need to obtain information that will help in the defense of the commandos sent by this organization, arrested during infiltration activities in the island.

"The organization I represent has taken on the responsibility of defending these men, particularly Humberto Eladio Real Suárez, who has been sentenced to death," said Sánchez. "At the moment, we are heading up a worldwide campaign to have his death sentence commuted."

Sánchez traveled to New York on Saturday evening, in order to meet with former Venezuelan president Carlos Andrés Pérez, with whom…

24 de febrero 2003.

Se le hace entrega al Sr. Elizardo Sánchez Santa Cruz, Miembro
de la Comisión de Relatoría de TODOS UNIDOS, de 100.00 U.S.
Dólares. Esta ayuda humanitaria la envían los hermanos de —
A.C.D.

Recibe Elizardo Sánchez Santa Cruz

2 de febrero 2003

or la presente se le entrega al Sr. Vladimiro Roca Antunez
iembro de la Comisión de Relatoría de TODOS UNIDOS, la canti-
ad de cien dólares 100.00 US.

sta ayuda humanitaria la envía desde el Exterior A.C.D. que
reside un patriota cubano en los EE.UU.

ecibe Vladimiro Rocas

Money sent from Miami to the mercenaries Elizardo Sánchez and
Vladimiro Roca by the Cuban Democratic Association.

February 24, 2003

We hereby deliver a sum of USD 100.00 to Mr. Elizardo Sánchez Santa Cruz, member of the Reporting Committee of EVERYONE UNITED, as humanitarian aid sent by the brothers of the C.D.A.

Received by Elizardo Sánchez Santa Cruz

February 22, 2003

We hereby deliver the sum of USD 100.00 to Mr. Vladimiro Roca Antúnez, member of the Reporting Committee of EVERYONE UNITED, sent from abroad, as humanitarian aid, by the C.D.A., headed by a Cuban patriot in the United States.

Received by Vladimiro Roca

Special reception given to the mercenaries at the Spanish Embassy in Havana. Raúl Rivero shakes hands with President José María Aznar. Beside him stand Gustavo Arcos Bergnes, Oswaldo Payá and Héctor Palacios, among others.

La Habana,19 de Octubre de 1997

A: SECCION DE INTERESES DE LOS EE.UU.

DE: P.P.D.H.C.

AVAL POLITICO

El Ejecutivo Nacional de nuestra Organización pacifista y Humanitaria le presenta el siguiente documento con el fin de comentar la —trayectoria desplegada por el Hermano RAFAEL GARCIA SUAREZ miembro activo desde el 16 de Mayo de 1995.

En las actividades que ha participado son en defensa de los Derechos Humanos y Civiles, cuyo afán es lograr una Cuba verdaderamente Libre y Democrática, siendo objeto principal de nuestro trabajo, entre —ellas están:

- Ha participado en el programa de ayuda a los presos políticos y —sus familiares con aporte de alimentos, medicamentos y dinero en e-fectivos.

- Ha difundido entre los activistas y pueblo en general la Declaración Universal de los Derechos Humanos proclamada en 1948.

- Ha participado en las misas ofrecidas en las distintas Iglesias de su provincia.

- Este Hermano ha sido detenido en reiteradas oportunidades por más de 72 horas en los años 96 y 97, recibiendo constantes amenazas por parte de los distintos Organos represivos del Gobierno.

Por todo lo antes expuesto es nuestro deber comunicarles y de ello somos testigos, que por sus ideales y actividades en defensa de los Derechos Humanos del Hombre es hostigado.

Dado en la Ciudad de la Habana, a los diecinueve días del mes de —Octubre de 1997.

Para su validéz y efectos posteriores, firman:

Odilia Collazo Valdés
Presidenta Nacional
P.P.D.H.C.

Cecilia Arza Collazo
Organizadora Nacional
P.P.D.H.C.

Horacio Casanoba C
Coordinador Nacional
P.P.D.H.C.

One of the endorsement letters written by Odilia Collazo, recommending the bearer for a U.S. visa, with its corresponding lies about "internal repression".

The national executive of our pacifist and humanitarian organization submits to you the following document, with the aim of detailing the career of our brother RAFAEL GARCÍA SUÁREZ, an active member of our organization since May 16, 1995.

Among the activities in defense of civil and human rights in which he has taken part, working for a truly free and democratic Cuba, he has:

- participated in the aid program for political prisoners and their families, contributing food, medicine, and money,
- distributed the Universal Declaration of Human Rights of 1948 among activists and the general public,
- participated in the masses held in different churches throughout his province.

On repeated occasions, in the years 1996 and 1997, he has been detained for periods exceeding 72 hours, receiving constant threats from the different repressive organs of the government.

Given everything hereto exposed, it is our duty to inform you, as witnesses, that as a result of his political ideals and his activities in defense of human rights, Mr. García Suárez is the subject of harassment by the Cuban government.

Issued in the City of Havana, on October 19, 1997.

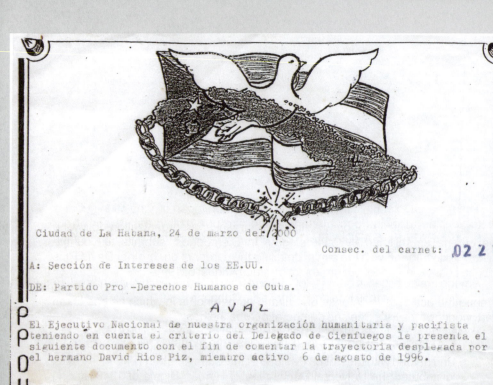

Ciudad de La Habana, 24 de marzo del 2000

Consec. del carnet: 0226

A: Sección de Intereses de los EE.UU.

DE: Partido Pro -Derechos Humanos de Cuba.

A V A L

El Ejecutivo Nacional de nuestra organización humanitaria y pacifista teniendo en cuenta el criterio del Delegado de Cienfuegos le presenta el siguiente documento con el fin de comentar la trayectoria desplegada por el hermano David Rios Piz, miembro activo 6 de agosto de 1996.

Entre las actividades que ha participado se encuentran las enmarcadas en la defensa de los Derechos Humanos y civiles del hombre.

Ha participado en el programa de ayuda a los presos políticos y ha ayudado en la Pastoral penitenciaria de la Iglesia católica.

Ha difundido entre los activistas y el pueblo en general la Delcaracion Universal de los Derechos Humanos.

Ha verificado y denunciado violaciones de los artículos de la Declaración Universal de los Derechos Humanos.

Fue separado de sus labores como trabajador por sus ideales políticos.

Por todo lo anteior es hostigado.

Dado en La Habana, a los 24 días del mes de marzo del 2000.

Presidente

Another "political" endorsement submitted by Odilia Collazo, recommending its bearer for a U.S. visa.

The national executive of our pacifist and humanitarian organization, following the criteria established by our delegate in Cienfuegos, submits to you the following document, with the aim of detailing the career of our brother David Rios Piz, an active member of our organization since August 6, 1996.

Among the activities in defense of civil and human rights in which he has taken part, working for a truly free and democratic Cuba, he has:

- participated in the aid program for political prisoners and their families and helped with the Prison Pastoral of the Catholic Church,
- distributed the Universal Declaration of Human Rights of 1948 among activists and the general public,
- verified and denounced the violation of articles of the Universal Declaration of Human Rights.

He has lost his job as a direct result of his political ideals.

Given everything hereto exposed, he is the subject of harassment.

Issued in the City of Havana, on March 24, 2000.

DENUNCIA DE VIOLACION DE DERECHOS HUMANOS

A OFICINA NACIONAL DE RECOPILACION E INFORMACION
DE VIOLACIONES DE DERECHOS HUMANOS
FAX-910557

Denuncia No _____

1- Quien cometio la violacio'n? _____

2- DE LA VICTIMA
Nombre y Apellidos _____
No de Identidad _____ Hijos _____ Nacionalidad _____ E.Civil _____
Ocupacio'n_____
Direccio'n Particular _____
_____

3- Violacio'n denunciada _____
_____
_____
_____
_____
_____
_____
_____
_____
_____
_____
_____
_____
_____
_____
_____
_____

Fecha _____ Lugar_____
_____
Testigos _____
Pruebas_____
4- Recursos agotados _____
5- Recursos por intentar _____
    Declaro que la informacio'n antes descrita es verdadera y correcta

6- DEL DENUNCIANTE
Nombre y Apellidos _____
No de Identidad_____ Fecha de formulacio'n de denuncia _____
Direccio'n Particular_____
_____ Telef_____

Lugar donde se redacta la denuncia _____
Afiliacio'n del denunciante _____

Firma del denunciante_____   (cualquier aclaracio'n anexa hacerlo al dorso)

Copy of a form used by "dissidents" to register a human rights violation in Cuba. The forms were designed and printed at the U.S. Interests Section.

Report on Human Rights Violations
National Office for the Gathering and Reporting
of Human Rights Violations

1. Who committed the violation?

2. Victim's full name:
ID Number: Children: Nationality: Marital Status:
Occupation:
Address:

3. Violation reported:

Date: Place:

Witnesses:

Evidence:

4. Appeals made:
5. Appeals to make:

I hereby declare that the information given above is accurate and true.

6. Informer's full name:
ID Number: Date on which the violation was registered:
Address: Phone Number:
Place where report was made:
Membership of the informer:
Signature of the informer:

Vicky Huddleston, head of the U.S. Interests Section, and Raúl Rivero, in the official residence of the U.S. diplomat.

Presentation of the book *Ojos Abiertos* (Open Eyes). Sitting at the table, from left to right: Victor Manuel Domínguez, Raúl Rivero and Gisela Delgado. To the right of them: Nicholas J. Giacobbe, James Cason (U.S. Interests Section) and the second secretary of the Swedish embassy, Fredick Floren, among others.

FUNDACIÓN

HISPANO CUBANA

D. Raúl Rivero Castañeda
Centro Habana (La Habana)
CUBA

Madrid, octubre de 2.002

Estimado amigo:

Me complace saludarle y dirigirme a Vd., en calidad de Patrono de nuestra Fundación, para comunicarle que, según consta en los archivos obrantes en el Registro de Fundaciones del Ministerio de Educación, Cultura y Deporte de España, recientemente ha caducado el plazo de vigencia de su cargo.

En este sentido, le rogamos se sirva efectuar las gestiones oportunas para proceder a su renovación, a fin de regularizar administrativamente su situación como miembro del Patronato de la Fundación Hispano Cubana.

Sobre este particular, le recordamos que, en virtud de lo dispuesto en el artículo 13.3 de la Ley española de Fundaciones,

"Los patronos entrarán a ejercer sus funciones después de haber aceptado expresamente el cargo en documento público, en documento privado con firma legitimada por notario o mediante comparecencia realizada al efecto en el Registro de Fundaciones. Dicha aceptación se inscribirá en el mencionado Registro."

por lo que le sugerimos que acuda al Consulado de la Embajada del Reino de España en La Habana con el documento adjunto firmado, a fin de que el Cónsul español -en cuanto fedatario público- legitime la referida firma y autentique el documento, con carácter previo a su remisión a esta Gerencia.

Quedando a su entera disposición para todo tipo de orientación al respecto, aprovecho la ocasión para enviarle cordiales saludos,

Atentamente,

Juan Morán
Director-Gerente

Renewal of Raúl Rivero's membership in the Board of Patrons of the Hispano-Cuban Foundation, an organization closely linked to the Cuban-American National Foundation.

Dear Friend,

I am pleased to extend my greetings to you, as a Patron of our Foundation, and to inform you that, according to the pertinent records in the Foundations Registry of the Ministry of Education, Culture and Sport of Spain, the validity of your membership has recently expired.

In this respect, we urge you to take the steps needed to renew your membership, so that we may once again legalize you as member of the Board of Patrons of the Hispano-Cuban Foundation.

Allow me to remind you that, according to article 13.3 of the Spanish Law on Foundations,

"The patrons will begin to exercise their duties only after having expressly accepted the post by means of a public document, a private document with a signature legalized by a notary, or in person at the Registry of Foundations. Said acceptance shall be inscribed in the aforementioned Registry."

We suggest that you visit the Consulate of the Embassy of Spain in Havana after signing the enclosed document, so that the Spanish consul may legalize your signature and authenticate the document, before remitting the document to our Office.

Should you have any doubts whatsoever with regards to this, I remain entirely at your disposal.

Sincerely,

Juan Morán
General Director

"El Heraldo" Contest
Independent Libraries of Cuba
Special Diploma
Granted to: Raúl Rivero Castañeda
As special recognition of his important work in the Independent Libraries of Cuba

"El Heraldo" Contest
Independent Libraries
Granted to: Raúl Rivero Castañeda
For his participation as member of the jury of this contest

The contest sponsored by the "Independent Libraries", the background to the book *Ojos Abiertos*.

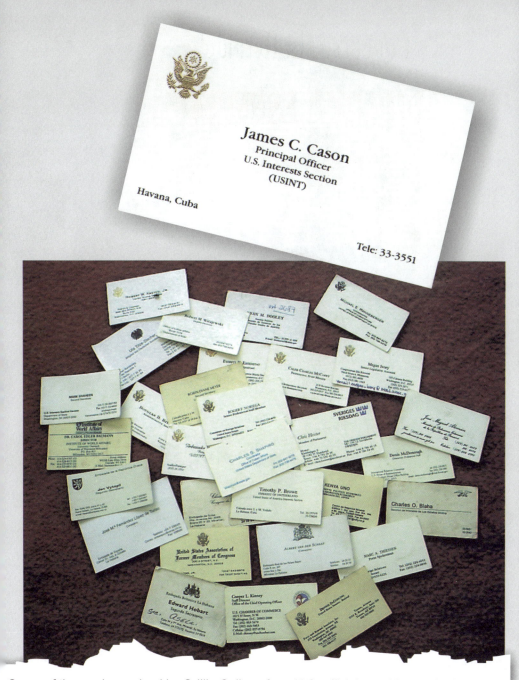

Some of the cards received by Odilia Collazo from U.S. officials working at the Interests Section (among them, that of James Cason), and from visitors from the United States and other countries whom she was instructed to meet with by the Interests Section.

At the home of U.S. Interests Section official Gonzalo Gallegos, Kevin Whitaker, head of the Cuba Desk of the U.S. State Department, meets with the mercenaries Rolando Arroyo, Gisela Delgado, Oscar Espinosa, and others. The meeting took place on December 18, 2002.

DIVISIÓN CUBAPACK
CORPORACIÓN CIMEX, S.A.
Calle 22 # 4115 % 41 y 47, Playa. Teléfonos 24 2134 y 24 2817

Servicio:	Mercado externo		Sello:	2200009670

Remitente:	FRANCISCO HERNANDEZ
Destinatario:	RAUL RIVERO
Dirección:	Calle: PEÑALVER entre FRANCOS Y OQUENDO Numero: 466 Apartamento: 9
Área:	Centro Habana Detalles: N/A

Agencia Mayorista:	ANTILLAS EXP. [IND]
Agencia Minorista:	ANTILLAS EXP. [IND]
Envio Mayorista:	M 22000204
Envio Minorista:	M 22000204
	Id Agencia: 105387

MODULOS

Código	Nombre	Cantidad	Importe
4	Modulo de Alimento 1	1	150

	Total:	150

ombre del distribuidor:		C.I. del cliente:
irma del distribuidor:		Firma del cliente:
echa de la entrega:		

Fecha: 28/03/03 Hora: 10:33:27 a.m.   Página 1 de 1

CUBAPACK DIVISION
Cimex Coorporation
Service: Foreign Commerce
Sent by: FRANCISCO HERNANDEZ
Sent to: RAUL RIVERO
Address: Calle PEÑALVER between Francos and Oquendo, #466, Apt: 9
Area: Centro Habana   Details: N/A

Code	Name	Quantity	Cost
4	Food hamper 1	1	150

MODULO DE ALIMENTO NO. 1
CODIGO:02010205
Noviembre/Enero 2002/2003

	U/M	Módulo no.1 Cantidad
Lata de luncheon de cerdo	425gr	4
Lata de perros calientes	225gr	2
Lata de jamón	454gr	2
Lata de chorizo en manteca	255g.	1
Lata de frutas en conserva	822g.	1
Puré de tomate	1000gr	1
Sardinas en aceite	425g.	1
Bolsa de leche en polvo	1000gr	1
Lata de leche evaporada	410gr	4
Lata de leche condensada	397gr	4
Pomo de mayonesa	470ml	1
Pomo de aceitunas	300gr	1
Aceite de cocina de Girasol	1lit.	4
Paquete de arroz	1000gr	4
Paquete de frijoles	500gr	2
Paquete de garbanzos	500gr	2
Paquete de espaguetis	400gr	5
Caldo de pollo o carne	10gr	100
Juego de especieros 6 tarros	1180gr	1
Paquete de café "Cubita"	230gr	1
Lata de fabada Asturiana	425gr	2
(se sustituyen por garbanzos)		
Paquete de macarrones	500gr	2
Lata de atún en aceite	1000gr	1
Lata de aceite de oliva	500ml	1
Lata de chocolate en polvo	800gr	1
Lata de salchichas	225g.	2
Ketchup	500g.	2
Paquete de fideos	400g.	2

Cubapack le obsequia una botella de sidra

Nota: Los productos establecidos para este tipo de módulo si fuera necesario sustituirlos se hará respetando el peso, calidad y precio del producto sustituido.

FOOD HAMPER No 1

CODE: 02010205
November/January 2002/2003

	Amt.	Quantity

Can pork luncheon meat
Can weiners
Can ham
Can chorizo
Can fruit cocktail
Tomato paste
Sardines
Bag powdered milk
Can evaporated milk
Can condensed milk
Jar mayonnaise
Jar olives
Sunflower seed oil
Package rice
Package beans
Package chick peas
Package spaghetti
Chicken or beef bouillon
Set of 6 jars assorted spices
Package "Cubita" coffee
Can Asturian bean soup
(Replaced with chick peas)
Package macaroni
Can tuna
Can olive oil
Can chocolate powder
Can sausages
Ketchup
Package noodles
Cubapack includes a complementary bottle of cider.

Note: Any replacements necessary will be of the same
        weight, quality and price of the original product.

Celebrating: René Gómez Manzano, Martha Beatriz Roque, Félix Bonne, Raúl Rivero and Elizardo Sánchez.

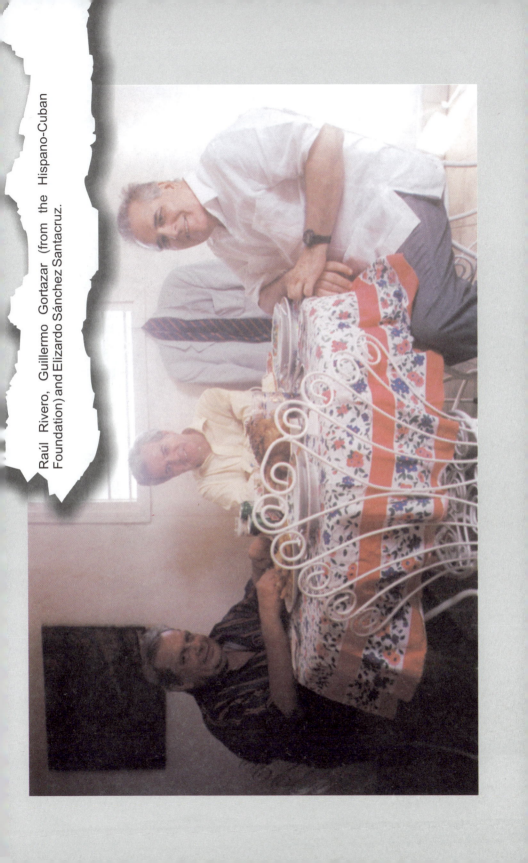

Raúl Rivero, Guillermo Gortázar (from the Hispano–Cuban Foundation) and Elizardo Sánchez Santacruz.

Oswaldo Payá, in Varadero, enjoying the money from his "awards".

A sequence, taken during his "discreet" vacation.

EMBAJADA DE SUIZA
SECCION DE INTERESES
ESTADOS UNIDOS DE AMERICA
SECCION CONSULAR

P A S E

UNIDAD: _____CONS_____

NOMBRE(S) Y APELLIDOS:

_____Oswaldo Payá_____

_____Antonio Díaz_____

CANTIDAD DE PERSONAS: _2_

FECHA: _abierta_

HORA : _abierta_

FIRMA: _____

Permanent pass given to Oswaldo Payá, granting access to the U.S. Interests Section. He may be accompanied by two other parties, on any day and time.

THE "DIPLOMACY" OF JAMES CASON

Chronological list of the activities of the Principal Officer of the United States Interests Section in Cuba (from September 10, 2002 to March 14, 2003)

2002

September 10:
He arrived in Havana at 3:30 p.m. He was received at José Martí International Airport by the Deputy Principal Officer of the Interests Section, Louis Nigro. During the welcoming ceremony, at 4:40 p.m. that same day, he announced to his employees that the aim of his mission was to accelerate the transitional process towards a democratic Cuba, and exhorted them to support anyone working toward that transition.

September 16:
Between 6:00 p.m. and 8:00 p.m., he held a meeting in his home with 17 counterrevolutionary leaders: Oswaldo José Payá Sardiñas (Christian Liberation Movement, Movimiento Cristiano de Liberación);

Héctor Palacios Ruiz (Center for Social Studies, Centro de Estudios Sociales); Gisela Delgado Sablón (Independent Libraries Project, Proyecto de Bibliotecas Independientes); Gustavo Arcos Bergnes (Cuban Human Rights Committee, Comité Cubano Pro Derechos Humanos); Víctor Rolando Arroyo Carmona ("Independent Journalist"); Raúl Rivero Castañeda (Cuba Free Press Agency); Félix Antonio Bonne Carcassés (Cuban Civic Current, Corriente Cívica Cubana); Juan Carlos Herrera (Young Democrats Movement, Movimiento de Jóvenes Democráticos), Rafael Ernesto Ávila Pérez (Young Cuba People's Party, Partido Popular Joven Cuba); Julio Ruiz Pitaluga (former counterrevolutionary prisoner); Pedro Pablo Álvarez Ramos (United Council of Cuban Workers, Consejo Unitario de Trabajadores de Cuba); Vladimiro Roca Antúnez (Social Democratic Party of Cuba, Partido Social Demócrata de Cuba); Osvaldo Alfonso Valdés (Cuban Liberal Democratic Party, Partido Liberal Democrático Cubano); Martha Beatriz Roque Cabello (Manuel Sanchez Herrero Institute of "Independent Economists", Instituto de Economistas Independientes Manuel Sánchez Herrero); Odilia Collazo Valdés (Cuban Human Rights Party, Partido Cubano Pro Derechos Humanos); René Gómez Manzano (Agramonte Union of Cuba, Unión Agramontista de Cuba); and Reynaldo Cosano Alen (Cuban Democratic Coalition, Coalición Democrática Cubana).

Also present were the Interests Section officials Louis Nigro, Deputy Principal Officer; Gonzalo Gallegos, Public Affairs Officer; Ricardo Zuniga, Deputy Political/Economic Chief; Francisco Sainz, Political/Economic Chief; and Susan Archer, Deputy Political/Economic Chief.

Cason expressed that his intention was neither to instruct nor lead the activities of the opposition, but rather to work toward implementing the policy announced by President George W. Bush. He asked what he could do to help the "opposition" and how beneficial the assistance provided by his office had been to that moment.

He declared that he was willing to grant access to both his home and the U.S. Interests Section headquarters to facilitate the meetings of "dissident" activists with diplomats from different countries. Félix Bonne Carcassés and René Gómez Manzano told him that no other diplomatic mission attended them the way this one did.

The head of the Interests Section expressed that he would continue with the work of his predecessor, and that he was planning a tour through the country to get to know, up close, the situation of the "opposition" groups. He also wished to take part in political activities, such as the Public Forums (Tribunas Abiertas), and to exhibit, in the offices of the consulate, the photographs and names of so-called political prisoners, so that visitors would see them and become aware of their situation.

He added that no proposal put forth by the "opposition" would be ignored, and that all of their concerns would be passed on to Washington.

At the end of the meeting, the participants were offered soft drinks, mojitos, steak sandwiches and ground beef turnovers.

The participants were also given copies of a book entitled *Martí Secreto* (The Secret Martí), containing 51 allegedly new reflections of the National Hero and contradicting the dictionary on José Martí recently published in Cuba by the Editorial de Ciencias Sociales. All visitors received white and yellow envelopes which had been previously marked with the names of participants. The counterrevolutionaries were finally taken to their homes in Interests Section vehicles.

September 17:
Between 6:00 p.m. and 8:00 p.m., Cason met with 18 mercenary counterrevolutionaries in his home, all of them involved with the "independent press": Manuel Vázquez Portal (Decorum Work Group, Grupo de Trabajo Decoro); Carmelo Díaz Fernández (Independent Trade Union Press Agency, Agencia de Prensa Sindical Independiente); Oscar Espinosa Chepe ("Independent" Economist); Miriam Leyva Viamontes (wife of Espinosa Chepe); Gilberto Figueredo Álvarez (*Cartas de Cuba* magazine); Manuel David Orrio del Rosario ("Independent" Journalists Cooperative,

Cooperativa de Periodistas Independientes); Luis García Vega ("Independent Journalists Cooperative"); Julio César Gálvez Rodríguez (Cuban Civic Press Agency, Agencia de Prensa Cívica Cubana); Beatriz Pedroso León (Cuban Civic Press Agency); Edel J. García Díaz (Centro Norte Press); Aleida Godínez Soler (Lux Info Press); Alicia Zamora Labrada (Lux Info Press); Claudia Márquez Linares (Decorum Work Group); Ángel P. Polanco Torrejón (Noticuba); Ángela Salinas Battle (wife of Polanco); Tania Quintero Antúnez ("Independent Journalist"); Omar Rodriguéz Saludes (New Press Agency, Agencia Nueva Prensa); and Ricardo S. González Alfonso (Manuel Márquez Sterling Journalists Society).

The Interests Section officials in attendance were Louis Nigro, Francisco Sainz, Gonzalo Gallegos, Ricardo Zuniga, Nicholas J. Giacobbe and Teddy Taylor, along with Cason's wife.

The meeting, whose principal aim was to introduce the counterrevolutionaries and to converse about issues of interest to the head of the Interests Section, was held in Cason's home library. Gonzalo Gallegos, the Public Affairs Officer at the Interests Section, served as moderator.

The participants spoke about Radio *"Martí"* and the "independent" libraries and press. Radio *"Martí"* was thought to be boring, and the interventions of counterrevolutionaries — who have limited their participation to soliciting material and financial aid — unnecessarily long.

The participants were offered sandwiches, turnovers, soft drinks, natural fruit juices and Cuban cocktails, which were served by the American officials, including Cason's wife.

At the end of the meeting, the guests were given copies of the "Varela" Project, *Cartas de Cuba* magazine, Amnesty International reports on human rights "violations" in Cuba, and the book by counterrevolutionary Hubert Matos, *Cómo Llegó la Noche* (How the Night Came). Also offered were the books *Escritos Cubanos de Historia* (Cuban Historical Writings), *Martí Secreto* (The Secret Martí), and *El Descubrimiento de África en Cuba y Brasil* (The Discovery of Africa in Cuba and Brazil), by Argentine writer Octavio di Leo.

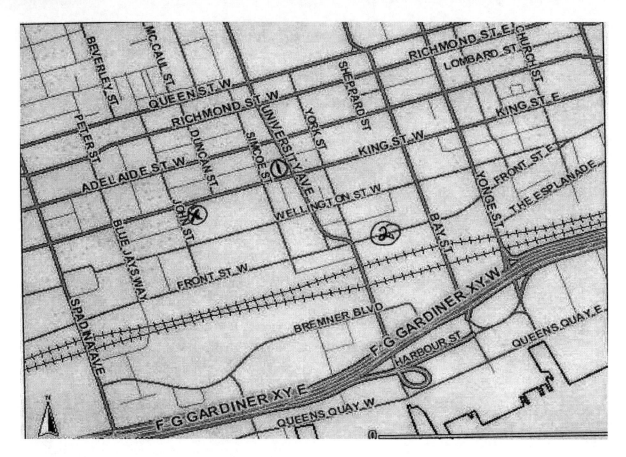

1 – St .Andrew Subway station (on University Line)
2 – Union Subway station (where University & Yonge line meet)
X – Metro Hall   55 John St / rooms 308-large hall & registration, 307-displays & coffee
and workshop rooms

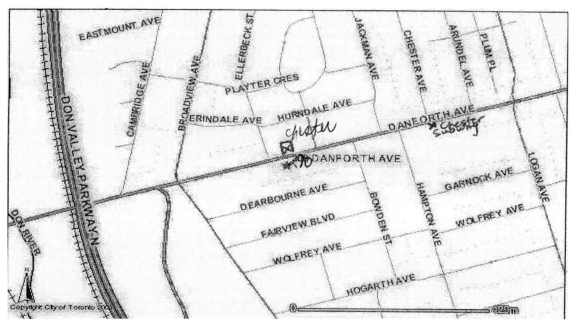

SUNDAY: To go the restaurants on the Danforth to eat supper & then return to 299 Danforth at 7pm
to attend the Convention Fiesta!   Live entertainment & cash bar for beer, wine, empanadas and
banana chips plus a $10 cover charge to help cover costs.
        Corner of John & King – go right along King St W to St. Andrew Subway.
Take subway train north to St. George Station. Use the stair/escalator to reach other level to catch the
Bloor/Danforth Line – take the train going east to the Chester Subway station.

SATURDAY – Reception **and meal** at the Residence of the Consul General of Cuba
46 Keane Ave.   7:30pm

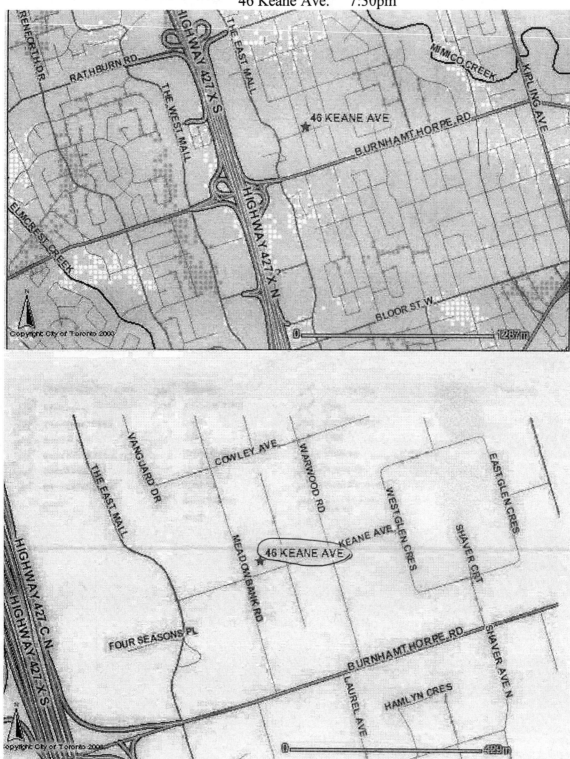

Corner of John & King – go right along King St W to St. Andrew Subway.
Take subway train north to St. George Station. Use the stair/escalator to reach other level to catch the
Bloor Line – take the train west to end of line – Kipling Subway station. Follow the signs to the Kiss &
Ride section. There you will be picked up & taken to the Consulate's residence at 46 Keane. And
afterwards returned to the subway station. [Ask for directions to get to the place that you are staying]
Those who are attending with their billeting hosts can leave with them.

October 19:
Cason visits the province of Cienfuegos. He was accompanied by Carmen Cason, his wife, and by Ricardo Zuniga. They arrived in the provincial capital at around 10:40 a.m. and toured the city until 11:00 a.m., when they visited the bishopric.

A short time later, they paid a visit to the home of the provincial leader of the Democracy Movement (Movimiento Democrácia), Pedro Castellanos Pérez, whom they asked numerous questions: When and how did he join the "opposition"? How is he able to transmit denunciations, is he called from abroad or is he responsible for doing this? How does he think the government will respond should it find out about this visit?

Next, they head to the home of Arturo Hernández (who is also linked to the Democracy Movement in Cienfuegos). They visit his "independent" library, which is located in his own home, and have lunch with both counterrevolutionaries. The conversation centers on the "independent" libraries, the rental of houses, entertainment for young people, the food situation on the island, and the people's reaction to these difficulties.

The officials address the issue of health. They claim that the Cuban government exports or capitalizes on medical services, alluding to the Cuban medical aid missions around the world.

They donate 20 radios, with their respective accessories, a rechargeable lamp, a number of flashlights, a pocket tape recorder, office materials, toys and a number of books, including some for learning English.

Cason invites the "dissidents" to visit Havana and dine at his home, in order to give them other books. They leave Cienfuegos at approximately 4:20 p.m.

October 30:
Cason receives 26 counterrevolutionaries in his home: Martha Beatriz Roque (Institute of "Independent" Economists of Cuba, Instituto de Economistas Independientes de Cuba); René Gómez Manzano (Agramonte Union of Cuba, Unión Agromontista de Cuba); Félix Bonne Carcassés (Cuban Civic Current, Corriente

Cívica Cubana); Arnaldo Ramos Laucerique (Institute of Independent Economists of Cuba); Francisco Pijuán (Institute of Independent Economists of Cuba); Jesús Zúñiga Silverio ("Independent Journalists" Foundation, Fundacion de Periodistas Independientes); María del Carmen Carro Gómez (Cuba Press); Edel José García Díaz ("Independent" Press Agency); Ramón H. Armas Guerrero (El Mayor Press Agency, from Camagüey); Néstor Baguer Sánchez Galarraga ("Independent" Press Agency of Cuba); Luis Viño Zimerman ("Independent" Press Agency of Cuba); Manuel David Orrio del Rosario ("Independent" Journalists Cooperative); Antonio Femenias Echemendía (Patria Press Agency, Ciego de Ávila); José M. Caraballo Bravo (Free Press Agency of Ciego de Ávila, Agencia Prensa "Libre" Avileña); Farah Armenteros Rodríguez (Union of "Independent" Cuban Writers and Journalists); Angel Pablo Polanco Torrejón (Noticuba); Mayelín Cedeño Constantín (Center of Information on Democracy, Centro de Informacion sobre la Democracia); Orlando Fundora Álvarez (Political Prisoners Association, Asociación de Presos Politicos); Fabio Prieto Llorente (Isla de Pinos Press Agency); Pedro Argüelles Morán ("Independent" Journalists Cooperative of Ciego de Ávila); Alina Rodríguez Carbonell (Santiago Press Agency); Alicia Zamora Labrada (Lux Info Press); Normando Hernández González ("Independent" Journalists College of Camagüey, Colegio de Periodistas "Independientes" de Camagüey); Amarilys Cortina Rey (Cuba Truth, Cuba Verdad); and Guillermo Gutiérrez and José Antonio González (Martha Beatriz' drivers).

They were there for a work meeting on the project known as the Assembly to Promote Civil Society in Cuba, organized and promoted by Martha Beatriz Roque. It began at 2:10 p.m. and lasted until 4:30 p.m. Seven officials from the Interests Section were present, Ricardo Zuniga, Nicholas Giacobbe and Susan Archer among them.

Cason welcomed the participants and said he was aware of the difficulties they had in meeting, which is why he offered his home to facilitate the gathering. He assured them that they could count on his material as well as moral support, as it was the aim of the United States government to bring "democracy" to the island. He regretted not being able to join them, due to other obligations at the Interests Section. The other officials remained at the meeting, as observers.

The officials served them coffee, lemonade and chicken, and handed each participant two bags containing radios, *Cubanet* pamphlets, two *Cartas de Cuba* magazines, the Universal Declaration of Human Rights, the book *La Conquista de la Naturaleza* (The Conquest of Nature), by Sergio Díaz, which presents a revisionist analysis of Cuban socialism, and various works by Carlos Ripoll.

November 2:
Cason and Ricardo Zuniga travel to Matanzas to visit the home of Félix Navarro Rodriguez, president of the Pedro Luis Boitel Democracy Party (Partido por la Democracia Pedro Luis Boitel). They were awaited there by Iván Hernández Carrillo, Tomás Fernández Tier, Sergio González Suárez Inclán and another 22 members of this group. Cason spoke of the virtues of the "Varela" Project and interviewed those present to gauge the acceptance and social impact of Oswaldo Payá's group. He was also interested in knowing the attention paid them by groups in Havana and abroad.

He mentioned he was touring the entire country in order to hear and see the true Cuban reality, not the version of reality promoted by the Cuban government. He felt that the diplomatic corps in Havana had a false conception of various aspects of life in Cuba. At the end of the meeting, he handed over four boxes of books, to furnish the "independent" libraries of Iván Hernández in the Colón municipality, Miguel Sigler Amaya in Pedro Betancourt, and Andrés Gobea Suárez at Central 6 de Agosto, in Calimete.

November 11:
A meeting with a delegation of 18 American activists who work in defense of black people's human rights. The meeting, which lasted approximately two hours, was held in Cason's home, and was attended by Oswaldo Payá Sardiñas, Osvaldo Alfonso Valdés,

Vladmiro Roca Antúnez, Oscar Elías Biscet González, and the latter's wife, Elsa Morejón Hernández.

In addition to the head of the Interests Section, officials Ricardo Zuniga and Gonzalo Gallegos were also present.

The aim was to promote the "Varela" and Everyone United (Todos Unidos) Projects, as well as to introduce the "opposition" members and the activities they carry out in our country.

At the end of the meeting, the diplomats presented the Cubans in attendance with two short-wave radios and a number of books; they were told by Ricardo Zuniga that they could take any books they wished from a bookcase set up for this purpose.

Lemonade, mojitos, crackers with ham, guacamole and fried plantain chips were offered during the gathering.

November 21:

Martha Beatriz Roque, promoter of the Assembly to Promote Civil Society in Cuba, called another meeting of her work group in Cason's home. The members of the Public Relations and Coordination and Organization Commissions made up the bulk of the Cuban participants; the American participants were Cason and Ricardo Zuniga.

The meeting began at 2:00 p.m. The diplomats were interested in meeting the members of the so-called Assembly, who presented them with letters of congratulations for the Republican Party's victory in recent state elections in the United States.

The hosts wanted to verify whether short and medium-wave radios were sold in dollar stores in Cuba.

Martha Beatriz asked the U.S. diplomats to contact the head of the United Nations Organization in Cuba, Luis Gómez Echevarría, to solicit a locale where they could celebrate their Human Rights Day on December 10. She complained that the official had refused to meet with her. Ricardo Zuniga said that, although he didn't know this official personally, he would help her get in touch with him to arrange to hold the activity there.

The diplomatic officials gave the participants four boxes containing copies of the Universal Declaration of Human Rights. James Cason asked them to gather photographs of "political" prisoners through the Assembly's History Commission, so as to exhibit them on what he termed the "Wall of Shame" located in the Interests Section.

The head of the Interests Section told them that in January of 2003, an official delegation of American doctors would visit Cuba, with the aim of meeting with those present.

The participants in the meeting were René Gómez Manzano, Félix Antonio Bonne Carcassés, Arnaldo Ramos Laucerique, Francisco Pijuán, Aleida Godínez Soler, Alicia Zamora Labrada, Rogelio Manuel Menéndez Díaz, María Valdés Rosado, Carlos Prades Herrera, Fernando Sánchez López, Yamira Jiménez and Juan Adolfo Fernández Sainz.

November 22:
From 10:20 a.m. until 11:45 a.m., counterrevolutionaries Orlando Fundora Álvarez, Yolanda Triana Estupiñán, José Barrero Vargas (Political Prisoners Association), Israel Picallo Ortiz ("Independent" Press Agency of Cuba), and another four unidentified people met in Cason's home.

They were welcomed by Rebeca Tobey, the wife of consul Laurence Tobey, who ushered them to a drawing room and offered them ham and cheese sandwiches, grapefruit juice, turnovers, coffee and milk. At the end of the meeting, she gave them a number of books and newspapers published abroad.

The meeting was called by Orlando Fundora to ask those invited, with Cason's permission, to gather information on people who had been allegedly harmed by the Revolution. The aim was to promote a legal action that would force the Cuban government to compensate those individuals and their families.

November 26:
Cason visits Camagüey. At 1:30 p.m., Cason knocked on the door of Alberto Hernández Frómeta's home. He was accompanied by Francisco Daniel Sainz. He was awaited there by Evelio Heredero, Eduardo Cedeño, José Antonio and someone known as Alexis, who claimed to be a cooperative member from the Sierra de Cubitas municipality. Frómeta's wife was also present.

Cason was interested in the following issues: the general public opinion in the province on the country's situation; the province's economic situation; the unemployment level in the province; how people managed to make ends meet if their salaries were insufficient (he proposed that a small, local survey be organized, to determine the unemployment levels in the province); general interest in the situation of "political" prisoners in the province, their numbers, means of communication with them, whether conditions in the prisons had improved, how they managed to get information out of the jails, and the response of the jail system; the support offered by the Catholic church and other churches to "dissidents" in the province, and whether they backed the "opposition"; the attitude of the masons with respect to the situation in the country; if the "opposition" groups in the province were united and gave each other mutual support; if the "dissidents" had grown stronger in the province in recent times; what level of repression was being exercised by the "Castro dictatorship" against the "dissidents", and whether this persecution was extended to their children as well. He inquired about the welfare of counterrevolutionary Humberto Real Suárez, given a life sentence, and the other members of the infiltration team that entered Cuba through Caibarién, as well as those jailed for acts of sabotage, whom he called "political" prisoners (he had a list of 16 names). He also asked those present if they considered the possibility that changes could be brought about; if they knew what had taken place at the University of Camagüey with members of the "opposition"; if officials from the U.S. Interests Section or any other embassy had ever visited their homes; if the group was receiving financial aid; and if they received medication sent from Miami by Frank Hernández Trujillo.

During the exchange held with the participants, the following was proposed:

To devote more financial resources to the cause of the alleged "political" prisoners, and to make photographs of prisoners available to the Interests Section, to be exhibited in its gallery; that the U.S. Interests Section would give them a video camera to film testimonies from the families of these prisoners.

In response to Frómeta's request for pens and paper, the officials said they could offer none at the time, but invited them to retrieve a number of boxes (four) from their car, containing pamphlets, books and newspapers.

December 19:

A "social" gathering held at the U.S. Interests Section. It lasted approximately two and a half hours. It was attended by James Cason and another 12 Interests Section officials, 10 diplomatic representatives of the embassies of the United Kingdom, the Czech Republic, Poland, Greece, Chile, Germany and Japan and 52 counterrevolutionaries from different groups: Victor Rolando Arroyo Carmona (an "independent" journalist from Pinar del Río); Pedro Pablo Álvarez Ramos (United Council of Cuban Workers); Aleida Godínez Soler; Alicia Zamora Labrada; Carmelo Agustín Díaz Fernández; Giraldo León; Juan Padrón; Arnaldo Pijuán Martínez; Odilia Collazo Valdés; Isabel del Pino Sotolongo; Reynaldo Cosano Alen; Félix Bonne Carcassés; René Gómez Manzano; Elizardo Sánchez Santacruz Pacheco; Marcelo Cano; Héctor Palacios Ruiz; Gisela Delgado Sablón; Gustavo Arcos Bergnes; Félix Navarro Rodríguez; Iván Hernández Carrillo; Jorge Olivera Castillo; Raúl Rivero Castañeda; Manuel David Orrio del Rosario; Julio César Gálvez Rodríguez; Beatriz del Carmen Pedroso León; Tania Quintero Antúnez; María de los Ángeles Menéndez Villalta; Miriam Leyva Viamontes; Oscar Espinosa Chepe; Ángel Pablo Polanco Torrejón; Ángela de las Mercedes Salinas Batle, wife of Ángel Polanco; Vladimiro Roca Antúnez; Ricardo González Alfonso; Osvaldo Alfonso Valdés; Claudia Márquez Linares; Manuel Vázquez Portal; an unknown counterrevolutionary from the Isle of Youth; Edel José García Díaz; Luis García Vega; Héctor Maceda Gutiérrez; Moisés Rodríguez Valdés; Ernesto Roque Cintero; Ana Rosa Veitía; Pedro Arturo Véliz; William Herrera Díaz; Adolfo Fernández Sainz and Elsa Morejón Hernández.

The meeting began without recourse to formalities as on previous occasions. No words of welcome or farewell were spoken, and each participant walked discreetly into the diplomatic venue where the reception was being held. They were free to eat and drink the food and beverages there, with no restrictions placed upon them, and to converse just as freely amongst themselves.

At the end of the meeting, each guest was given a bag containing the following items: three VHS tapes, with the three parts of *Una Fuerza Poderosa* (A Powerful Force); the digital version of the book *Cómo Llegó la Noche* (How Night Fell), by the terrorist Hubert Matos; *Temas Clásicos* (Classic Themes), by the counterrevolutionary Carlos Franqui; the Universal Declaration of Human Rights and a portable radio with accessories.

2003

January 9:

A trip to Pinar del Río had been planned. Cason was to travel with a group of officials from the Interests Section, but the Cuban Ministry of Foreign Relations denied authorization for the visit. Regardless, at 1:50 p.m., a white station wagon with license plate number E(201)031, carrying two Cuban citizens and traveling on the Seis Vías highway toward Pinar del Río, is seen to turn onto the bridge at Las Ovas, headed toward the city.

—3:32 p.m.

They park outside the bishopric of Pinar del Río. The driver delivers a cardboard box and two packages. Dagoberto Valdés was inside the bishopric when the visit took place.

—3:45 p.m.

A cardboard box is delivered to a private residence, with material to furnish the "independent" libraries of Reynaldo Núñez Vargas – known as the Ileana Ros-Lehtinen Library — and of René Oñate. They delivered 1,000 copies of the Universal Declaration of Human Rights, 50 books and two thousand sheets of paper.

—4:12 p.m.

The car stops outside the home of counterrevolutionary Víctor Rolando Arroyo Carmona's mother. They unload a medium-sized box. They delivered 1000 copies of the Universal Declaration of Human Rights, 60 books and one thousand sheets of paper.

January 16:

Cason takes part in an activity held at Héctor Palacios Ruiz's home to present the book *Ojos Abiertos* (Open Eyes), an expressly counterrevolutionary work which gathers some of the award-receiving pieces from the *El Heraldo* contest for the so-called "independent" libraries. Twenty-three "dissidents" attended the activity: Elizardo Sánchez Santacruz Pacheco; Vladimiro Roca Antúnez; Osvaldo Alfonso Valdés; Claudia Márquez Linares; Raúl Rivero Castañeda; Blanca Reyes Castañón; Félix Bonne Carcassés; Ricardo González Alfonso; Omar Rodríguez Saludes; Diana Margarita Cantón; Isabel Ramos Martínez; Héctor Palacios Ruiz; Gisela Delgado Sablón; Adela Soto Álvarez; Jorge Olivera Castillo; Víctor Manuel Domínguez García; Miguel Galván Gutiérrez; Pedro Pablo Álvarez Ramos; Oscar Espinosa Chepe; Juan Padrón; Gustavo Arcos Bergnes; María de los Ángeles Menéndez Villalta and officials from the accredited diplomatic corps in Cuba. Three Swedish emissaries who were visiting our country, as well as a CNN representative, also attended.

The presentation, which began at 3:00 p.m., was organized by Rivero Castañeda, Gisela Delgado Sablón, Víctor Manuel Domínguez García and Hugo Araña.

January 20-23:

A tour through Santiago de Cuba. James Cason and Ricardo Zuniga visited the homes of four leaders of counterrevolutionary groups, and met with a total of 18 individuals, including nine group leaders, three representatives of the so-called "independent" libraries and press, and six active members of the following groups: Christian Liberation Movement (Movimiento Cristiano de Liberación), Voice of the East Press Agency (Agencia de Prensa La Voz de Oriente), Independent Libraries Project (Proyecto de Bibliotecas Independientes), Transition to Democracy Group (Junta de Transición a la Demócracia), Followers of Chibás Movement (Movimiento de Seguidores de Chibás) and Carlos Manuel de Céspedes Group (Junta Carlos Manuel de Céspedes).

During their meetings, Cason and Zuniga said that the Spanish embassy had recently received a container with more than 5,000 books that would be distributed throughout the country; that Cason's trips throughout the island, and all of his movements, had to be coordinated with the Ministry of Foreign Relations, reporting the time, date, place, and route to this ministry, or otherwise these trips could not be undertaken, which is the reason why they established the same regulation in the United States; that the U.S. officials needed to know the present situation of the "opposition" to be able to offer aid; and that they were satisfied and impressed with the great amount of propaganda posted on the inner and outer walls of the home of "dissident" Jesús Mustafá Felipe (a member of the counterrevolutionary group Christian Liberation Movement), since this was a clear indication that the group is working.

Cason made offensive remarks about President Fidel Castro and mentioned the expulsion of four Cuban diplomats in Washington. He offered the use of his own home for anything they needed and instructed the participants to carry out acts of civil disobedience. They delivered four boxes of books, radios, crayons, pens, toothpaste and toothbrushes, office materials and subversive pamphlets.

February 2:
Cason held a "Cuban cultural evening", which was attended by representatives of the accredited diplomatic corps in Havana, members of the foreign press, representatives of the Cuban cultural sector, and a select group of counterrevolutionaries. Also present were representatives of U.S. businessmen based in Washington and other Americans who attended the Havana International Book Fair.

Among the counterrevolutionaries present were Elizardo Sánchez Santacruz, Oswaldo Payá Sardiñas, Vladimiro Roca Antúnez, René Gómez Manzano, Martha Beatriz Roque, Gustavo Arcos Bergnes, Félix Bonne Carcassés, Oscar Espinosa Chepe, Pedro Véliz and Odilia Collazo Valdés.

February 7:
A reception is held, attended by representatives of the Cuban cultural sector, members of the accredited diplomatic corps in Ha-

vana, and 21 counterrevolutionaries: Elsa Morejón Hernández, Vladimiro Roca Antúnez, Elizardo Sánchez Santacruz, Martha Beatriz Roque, Félix Bonne Carcassés, René Gómez Manzano, Oswaldo Payá Sardiñas, Osvaldo Alfonso Valdés, Manuel David Orrio del Rosario, Luis García Vega, Julio César Gálvez, Beatriz del Carmen Pedroso León, Odilia Collazo Valdés, María de los Ángeles Menéndez Villalta, Arnaldo Ramos Lauzerique, Oscar Espinosa Chepe, Miriam Leyva Viamontes, Claudia Márquez Linares, Marcelo Cano Rodríguez, Francisco Pijuán Martínez and Pedro Véliz Martínez.

The activity was of an informal nature. Sausage rolls, pizza, soft drinks, pastries, mixed drinks, rum, beer and juice were offered.

February 24:

Between 10:00 a.m. and 11:00 a.m., the 24th of February was commemorated at the home of Martha Beatriz Roque. Forty-four people participated, including U.S. diplomats James Cason, Ricardo Zuniga and Gonzalo Gallegos, seven representatives of foreign press agencies, and 34 members of counterrevolutionary groups: Martha Beatriz Roque, René Gómez Manzano, Félix Bonne Carcassés, Manuel S. Cuesta Morúa, Juan C. Linares Balmaseda, Noris Durán Durán, Isabel Ramos Martínez, William Toledo Terrero, Raimundo Jorge Martínez, Elsa Morejón Hernández, Nelson Aguiar Ramírez, Delia Leal Francisco, Fernando Sánchez López, Adolfo Fernández Sainz, Ángel P. Polanco Torrejón, Ismael Salazar Agüero, Tania Quintero Antúnez, Alicia Zamora, Nelson Molinet Espino, Belkis Bárzaga, José A. Gónzalez Torriente, Manuel D. Orrio del Rosario, Jesús García Leyva, Nelson Vázquez Obregón, Edel J. García Díaz, Yamira R. Jiménez Casal, Frank Delgado Macías, Manuel León Paneque, Manuel Fernández Rocha, Mijail Bárzaga Lugo, Armando Barreras, Marcos González, Orlando Rubio and Carlos Grandal.

The meeting was started by Martha Beatriz, who thanked the foreign press and the officials from the U.S. Interests Section for their presence, and regretted the absence of the European diplomats she had invited.

She explained that the meeting was held to celebrate the 108th anniversary of the War of Independence, as well as the anniversaries of the downing of the planes belonging to the organization Brothers to the Rescue (Hermanos al Rescate) and of the Cuban Council.

Without prior announcement, the head of the U.S. Interests Section, James Cason, offered a sort of press conference to the foreign and "independent" journalists present, where he affirmed that: "the revolution towards democracy is underway, and we want you to know you are not alone, that the whole world supports you." On being asked by a journalist about the possibility that the Cuban government could interpret his participation in the activity as an unfriendly gesture, the head of the Interests Section answered that "he was not afraid."

March 4:

Cason visits the province of Pinar del Río. He was accompanied by Ricardo Zuniga and Nicholas Joseph Giacobbe. In the morning they visited the bishopric, where they delivered two packages of paper, and the home of counterrevolutionary Víctor Rolando Arroyo Carmona's mother, where they delivered nine cardboard boxes and a package.

After having lunch in a *paladar* (privately run restaurant), they returned to Arroyo Carmona's mother's home and then went with him to his own home. Here they met with another 10 counterrevolutionaries previously summoned.

The meeting began at 1:30 p.m. Cason spoke of his experiences during his tours through the central and eastern regions of the island. He mentioned that Fidel was now touring Asian countries that perpetuate socialism in their own way, which made him suspect that he might alter his policies on returning from those countries.

He urged those present to seek aid at other diplomatic missions (without indicating which), "because the will to aid and support you exists, and you are not taking advantage of it."

He mentioned how he recognizes that the Cuban government is coherent in some respects: for instance, the flexibility it shows in allowing the Interests Section and its guests to meet counter-revolutionary groups. He cited the examples of the visit paid to Oswaldo Payá by two congresspeople and his personal relationship with Martha Beatriz Roque, although a container of books was seized on one occasion.

He was also interested in their use of the Internet, their contacts with their "brothers in exile", and the number of young people who spoke the English language. Once again, he touched on the changes that the Cuban president could bring about on returning from China.

He was concerned about the different projects being undertaken at the moment, the medical supplies being received, and the work carried out by the Dissidence Support Group (Grupo de Apoyo a la Disidencia, GAD). He also asked for a list of the medicines most urgently needed in the country. He mentioned that a more severe crisis was nearing for Cuba, and that his government was circulating a document claiming that millions of dollars were invested by the former Soviet Union and no one knows what they were used for. He spoke of long-distance education courses offered to "opposition" members through the Internet and of human rights issues. He concluded by saying that radios and other work supplies would continue to be sent.

At the end of the meeting, they distributed a box of books among those present and took a group picture.

Afterwards, accompanied Víctor Arroyo and the painter René Oñate Sixto, they headed to the home of the latter, where they took photographs of some his works. They returned to Havana at 3:30 p.m.

March 12:
Orlando Fundora Álvarez and other members of his group visited the home of head of the Interests Section to discuss the status of the project known as "I Demand" (Yo Demando). They were there from 11:00 a.m. until 4:00 p.m.

The meeting was held at the apartment adjacent to the home of the American diplomat, and they were received by Rebeca Tobey, wife of the consul Laurence Tobey.

The activity began with a presentation by "independent" journalist Israel Picallo Ortiz, who explained in detail what the aforementioned project consisted of. Forms were handed out to gather signatures in support of the project.

The American limited herself to listening in on the meeting and gave each of them two books, one on Cuban history and another on the Constitution of 1940, as well as a portable short-wave radio. Natural fruit juices were served.

At the end of the meeting, the participants were clearly un happy unsatisfied with the treatment they had received. They complained that no official from the Interests Section had attended the meeting, and that only juice had been offered despite the remoteness of the meeting place; they had apparently expected to be served lunch.

March 14:

A Workshop on Journalistic Ethics, promoted by Manuel David Orrio and Martha Beatriz Roque, was held at the home of James Cason. Thirty-four counterrevolutionaries linked to the so-called "independent" press were present, as well as 21 journalists from ten accredited foreign press agencies and five officials from the Interests Section.

Between 9:30 a.m. and 10:25 a.m., the "independent" journalists arrived at Cason's home. All of them came in taxis (Panataxi) and rented cars. They were received by Rebeca Tobey, who was monitoring the arrival of the participants, supervised by the deputy public affairs officer, Nicholas J. Giacobbe.

Before beginning the activity, the participants were offered a snack consisting of: coffee (of poor quality), milk, cupcakes with raisins, water and lemon-flavored soft drinks.

Before the "work sessions" were started, Public Affairs Officer Gonzalo Gallegos ratified their "willingness to collaborate with and support not only the 'independent journalists', but rather all those who, in one way or another, defend their rights as citizens of this country full of restrictions and censorship."

At approximately 11:00 a.m., the guests divided themselves into four work commissions: the Photojournalism Commission, run by Alicia Zamora Labrada and Israel Picallo Ortiz; the Interview Commission, with Jesús Zúñiga Silveiro and Olga Rita Ramírez Delgado as leaders; the Analysis, Conflicts and Interests Commission, headed by Manuel David Orrio del Rosario and Aleida Godínez Soler; the Commission on Relations between Journalists and Editors, directed by Néstor Baguer Sánchez Galarraga and Adela Soto Ascuy; and the Commission on Journalistic Language, with Luis García Vega and Ángel Pablo Polanco Torrejón.

After the work sessions, they broke for lunch, which included buttered white rice, rice and beans, roasted pork chops, beef stew, pasta salad, tomato salad, lettuce, carrots, sautéed eggplant, pudding, turnovers, water and soft drinks.

Finally, the conclusions arrived at by each commission were announced, the agreements reached were adopted, and the situation with Radio "Martí" was discussed once again. Apparently, Nicholas Giacobbe made a telephone call to the U.S. State Department to express the concerns of the participants.

At the end of the discussions, the participants received a diploma for having participated in the workshop, which was signed by the journalists Manuel David Orrio del Rosario, from the Federation of "Independent" Journalists of Cuba (Federación de Periodistas Independientes de Cuba), and Farah Armenteros, for the Assembly to Promote Civil Society in Cuba project.

March 14, 2003: Journalistic Ethics Workshop, held in James Cason's home, and chaired by Agents Miguel and Vilma.

CONTENTS

IMPRENTA
ALEJO CARPENTIER